DeForest Kelley
Up Close and Personal

A Harvest of Memories from the Fan
Who Knew Him Best

By
Kristine M. Smith

Black and White EDITION
ISBN-13: 978-0692607206 (Custom)
ISBN-10: 069260720X

This book is printed on acid-free paper.

This is an enhanced version of the author's previous 2001 title **DeForest Kelley: A Harvest of Memories, My Life and Times with a Remarkable Gentleman Actor** with more than fifty-five pages of additional anecdotes and dozens of previously-unpublished images.

Illustrations by DeForest Kelley. DeForest Kelley's poetry, notes, letters and personal home photographs reprinted by permission of Carolyn Kelley. Photographs: William Dow, Carolyn Kelley, Dorothea Smith and the author.

STAR TREK™ is a Registered Trademark of CBS Studios Inc.

Professional studio images courtesy of CBS Home Entertainment

Printed in the USA

Yellow Balloon Publications – rev. December 18, 2015

DEDICATION

Dedicated to the memory of my beloved "serval son" Deaken because DeForest Kelley believed he richly deserved a book dedication.

Dedicated also to <u>you</u>, whose love for DeForest Kelley will endure as long as your memories of him last.

I trust that many of the memories in this book will become yours.

I am *beyond happy* to bequeath them to you!

FOREWORD

"The evil that men do lives after them;
the good is oft interred with their bones." - Shakespeare

If Shakespeare's quote is true—as sadly, it usually is—this book wouldn't have been written, couldn't have been written. DeForest Kelley was never a bad guy, except in movies and hundreds of television series episodes.

At his memorial service on June 22, 1999, on the verge of tears, I stated, "In my opinion, DeForest Kelley was the kind of man God had in mind when He created Adam. If this sad old world could boast a much larger population of DeForest Kelley types, it would be the paradise we all wish it was."

DeForest Kelley—the person, not the actor—became such a monumental part of my personal architecture that I'd crumble without his spirit and legacy to support me. I'm not built, or even retrofitted, to withstand a 10.0 magnitude fracture to my superstructure. "De" was a mentor, a guardian, and a devoted friend. I respected him, treasured him, and honored him. His goodness continues.

After reading this book, you will understand all this. He was a decent, gentle, kind human being. He was all of these things, nearly all of the time, which comes close to qualifying him for sainthood in my judgment. You will also understand, I think, why De laughed so heartily all those times I tried to cajole him into writing his autobiography "before it's too late". I joked once, "You know, De, if you don't write it, and I end up writing, it may inadvertently launch a new world religion!"

All this might lead you to wonder if he was perhaps too kind for his own good—so kind as to be ineffective when toughness or tenacity mattered. Not so. He was effective and tough in the ways that matter in life. I learned a lot watching and listening to him. I sincerely hope some of it rubbed off.

De and I discussed, numerous times, the possibility of my writing his biography. De wanted to be involved in any such recounting of his life and times—with which I heartily concurred. Toward the end, with more pressing concerns occupying our time and minds, we eventually understood and accepted that he'd never be able to concentrate on the monumental task of reflecting publicly and extensively on his life. He then gave me permission to go ahead and write anecdotally about him; a huge and marvelous gift. (De's bio became the work of Terry Lee Rioux.)

This particular effort is my public salute to De, the man I knew and loved through the best of times and the worst of times. De showed us how

4

to live, and he showed us how to die. He did both with grace, humor, hope and endlessly enduring love.

What follows are my own personal life and times with DeForest Kelley, from the first time I met him as a teenager in Washington State in May, 1968, until his last day on earth, June 11, 1999. Although this narrative is mostly upbeat, fun, poignant, funny, and heartwarming—which was what 98% of being in De's company was all about—the final days may upset you in some places. It is quite likely that you loved DeForest Kelley wholeheartedly, whether as a personal friend, business associate, or from afar, in the outermost reaches of fandom. I have been honest throughout. I have also taken great care to be sensitive to your needs as fans and readers so that I would not unduly upset you when delving into end stage events. I know you want the truth. The truth is he was magnificent. The world is a better place because he trod here mindfully with the indwelling gentleness of a true spiritual champion.

Kris Smith Tacoma Washington
December 15, 2015

DISCOVERING DeFOREST KELLEY
1968-1993

September 8, 1966. Star Trek, the first televised space travel series to take itself seriously, debuted. On the bridge of the Starship USS Enterprise were Captain James T. Kirk, First Officer Mr. Spock (a Vulcan), and a cadre of others who would become as well-known and well-loved to many of us as our own families and dearest friends.

I was fifteen. I first noticed Star Trek because my Dad and twelve year old cousin, Tim, were absolutely crazy about it. When the theme song came on, the order went out to "Shut the hell up!" It seemed certain that anyone who dared utter a word would be banished from the house, disinherited, drawn and quartered, and made to suffer in countless other hideous ways, if even a single word of dialogue was obscured by mindless babble—or even a sneeze. So I had two options: shut up and watch, or find something else more interesting to do. I never found anything more interesting than watching the episodes, waiting for the commercials, and then jibing Dad for "being in love with the green man with pointed ears." Dad and I didn't get along in those years; Star Trek was pretty much all we had in common, and even that was simply because it gave me a chance to make him miserable four times an hour. He usually had the upper hand in making misery.

But the show pulled at me like a tractor beam. The fellow I felt most drawn to was Doctor Leonard "Bones" McCoy, partly because he was such an asset to his shipmates and to his profession, and partly because I felt he was nearly always right. But sadly, he was even less adept at winning arguments with his nemesis, Spock, than I was with the irritants in my life. Someone else always seemed to be getting the last word. Mostly I loved McCoy's innate decency and obvious compassion. He looked as though he belonged on a gentleman's farm in rural Georgia, and seemed to feel that way, too. When confronted by some new alien race he reacted the way a person could be expected to react, rather than as if this was business as usual. It was all new to him! You could see it, feel it, go with it. You knew you could rely on him to be honest even when it wasn't particularly wise or logical. His heart—his humanity—usually led the way. Oh, sure: Spock could rattle his cage on occasion, turning him into an irascible curmudgeon, but good friends have a way of doing that to each other when they're in a low mood, so that seemed to fit, too.

Just as soon as I began enjoying the show, I began writing Enterprise-based stories as creative writing assignments for English class; I began portraying various crew members in Drama class. I began to actually believe in the dream Gene Roddenberry and his cast had created, as it seemed a much nicer place to play than our own planet with its racism, barbarism and

6

paranoia about differences. On the second day of May in 1968, I was thrilled to learn that DeForest Kelley—my beloved "Bones"—would be appearing in the Wenatchee Apple Blossom Festival on May 4. I raced to Mom and Dad, imploring them to drive me there from Cle Elum—two hours away—to see him. They told me that was impossible; they had to plant the field. "But if you want to go, you have your driver's license now. You can take the car."

Take the car? I was a novice driver! I had never driven in a town larger than Cle Elum, population 1600, without Mom or Dad at my side. Wenatchee was a big city! Lord God Almighty. It was the scariest thing I had ever considered doing in my life.

I quickly called my best friend, Corean Scott, and asked if she would accompany me to Wenatchee to see the Wenatchee Apple Blossom Parade and DeForest. She could tell I was petrified and that I needed moral support. She quickly asked her mom and got permission. We spent the next day whipping up some placards with DeForest's photo on them. One said, "HI, BONES! WE LOVE YA!" We bought autograph books, too, just in case. Neither of us thought we'd actually get near enough to meet him, but as eternal optimists we decided to prepare for every possibility.

The next morning we headed over the pass at 6:30 a.m. It was dark and the road was still slippery in places with black ice. Nervous Nellie that I was, I wasn't as concerned about the pass as I was about driving in heavy traffic on four-lane boulevards! When we got to Wenatchee, a full two hours ahead of the scheduled parade kick-off, I found the first parking lot available, parked the car, and released a huge sigh of relief. As luck—fate…God—would have it, we were just two blocks from the parade route. We quickly discovered that we were also on the same block where the limousine for Mr. and Mrs. DeForest Kelley was parked! Corean and I looked at each other, stunned. I finally said, "You know, if we play our cards right, we might get a chance to actually meet DeForest, not just watch him go by." I told her, "Here's Mom's movie camera. I'm going back to the car for the autograph books. If anything happens while I'm gone, be sure and film it!"

I raced back to the car, grabbed the placards and autograph books, and raced back. Luckily, I hadn't missed anything. We loitered shamelessly, pretending occasionally to window shop. Suddenly, I heard Corean gasp, and then she said, "Oh, my gosh, there he is!" I followed her gaze and just about fell over. I had never, until this moment, been overly impressed with DeForest's looks. Not that I thought he was unattractive; I just had never really considered him "drool material," and neither had Corky. We were both unutterably stunned to see how extraordinarily handsome he was in the flesh. And he was smiling, even grinning! This was not what we had expected in "our" Dr. McCoy!

I said, "Geez, Cork, he's adorable!"

"What do they do on Star Trek to make him look so…plain?" She asked.

I shrugged my shoulders and said, "I don't know…but they should stop it. He's gorgeous!"

The Kelleys got into the limo. Surprisingly, the driver didn't start the engine and take off right away. A few other passing fans spotted their vehicle and approached it. We stayed back for a good ten minutes, watching. I was a little apprehensive that I might find him disinterested in his fans, but it quickly became apparent that this wasn't the case at all. He was genuinely appreciative of their attention, and spoke easily with each of them, thanking them for their interest in and support of Star Trek. Butterflies inhabited my innards. I wanted to go to the car and greet him but was afraid I'd make a fool of myself if I tried. I held back hemming and hawing so long that finally Corean elbowed me and said, "Go on over and get his autograph. I'll film it." I took a big breath and said, "Ho-kay. If I survive it, it'll be a miracle." I stepped up to the car. Mrs. Kelley spotted me first, looked up and grinned, "Hi!" she said.

I muttered, "Hello…" and took a step back to recover.

"De," Carolyn said, "over here."

DeForest looked over at me, grinned. "Well, hello, there!"

"H-hi," I managed to stutter. "May I have your autograph?" "Certainly!" he responded.

I handed him the autograph book and the pen I had. He began to uncap the pen, but it was a kind he wasn't familiar with. I watched him start to uncap it the wrong way. The last thing I wanted to do was correct him, so I just watched as he fumbled with it. I felt embarrassed for him and for me.

"What's your name?" he asked, still trying to find his way into the pen.

"Uh…Kristine. With a K," I said

He finally got the pen figured out, and then asked, "Kristy?"

"No, Kristine." I spelled it.

"That's one of my favorite names," he said.

I blushed. He signed the book and handed it and the perplexing pen back to me.

"Thank you," I said.

"You're very welcome."

My trial over, I stepped back to the sidewalk. Corean was thrilled. She had captured the entire thing on film. It was then that the driver started the car and pulled away from the curb to get into line for the parade. Corean and I discussed how nice he seemed. I was on cloud nine. I had not expected him to be quite this amazing as a human being. He had class and charisma and an elegance about him that was breathtaking. I had never met anyone as classically "Southern gentleman" before. It was as though he respected me enormously, as scared witless as I was! Not long after the parade began, and as it proceeded down the street toward us, I grabbed the camera, handed the placard to Corean and said, "They're going so slow, you can take this out to his car and show it to him. Perhaps he'll sign it for you. Go on!"

Corean carried the placard out to the car, which was surrounded with young, fresh-faced Kelley fans. He was signing as fast as he could. When he spotted the placard he grabbed it, held it up for the TV cameras, grinned, and then told Corean, "This is terrific! Thank you!"

She said, "Thank you! Would you mind signing it for us?"

He said, "Not at all," and signed his name to it.

Corean came back to the sidewalk, grinning ear to ear, sighing, "He is so nice! Gosh, I just love him!"

We watched the parade until our own Cle Elum Marching Band went by and then got into the car and headed for home. I no longer worried about driving or anything else. We drove home in a cocoon of affection for the man, expressing over and over how nice he was, how well mannered, how appreciative...how handsome.

That night, I wrote an essay titled "The REAL McCoy" and submitted it to my English teacher on Monday. Mr. Dobbs was impressed with a capital I. He had me read it in class and then, after the session, suggested that I send the essay to Mr. Kelley. I paled and balked. I sputtered, "Oh, no. No way! I don't write to movie stars."

He said, "Look, if you impressed someone as obviously as he impressed you, wouldn't you want to know?"

"Sure," I replied, "—but he's an actor. He probably hears stuff like this ten times a day."

Mr. Dobbs practically ordered, "Send him a copy."

Since he was my teacher and had a say in what my citizenship grade would be, I agreed. Besides, I told myself, Kelley's secretary would see the essay and she would probably toss it long before he ever laid eyes on it, so I figured I really had nothing to fear.

School let out shortly thereafter for the summer. I promptly forgot all about the letter and essay to DeForest, what with the assassinations of Dr. Martin Luther King Jr. in April, and Robert F. Kennedy in June, holding center stage and my heart that summer.

Then one day in August an envelope arrived from Paramount. "Oh, my gosh..." My heart climbed into my throat as I opened it. Inside was a brief letter—one that would change my life forever. **(See images.)**

My parents and sisters had to peel me off the ceiling several times a week for the next several months as I awaited the debut of my first-ever published article, about my favorite actor, submitted by my favorite actor! I sent another letter or two thanking DeForest for thinking enough of the article to submit it for publication with such a well-known New York publisher. I had been writing since age six, but didn't have the confidence to actually submit anything for publication; DeForest had gone ahead and done it for me. It was the greatest thing imaginable. I was so happy, felt so lucky—and Mr. Dobbs made sure to let everyone know when school reconvened, via news reports in the local and regional newspapers.

Shortly before the article appeared in the Holiday/January '69 issue of TV Star Parade, I again wrote DeForest thanking him for the boost in launching my writing career.

When the article appeared, the entire school more or less declared a Kris Smith Day. Lots of classmates purchased the issue and asked me to personally autograph the cover or the inside story.

Shy as I was, I was mortified by all the attention but I was also enormously proud. Not one word of the essay had been changed by the New York publisher, which I had dreaded might happen. After all, I was just a kid from the sticks. I'd been given encouragement and a two-year subscription to a writing magazine by my seventh and eighth grade English teacher, Mrs. Alpha Rossetti, who believed, but come on! I never thought I could actually write anything publishable. I wrote one more letter to Mr. Kelley, letting him know the outcome of my "adventure in celebrity." I was going to write still another, but my parents derailed the plan. Mom explained: "Kris, the man has been very kind to you. Don't drive him crazy with your incessant letters. Leave the poor fellow alone, now." I figured she was right. I always had gone overboard writing letters, which is why I had about 25 pen pals at the time, and it seemed predictable that had I continued to play pen pal with Mr. Kelley, I would have worn out my welcome. So I stopped. Cold turkey. Just like that. For seventeen years.

But I never truly let go.

My heart and soul knew better, somehow.

REUNION
1971-1978

After a couple years of college, I hired on as a secretary and laborer in my folks' construction company. They had a fifth wheel trailer and were building and remodeling restaurants all across the mid- and southwest and I thought that would be a wonderful way to see the country: stay 30 to 90 days in each region, meet folks, learn customs and habits and idioms. Of course, during all this time (1971-78) we had no real address; we were "living like turtles" as Mom put it. I was out of the loop with all things Trek and didn't have the slightest indication that it was anything but "dead, Jim."

I continued to write in my journals, but professional writing was impossible during that period of time. After my stint as a construction worker, I began working in the animal welfare field. Animals had always been a passion, and I felt I could contribute to their well-being with my activism and writing abilities, so I studied wild animal behavior and training, worked for a wildcat sanctuary, and later for an international animal welfare agency.

The strangest thing was going on during all these in between years. It was so strange that I was hesitant to discuss it with anyone. In fact, up until now, only two others have known about it. I was having dreams—lucid, detailed dreams, recurrent, evolving dreams—about DeForest and Carolyn Kelley! It seemed strange even then. After all, I had only been with them— what?—perhaps ten minutes in my entire life. I had left Star Trek behind three years previously, along with any plans about becoming a professional writer and was now working in endeavors that had n o t h i n g to do with the Kelleys. I was so "out of the loop" I never even turned on a television set for close to ten years. So, I was intrigued and confused by what I considered this subconscious obsession with the Kelleys.

The first dreams always began almost mid-mission. I was plopped down in a strange Southern California neighborhood; I had a message in my hand from DeForest that I was to give to Carolyn. The problem was that I didn't have the address to the Kelley's house. The only thing I knew about it was that in the back yard there was a desert tortoise (Myrtle). So, throughout the dream, I was walking up and down sidewalks, looking over fences and block walls, trying to spot Myrtle.

After several recurrences of this dream, I began to dream that no matter where I was, no matter where I went in my dreams—to a lake, to a fair, to a farm—Myrtle would be there. So, now my dreams had evolved to the point where I had found Myrtle, but alas—no De or Carolyn! This dream continued for some time. I would wake up, scratch my head, wonder and wonder, but my intuition offered nothing in the way of clarification. It was just one blasted Mystery to me why I should be obsessing over things Kelley!

Then a dream appeared that persisted for years. I was in a familiar living room—mine or another—chatting with the Kelleys as if we were family. Chatting to them about my writing, De's work, the state of the world, and even about the most mundane things imaginable, the way we often do with trusted family members. It was as if we had been together our entire lives. I loved this dream. The many years of searching dreams were over, and never came again. In these new dreams I had located the Kelleys at long last, and we were as comfortable as three bugs in a rug.

There was talk and laughter and the most pervasive and relaxing feeling of peace I had ever known, in the dream state or awake.

I wanted life to be like this. Of course, then I would wake up, the dream would vanish, and I would be plopped back into the real world where I had no contact with the Kelleys. Still, I felt I did. My dreams kept it all alive for me.

Between 1972 and 1985, whenever I wasn't working in construction, I worked in animal welfare. I worked with a veterinarian, spoke at rallies against unnecessary animal research (advising doctors and researchers of alternative, non-animal methods of research), "babysat" cougars and leopards, and wrote about crises facing wild and domestic animals (among them puppy mills, leg-hold traps, seal-clubbing and the like). In 1979 I adopted a week-old, weak-boned serval kitten. His name was Deaken (nickname DeDe or just plain De at that time). He eventually lost a rear leg due to weak bone syndrome, after which I sometimes wryly referred to him as Tri-pawed. My animal welfare articles appeared in dozens of newspapers and magazines between 1981 and 1985. They were a source of enormous pride to me, because I felt that they would help foster a new awareness of each animal's intrinsic importance to this planet. I was using my skill as a writer for a very great cause and felt that if I accomplished nothing else as a writer, this would be quite enough. I also felt I was finally paying back folks for their faith in my ability to string words together.

In 1986, after five years of living in the Sacramento area, I returned to Washington State and began living in a guest house at my parents' place in Eatonville. Out the front window was the most gorgeous view of Mt. Rainier that ever existed. I could hardly stand to drag myself away from home; it was in a rural area, surrounded by woodlands and populated by deer, raccoons, elk, squirrel...the whole repertoire of Pacific Northwest wildlife. We could easily visit the magnificent wildlife park called Northwest Trek. After five years of living in a big city, this was more like home, and it felt just right...except that I was almost dead broke, had a job that paid next to nothing, and had bills from Sacramento which threatened to bankrupt me. So I was in a paradise, yet living under a great deal of stress. Dad and I had converted an outlying garage into a very nice unit for my "serval son," Deaken, who was now six years old and the apple of my eye.

I began to write again to try to supplement my income in a last-ditch effort to get the damnable bills paid off and still eat and pay my parents at least something for putting up with me again.

In early August, I learned there would be a twentieth anniversary Star Trek convention in Spokane. Spokane was at the extreme end of the state from Eatonville, and I had never been to a convention. In fact, after seeing news coverage on television regarding Trek cons, I never wanted to go to one. Based on media coverage, I was under the impression that only "Trekkies" populated these events, pretending they'd just beamed down from some starship. In short, I thought only show-offs or true fanatics went to Star Trek conventions. I thought long and hard about driving all the way across the state for a "Trekkie" gathering, let me tell you! It seemed a rather terrifying prospect.

But! Wait! Hold it now! I couldn't get it out of my mind: DeForest Kelley was appearing at this convention, the man who had been appearing regularly in my night-time dreams for seventeen years! I was awfully sure that, with his integrity, he'd never agree to attend any event at which he had to address a roomful of nutcases. Plus, Gene Roddenberry would be there, as would other essential Star Trek people. So I felt safe. Hey, I thought, it might even end up being a relatively profound experience.

So I wrote Mr. Kelley a brief jovial note telling him that I would be in Spokane because "I owe you a long overdue hug for launching my writing career." I reported to him that I had since become a freelance writer and that I had numerous articles to my credit. I also enclosed a copy of "The REAL McCoy" to refresh his memory, along with a few of photos of my folks' chalet, Deaken, and my other domestic kitties. I signed off with, "If not for you, I would probably never have considered myself 'good enough' to call myself a writer."

The moment I mailed that note I again panicked, just as I had when I'd sent "The REAL McCoy" to him the first time. I crucified myself with such pleasing comments as, "You lunatic! He's an icon these days! A household name! You're 35 years old! You sounded like a 17 year old! 'I owe you a long over-due hug'! Fer gosh sakes, have you lost every marble you ever had! Jesus, Joseph and Mary! Get a grip!"

Plus, I was broke. What was I doing driving across the state—using gas, paying convention fees—when I didn't even have enough money to buy groceries at times? I was being the most thoughtless, selfish, stupidest woman the planet had ever known! I jumped all over myself in the worst ways possible. In fact, I actually talked myself out of going! But Mom and

Dad, noticing my depression over bills, thought the convention might be something that would pick me up a bit. They encouraged me to go. They offered me their truck so I could carry camping equipment in it and stay at a campground when I got to Spokane. Still, I hesitated.

Then the envelope arrived. Inside, the note read, "Enjoyed the photos of your pretty house and pets. Wishing you continued happiness. DeForest Kelley."

What did it mean? Was he looking forward to seeing me in Spokane? No promises there, just a polite note of thanks for the communication. So I felt off the hook if I really didn't want to go.

Still, I said I'd be there to give him a silly hug and just suppose he looked for me and I didn't show up?

Yes, I realized I was probably fantasizing. I was trying to make something out of a note; trying to read some between the lines statement.

He wanted to see me again!

No. That was me wanting to see him again.

No, it was him. That's what he had meant.

No, Idiot, it isn't what he meant. In fact, since he didn't mention the convention at all, he doesn't have any desire whatsoever to see you again. You're making it all up, and if you go, and he doesn't say hello, you'll be even more depressed than you are now! So, save yourself additional heartache and forget it, girl!

But what if —?

I went back and forth like this for days. I backed out a dozen times. The convention was three days away. I needed to make a decision!

Aw, what the hell, just go. See what happens. Just go and try to have a good time.

I called my sister Jackie and asked if she would loan me her eleven year old son, Philip. Philip was my "Trek buddy"—he loved Star Trek as much as I had. I needed a decoy, a reason to go to a convention with Klingons and Andorians and Starfleet Academy cadets. I figured I could tell folks I was escorting my little nephew….

Jackie agreed, Philip was ecstatic, so now I couldn't back out. I'd disappoint my beloved nephew! We drove over on a Thursday afternoon, checked into a KOA Campground then pitched the tent. The convention would begin the next day. Philip and I toasted wieners and ate marshmallows and chatted about what the next three days might bring. He had more hopes than I did. I tried to keep a lid on his expectations, since nothing was truly likely to happen, but his enthusiasm kindled my own hopes, and I don't think I slept more than two hours all night long. We got up, took showers, dressed, and drove to the convention hotel. I had an original copy of "The REAL McCoy" along, just in case I actually got a moment with Mr. Kelley; perhaps I could have it signed.

When we walked into the teeming lobby Trek fans were everywhere and, amazingly, most were dressed just like I was. There were very few "aliens" or Starfleet officers there. In fact, until I finally saw a Trek fan in a costume, I worried that perhaps we were in the wrong hotel.

I had prepared a note for DeForest, and asked a desk clerk at the convention hotel if he could deliver it to Mr. Kelley. Not another one, he probably thought. "No, ma'am, I can't. I have no idea what hotel he's staying at. There's no way I can deliver notes to any of the Star Trek stars." He'd said it a million times already; I knew there was no way an appeal at this point would do any good. I said, "Thank you. I understand"—which I did. Philip and I left the desk.

Philip looked up at me and said, "What now?"

I said, "Let's go find some fun to get into."

We walked down the hallway, signed in, and volunteered for some convention duties. There was really nothing I wanted to do there except hear DeForest's presentation, and the program indicated that he wouldn't be speaking until Sunday. I figured we'd volunteer to help the convention managers, earn a SPOKANE STAR TREK T-shirt in the process, and pass the days until DeForest would appear.

Unbeknownst to me, the Kelleys were trying to locate me. They called around, trying to find my room at the convention hotel. When that failed, they called other hotels in the area in an attempt to track me down. When nothing came of their efforts, they decided I had probably been unable to make it and dropped the idea of meeting with me.

Phil was placed at the book-selling, book-signing table with David Gerrold, the author of The Trouble with Tribbles.

As luck would have it, Gene Roddenberry's son Rod Jr. was assigned to the same book table. Both kids were 11 years old, so they hit it off and enjoyed Friday and Saturday together. I was assigned nearby. I don't recall what my tasks were. I know I earned my twelve hours, as did Phil, and we both received convention T-shirts as a reward. I told one of the convention managers that we wouldn't be able to volunteer during DeForest's appearance because that was the entire reason we had come to the convention. She nodded her understanding and said, "That's no problem. When De speaks no one will be buying anyway. We'll all be in there!"

While wandering around, looking at dealer's tables, I spotted a flyer for the DeForest Kelley Fan Communique, a fan club by Sue Keenan. I picked it up, folded it, and tucked it into my satchel. "Just in case I decide to join a club," I told myself silently.

Friday and Saturday sped by. I met Sammie Portman, a computer programmer from Seattle who was a big DeForest Kelley fan. She was fascinating. I didn't have a computer yet but I listened to all she had to say about the subject. I just knew someday I'd be as enamored of my PC as she was of hers.

On "De Day" we arrived early and got seats as close as we could to the stage. De was almost the final speaker of the day. We were back a good fourteen rows but within view of the podium and on the center aisle, so I considered us pretty lucky.

As the time approached for his appearance, I noticed that the aisle was beginning to fill with fans, so I told Phil, "Let's get up there and sit in the aisle, to get as close as we can."

Phil seemed uncomfortable doing that, and said, "No, I'll stay here and keep our seats. If the fans in the aisle get sent back, you will still have a place to sit that's close."

"Are you sure?"

"Yes."

"That's really good thinking, Phil."

I walked to within about fifteen feet of the stage and then sat down in the aisle. The Fire Marshall didn't object, so that's where I stayed.

Just before DeForest's name was announced, my heart was beating so hard and so loudly that I was embarrassed that someone sitting next to me might hear it.

The thunderous applause and the standing ovation he received didn't make me feel much better. I was truly in the midst of a throng which quite obviously adored DeForest Kelley. His talk was interesting, fun, poignant, sweet...it mesmerized me. Then he opened up the appearance for questions or comments from the audience. A thousand hands went up.

He continued to choose hands and answer questions. After about fifteen or twenty minutes of that I saw him looking at his watch, so I knew his time was coming to an end. I squirmed uncomfortably inside my own skin. Okay, Kris, it's now or never. It'll only take five seconds. Do it, or you'll lose the chance forever.

I raised my hand into the sea of outstretched hands and—call it a miracle—DeForest picked it. I could not believe it. He looked at me and said, "Yes? You."

I rapidly stated, "I just wanted to thank you for launching my writing career."

De looked at me and asked, "Are you Kris?"

I just about fell over. "Yeah," I muttered.

"Well, I've been lookin' all over for you!" I just about fell over again. Oh, God…

De continued with the audience, "Well, I want to tell you, this young lady wrote me a letter a long, long time ago…" To me, "What year was that?"

"Uh…'68."

"'68 it was. And you presented me with a story. I was so impressed with it that I sent it to a movie magazine, and they published it for her." To me, "Would you stand up?'

Under my breath I muttered, "Oh, Lord." I stood up. The audience began to applaud. De then joked, "She was about this high at the time." He indicated waist high.

Then he said to me, "And thank you for the beautiful photos you sent me of your home here in Washington. That's beautiful."

At this point, a convention manager with a microphone came to me and thrust the instrument in my face, expecting me to react in some way to De's nice comments. I was speechless and my cheeks were flushed with embarrassment. I didn't know what to say, and I certainly didn't want to say in public what issued from my lips, so I kind of whispered it: "May I give you a hug?"

De said, "You certainly may. Come on up here!" I stepped forward—the fans ahead of me parted so I could get through—and I leaped onto the stage. There was pleased laughter from the crowd, and flashbulbs were going off, blinding De; my back was to the audience. I gave him a long, heartfelt hug…then another…then patted his back saying, "Thank you so much."

He said, "We're proud of you. Keep up the good work."

I said, "I will. Thank you again, so much."

I left the stage and walked back to my seat to join Philip, who looked awe- struck. De was saying, "There! Now we have a writer to our credit." De went on to another fan.

Philip looked up into my eyes and asked me, "Did you cry?"

"No," I said. "Almost, though." I waited a second or two and then asked him, "Were you embarrassed when I asked him for a hug?'

"No!" he said resolutely. "I was proud!"

A few minutes later, De's appearance ended. I told Phil, "If we're fast, maybe we can get over to the exit door from the stage and have a picture taken with him."

Phil nodded, "Okay!" and we hurried toward the rear of the auditorium, took a sharp right, and headed to the stage area exit door. Sure enough, DeForest came out. He spotted me and grinned, and I said, "Hello, Mr. Kelley. I don't want to impose or slow you down—"

"Oh, no, not at all, Kris."

"Would it be possible to get a picture with you?"

"Certainly."

I gave my camera to Philip. He fiddled with it a little bit, trying to put it into focus. He was nervous and so was I, standing there arm in arm with De. A fellow fan, about thirty, offered to take the camera from Philip and do the honors, so Philip gratefully relinquished it. The picture was taken.

I shook De's hand and he said, "Stay in touch."

I said, "Okay."

Philip and I wandered around for a while then prepared to leave. Then Philip tapped me and said, "Aunt Kris, DeForest is sitting with Gene Roddenberry in the restaurant!" I looked, and sure enough, there he was, with wife Carolyn, Gene's wife Majel, Nichelle Nichols, George Takei, and others. I said, "Oh, dear…"

Philip said, "I'd like to get his autograph."

I said, "I know, sweetie, but I don't think we should interrupt their dinners. That would be rude."

He said, "I know it."

We hung around a little bit longer. DeForest stood up and headed into the men's room. Phil brightened considerably. I countered with, "No way. You can't go into the bathroom to get his autograph."

He said, "I wasn't thinking of that! I could go stand outside the door and ask when he comes out."

I sweated. Finally I said, "Okay, but I'm going around the corner and hiding. I don't want him thinking this was my idea!" I figured DeForest would accept this ambush from a little boy and let Philip go ahead. I fled around the corner and waited. And waited. And waited. Finally, Philip came back, beaming, showing me his paper. "I got it!" Then he announced proudly, "He wrote Phil on it!"

I said, "OK, Phil, we're both happy now. Let's get out of here."

As we walked down the hallway, he confessed to me, "When DeForest came out, I made a mistake. I told him, 'Hi, I'm Kris's aunt!'"

I laughed then said, "And what did he say?"

Phil reported, "He said, 'You are?'" Then I said 'I mean, Kris is my aunt' and he said, 'That's what I thought you meant.' And then, after he signed his autograph, he asked where you were. I told him you were hiding around the corner!"

I said, "Oh, great going, kidlet!"

Philip and I spent the last night at the KOA and then, on the way out of town, we decided to stop one last time at the convention hotel. We'd had such a good time that we weren't quite ready to consign it to memory.

I parked the truck and we started to walk in. Mark Lenard, who played Sarek (Spock's father) was standing outside, and we spoke with him for a few minutes. He seemed very shy and a little bit haunted, but he was very,

very nice. Then we went inside and I spotted my new computer programmer friend, Sammie, from Seattle. She, of course, had seen De's appearance and was very happy for me, and even shed a few tears while remembering it.

The three of us were off in a corner, chatting in the hotel lobby, when suddenly the whole crowd seemed to experience a communal intake of breath; then I heard exclamations of, "There he is!" We glanced across the crowd in the direction of everyone's gaze. DeForest and Carolyn Kelley were entering the lobby on their way to the limousine which would carry them to the airport. We were as far away from the Kelleys as it was possible to get, which I was plenty happy about, since Philip had divulged the fact that I was hiding around the corner when De was accosted for yet another autograph request the night before. I held back, thinking that now it was time for other fans to have their special moments to see and speak with De.

De lingered for a few moments, and then glanced across the lobby and spotted me. He called out, "Kris! Good morning!"

I waved a "Good morning!" wave and smiled. De grabbed Carolyn's hand and started through the throng in my direction. I about had a heart attack. I could not believe he was coming over yet again to see me. Stunned, but recognizing my responsibility, I started across the lobby toward the Kelleys so it wouldn't be such a trek for them.

We met in the middle of the throng, which was respectful and didn't crowd us much. De said to me, "Do you remember Carolyn?"

I said, "I sure do! Hello!" and reached out to shake her hand.

But she took both of my hands in hers and said, "Kris, it's so nice to see you again! We always wondered whatever happened to the little girl who wrote so well!"

I muttered and sputtered, deciding not to tell them the truth. How would they have reacted to a 35 year old telling them that "Mom and Dad told me to leave you alone; not to drive you nuts anymore"? Instead, I told a slightly convoluted, but equally true, story: "My folks and I spent a lot of years building and remodeling restaurants all over the country. We really didn't have an address, to speak of. So I lost touch with everybody, not just you."

De said, "Well, we're glad you're back in touch."

Carolyn added, "Yes. Now, don't be a stranger. Send us some of the articles you've had published."

I said, "Okay."

Carolyn repeated, for emphasis, "We mean it. Stay in touch."

I said, "Okay," yet again, then, "Thanks!" and we parted.

I still had money problems, and I still had a pitifully paying job, but I was re-born. My spirits lifted; I saw a light at the end of the tunnel. Once

19

again, I had some faith in myself. The long nightmare was finally ending. I was out of the self-pity business entirely.

When I got home from the convention, I re-invented myself. I mailed off the flyer to Sue Keenan and signed up for a year of the DeForest Kelley Fan Communiqué. The first thing I did was write a report of the convention and submit it to her for her newsletter. Then I got silly and started writing other humor pieces about the "adorable" De Kelley, all of which she published. I had by now sent the Kelleys copies of many of my articles which had been published, and since most of the articles related to animal welfare I was delighted to find that the Kelleys were big animal lovers, too. In fact, De's official charity was the North Shore Animal League.

Since the subject matter of my non-fiction, animal welfare articles was pretty heavy and dealt with unhappy topics, I made sure that the letters accompanying them were as wild, wacky and funny as I could possibly make them. I certainly didn't want them thinking that I was an always - serious, over-zealous, ever-crusading animal savior every waking moment of my life. In fact, I had already distanced myself from much of that endeavor, since I realized the intense involvement was contributing to a tendency toward depression. I was temporarily burned out on trying to save the animal world, and I wanted them to be uplifted when they got letters from me.

De's next convention would take place in Dearborn, Michigan. I made arrangements to stay with a pen pal, Jeannie Armstrong, and then I had a T-shirt especially made to wear for the occasion. After that, I informed my boss when I would be using my vacation time, and for what reason. Yikes! Unfortunately, our store was having its annual Tent Sale—the biggest sales event of the year—and so he refused to let me get away. Heartbroken, I called Jeannie and told her that I wouldn't be able to attend, but said I'd send the T-shirt, and she could wear it to the convention. The T-shirt read: "NO BONES ABOUT IT: I'm a DeForest Kelley Fan!" and had "DeForest" and "Carolyn" written down each sleeve, with hearts where the O's belonged. It was one cool-looking shirt! I wrote to the Kelley to be looking for the lady with the most terrific Kelley shirt on the planet.

Amazingly enough, De did look for the T-shirt, had Jeannie model it, and then explained how he had met me twenty years earlier. At that point, he got nostalgic or tickled or something and said, "I get a lot of wonderful mail, and I read it all—I want you to know that—but it is impossible for me to become a pen pal." Everyone laughed at that, of course understanding. Then he said, "If there's anyone I should write to, it should be Kris… and I have, on occasion…" Then he half-laughed, "I've had to answer her a couple times. But it's impossible, even with her, even those we have some kind of personal situation for…" and he trailed off without finishing the thought. Well, Jeannie sent me a videotape of that appearance, and when I watched it I was so touched. Then I suddenly felt guilty, thinking he really might be sitting up nights feeling badly that he wasn't writing as often as I was (although Carolyn was certainly doing her best to keep up with me all along). So, I took out a pen and I wrote a heartfelt letter telling De that he didn't owe me a thing–that it was me who owed him.

Well, enter "Krazy Kris". For some reason, the day I knew the note had to have reached him, the mischievous side of me got inspired! (Thank You, God!) I started to giggle, and I started to type. (Or, rather, Krazy Kris did.) I pictured him at home, reading this heartfelt, "don't feel guilty" letter, while Krazy Kris was writing:

Dear Penpal,

Why haven't you written?! I've been sitting here looking forlorn for almost a year now. (Okay, so it's only been seven months. Time FLIES when one is forlorn.) I'm not one to notice these things, and I know how busy you are, but WHERE'S MY AUTOGRAPHED PHOTO? [I had never even asked for an autographed photo!] I am incensed! I have an empty spot on my wall – there's only one small empty spot left – that's just the right size for a photo of—who? But, of course, I suppose I could put a photo of SPOCK there—but it wouldn't go with the rest of my De-cor, if you get my drift.

So, if you want to stay in my good graces (and good gracious, of course you do!) SEND ME A PICTURE! And sign it something short and sweet like "To My Dear Penpal (who belongs in a pen!) with warmest regards and hugs and kisses and Saurian brandy, Bones." (And don't worry if you can't see the picture afterwards. I have plenty of pictures, but no signed ones!)

Grin! It looks great on you!
XOX

Krazy Kris
P.S. I lock her up when I see you. Aren't you glad???

Within days, I received a teensy weensy, smaller-than-wallet size photo of De with a bouquet of roses. "Maybe this will shut you up until I can get a big one for your wall DE-cor. DeForest. P.S. Stick it in your wall-et.

I roared. A major breakthrough! Gone were the social amenities. And gone was the "Kelley" from his name! I interpreted this as a near-miraculous leap forward. Needless to say, Sane Kris seldom wrote after that, except to Carolyn on business regarding articles I was writing on De for publication.

THE ADVENTURE CONTINUES....
1987-1990

The next convention that featured De was in Los Angeles in October '87, so that became my next goal. I called Sue Keenan, De's fan club president, and asked her if she knew of a roommate I could share with, to cut down on expenses. Sue wrote back and said, "I have the perfect roommate for you. Her name is Kat Lane. I know she's perfect for you because you are both certifiably nuts!" My eyebrow went up at that.

When I arrived in Los Angeles, Sue expected a wacky broad, I'm sure. She got one. I expected Kat Lane to be a wacky, lustful broad, as we had been writing for a few weeks by this time and she had been proclaiming to all what I had only alluded to previously to a few comrades: De was sexy! So, Sue invited the two of us, not really knowing either of us, and then had crossed her fingers hoping (I'm sure) we wouldn't become a pain in the butt to De.

The chemistry was truly atomic.

Kat and I spent so much time laughing at and with each other day and night even before the convention got underway that we were half sick—and very sore (laughing non-stop becomes painful!)—when we finally made it to the auditorium to see De's appearance. At times, I wasn't even sure Kat would make it to De's appearance, she was so sore and sick from mirth. I plied her with orange juice to bring her sugar levels back up to "functional," and off we went, never quite certain she'd survive it.

So there we were in L.A. We were so excited to see De again that we didn't eat and seldom slept all weekend. We just sat up most of every night laughing and philosophizing and kidding and laughing some more. Finally, when we were completely and utterly exhausted, with our sides aching beyond endurance, we retired. Just before drifting off to sleep, I heard Kat say what I thought was, "Good night, dear." I was so touched to know that someone so new to me considered me dear, and I responded, "Goodnight, Kat." She started howling and pounding on the bed and crying because it hurt so much to still be laughing.

I asked, "What's so funny?!"

She told me: "I said, Goodnight DE!"

I cracked up, then! I said, "Well, he's at least 20 miles from here, so you'd better say it a hell of a lot louder than that!"

Carolyn wasn't at the convention because Fancy (the Kelleys' Lhasa Apso) was ill and she was at home with her. I behaved myself in the auditorium during De's appearance. (DE didn't, but I did.)

On Saturday, De introduced me as "Krazy Kris" for the first time, and it stuck in DKFC members' minds. And that's when I decided that, at some point in the future, I would get even with Mister Kelley publicly for "DE-faming" me.

When I got home from the convention, I blasted him with a pseudo-outraged letter regarding his impertinence. A sticker at the top hinted at what might follow. It read: "CAUTION: Contains material that may be offensive to persons lacking a sense of humor."

The letter went like this:

JACKSON DeFOREST KELLEY! (The sound of thunder or growling goes here.) (Ooh—doesn't that just make the hair on the back of your neck rise? Why, whenever I heard my full name used in that tone of voice, I knew I was in Big Trouble. I only heard my full name used TWICE in my life – once, when I went inner-tubing in Spanaway Lake before I knew how to swim (unaccompanied), and once — but I digress: This is your chewing out, not mine!!)

("Yes?") You are in Big Trouble! ("I am?") Yes! You! ("What did I do, pray tell?")

Well, if you don't even know, I am outraged! ("So, clue me in, will you?") You called me KRAZY KRIS in LA and now everybody is doing it—all these people who used to think of me as sane, sensible, reputable, dependable, intelligent, and professional. Stop laughing now! There were a few misguided souls who really felt that way!

Krazy Kris was a secret—didn't you know?! No one was supposed to know she existed; I had managed to keep her under wraps for 36 years and then you had to open your big mouth in LA and let the cat out! Well, as you no doubt guessed, the DKFC reporters (your stooges, particularly the Top Stooge, Sue Keenan) picked it right up, and now it is INTERNATIONAL news! What am I supposed to tell my Trekkie boss who, up until now, thought I was safe to have around? "It was a case of mistaken identity?!" You blew my cover! Okay, two can play this game. Don't expect me to run interference for you ever again. If I see you sneaking down the street in Spanaway or anywhere else in the world in your movie star "They'll-Never-Recognize-Me-In-This-Get-Up" glasses, will I just nod to you and pass by, keeping it under my hat that I know who you are? Not on your life! I'll shriek at the top of my lungs, "Hey, there's DeFOREST KELLEY!" and while everyone on the block is thinking, "Gee, where do I know that name from? It seems so familiar…" I will add, "DR. McCOY, you guys! Get with it! Mob him!" You'll never have another moment's peace, if I have anything to say about it! I considered punishing you by not writing at ALL this month, but then I decided, hey, the best punishment of all is writing to him! Make him suffer for the indignities he has caused me. The mental anguish, the guffaws of my co-workers, WHO I WAS TRYING TO INSPIRE AND LEAD, for heaven's sake! What you have done is the equivalent of calling Captain Kirk a lunatic in front of the Klingons! It will never be forgotten! I am ruined!

If I need a new job as a result of all this, I hope you will be kind enough to write me a letter of reference, leaving out anything you might know about me that would indicate I am not working on all thrusters. (No matter how little that leaves to talk about.)

Sincerely yours, (Hah! More like, "Go milk a duck, Bones!") ("Go milk a duck, De," sounds a bit too harsh. Bones can take it, though!)

The One Who Shall Remain Nameless, Faceless and Incognito to protect what's LEFT of her shattered reputation!

HAPPY BIRTHDAY TO YOU

In November, Kat and I planned our next adventure. I would fly to Tampa to De's next convention, in January.

Then my car broke down and I didn't have enough money to fix it and then fly to a convention. I was distraught. But I was resolved not to let this little (Arghh!) tragedy kill me. The week before the con, I went to the dentist for a check-up and this experience loaded me with all the ammunition needed for the next funny letter to the Kelleys (which Kat knew nothing about, as far as I knew).

I wrote:

Dear Ones:

I want to pass along to you some vital professional advice. It's revolutionary.

Up until today, I thought I had heard it all. But I was wrong.

Today I went in for my regular dental check-up. The dentist looked around in my mouth and couldn't find anything on my teeth worth complaining about, so he asked, "And do you also brush your tongue?"

???????????????

If he hadn't had both hands and some sort of lethal-looking metal device shoved halfway down my throat, I would have laughed. Instead, I almost choked. When he let me up for air, I said, "You have got to be putting me on!"

"No." He was serious! He said that people who brush their tongues taste food better. He said that bacteria found on the teeth are also found on the tongue; it only made sense that they should receive similar treatment. O.K. I accepted that; it sounded logical.

But that led me to ask, "But—how do you brush your tongue without gagging?"

He had an answer for that, too. "Stick your tongue out and pant while you brush."

I was beginning to wonder if I had perhaps run into one of those dentists you're not supposed to trust as far as you can throw them. (I'm still not sure I didn't!) But now I am dutifully brushing my tongue, as well as my teeth. And it gags me every time, because I refuse to pant in a house where others live and where the walls are thin. I mean, can you imagine?

"What's she doing in there?'

"She's brushing her tongue."

"I see..." (long pause) "I told you we should have had her confined when she started talking to animals, but no! You said she'd outgrow it!"

But the dentist is right. Food does taste better! (Just what I need, is for food to taste better! I'm already 30 pounds overweight!)

I have been thinking about this conversation ever since. And I thought, Well, I bet this is something Carolyn and De haven't been written to about before. (It's not easy coming up with a Letter of the Month to you that won't end up sounding like old hat. I mean, don't you get tired of hearing how wonderful you are, how you have changed people's lives? All that serious, mushy stuff? Isn't it refreshing to know you can count on me to update you on oral hygiene advances now and then?

Love you,
Krazy Kris (pant, pant)

I sent that letter off on a Monday, the week before the Tampa convention weekend. I didn't figure they would even receive it until after the con, so I wasn't expecting anything the day Kat called to give me the lowdown on what was happening back there on the east coast. She floored me by saying, right off the bat, "Oh, Kris, the most awful thing happened." My throat felt into my shoes.

"What?!" I cried.

Kat said, "My car broke down on my way to the convention, and I missed De's appearance completely!"

I was so upset by that, I started saying, "Oh, no! Oh, no!" so much that she finally had to tell me to shut up so she could complete her story.

"But I did get to see him after his appearance!" she finally managed to say.

"Oh, super!" I said, delighted. "Where was he?"

"He was in the bathroom—brushing his tongue!"

I screamed, probably deafening Kat for a beat or two. I couldn't believe it. Kat didn't know anything about my visit to the dentist. I knew right then and there that there was more—much more—to this story than met the ear piece.

As it turned out, Kat had seen De, and had wound up on the same shuttle flight between Tampa and Fort Lauderdale. De had invited her into first class to sit with him and Carolyn, and they had gotten to talking about this goofy letter I had sent them, and De had decided to have Kat play this joke on me!

Now, remember, I still hadn't (up to this time) spent more than fifteen minutes with them over the course of eighteen years. I couldn't believe that they would go out of their way like this to make me feel a part of the con that they knew I was so heartbroken over not being able to attend! Because of their thoughtfulness, I feel to this day as if I was in attendance at that Tampa-Fort Lauderdale convention.

Kat called me all weekend long to tell me what was happening. That night while they were at dinner, she and De and Carolyn actually came very close to calling me on the phone, except that the restaurant was very crowded and they were hidden back in a quiet alcove. De would have had to risk being spotted when going to the phone, thereby turning the whole dinner into an unscheduled personal appearance. Reluctantly, he finally vetoed the idea—much as he liked it—saying that since he preferred to remain incognito as much as possible, "You'll have to tell Kris that it's the thought that counts in this instance!"

And of course, it was everything. I'll never forget it. (I'm also very glad for another reason that he didn't call. At that stage in our association, I would probably have been a complete nerd over the phone and they might have written me off as too weird to tolerate!)

The next convention was two months later, in Denver. Kat had joked with De at the Florida convention dinner, "Well, I drove all the way here to spend your birthday with you, so now we will fly to Denver in March so you can spend our birthdays with us."

De asked, "Your birthdays are in March?"

Kat said, "Uh-oh. Yes."

De said, "I won't forget that, you know."

We started fantasizing: "What might he mean" by "I won't forget your birthdays"?

At one point, I kidded with Kat, "Gee, maybe we'll wind up at dinner!" (I was sad because I had missed the one in Florida, needless to say, so it was on my mind.) Then I added, "I'd even be happy to pay for it, providing we go to McDonald's—they have birthday balloons."

Well, that scenario hit Kat like a ton of bricks, and we started writing skits in which we wind up at McDonald's in Denver with De and Carolyn. The skits had De posing beneath the Golden Arches until he's frozen half to death so we'll have our birthday on record; they have De sucking the helium out of balloons and yelling, "He's Dead, Jim!" in a falsetto; and all sorts of weird, riotous stuff…You get the idea, right?

Kat wrote to the Kelleys and told them just enough about the skits to let them know the basics, then sent McDonald's gift certificates to them and asked if they might enclose them in a birthday card to me. De did better than that: on a post-it note he added "maybe you can use these in Denver!"

I haven't the faintest memory what else I received that year for my birthday, but that will never be forgotten!

HAPPY BIRTHDAY TO ME

Three weeks after my birthday, Kat and I wound up in Denver and were invited (via Sue) to dinner with the Kelleys. This was my first actual, sit-down-and-chat meeting with them, and I was so nervous that before we headed into their suite that I pleaded with Kat "Sit right next to me all night long, and if they ask me a question, you answer it!"

When you find yourself in an overwhelming situation like this one, you want to be at your best. You want to make a good impression; above all, you do not want to come across looking like Garfield's little buddy Odie! On the other hand, you don't want to look as if you're having an audience with the Pope. Something right smack in the middle seems about right...but I was nowhere near certain I could handle a middle-of-the-road approach. So I was nervous.

No. I was petrified.

I followed Jackie, Kat and—all of whom were cool, calm and collected by all appearances—into the Kelleys' hotel suite, where we were to meet, and I managed, for a moment, to present myself as normal. I hugged Mrs. Kelley and said, "Hello." Then I went over and shook hands with De. So far, soooo good...

Alas, how quickly I went downhill from there, inside my nerve-wracked body...

We stepped over to the couches and prepared to sit down. De asked us if he could take our coats. Now, if anyone else on the planet had asked me that question, an easy answer would have been yes or no, right? I mean, he wasn't asking my opinion on whether the U.S. should get out of the United Nations; he was just asking if I cared to give up my coat for a while. I gave it serious thought. I thought, What does he want me to say? Should I say yes? Will he be upset if I say no? Finally it occurred to me that he didn't give a fig whether I said yes or no, just so long as I said something, so he could sit down! So, I said no. That seemed to satisfy him, but not for long. Next he wanted to know if we would like drinks. I don't drink, so naturally I said yes. (Well, I had just told him no on something else. I didn't want him to think I was a bitch.) So, I said yes. Then he wanted to know what I would have. Oh, boy. He had me there! He was pitching these incredibly difficult questions at me and I was unable to field them!

"Oh...whatever!" I finally decided, hoping that would end the interrogation. Mrs. Kelley probably recognized the fact that I had slipped into the much-dreaded Idiocy Mode (a common affliction of fans) and tried to help me out. She suggested that I try a "DeForest Kelley." I looked at her, and I thought, *Gee, that is a very generous offer!* But I realized I wasn't getting the proper picture. She explained to me that a DeForest Kelley was a drink known to all of fandom--except me, obviously. "Oh, fine. I'll have one of those…"

Well, after a couple of DeForest Kelleys (vodka and water with a twist of lemon), I felt calmer. No one had raised any other controversial questions similar to "Can I take your coat?" in quite a while, so I was just sitting back and listening and watching everybody talk and laugh and have a good time. Not much later, we went downstairs for dinner.

De sat at the head of the table. To his right sat Sue Keenan, and to her right sat Jackie Edwards. To De's left sat Kat, then Carolyn (Mrs. Kelley), then me. There was nobody on my left for a hundred miles. I quickly lost my nervousness sitting next to Carolyn, because she is a doll—so nice, and so much fun. She could calm a jackhammer. I know, because she calmed me, and I'm the greater challenge! We lost ourselves in some conversation about having both been raised in the State of Washington.

At one point I was explaining something to her in great detail, and a fold or a crease on my left sleeve popped me with a great deal of force and I stopped in mid-sentence and turned around to my left, fully expecting to find a waiter or someone who had come along to ask me a question. There was nobody there! I panicked. I thought, *Okay, Kris…How are you going to handle this dilemma?*

Well, I had two choices. I could turn back to Carolyn and just continue the conversation as if nothing at all had happened, or I could explain what happened. Well, naturally I opted for the truth, but I forgot to provide a complete explanation. Instead of what I just told you, I turned back to Mrs. Kelley and I said, "Strange. I could have sworn somebody just tapped me on the shoulder." Carolyn accepted this bizarre information calmly. She looked at Jackie. Jackie looked at her. They both studied their salads for a while and said nothing.

I'm amazed the Kelleys didn't signal someone to bring a butterfly net!

It took me over a month to remember all the stupid things I said and did at dinner that evening. I found it comforting, at a later date, to learn that other fans admitted experiencing similar difficulties the first few times they were faced with actually trying to communicate with the objects of their affection.

After the convention (at which I had "debuted" as a stand-up comic, swooning over McCoy) Kat and I, by happy coincidence, were at the Denver Airport at the same time the Kelleys were, waiting for flights. Kat came over to the United terminal with me, since her flight was delayed for several hours, and we wandered over to the United gate that had a departing LA flight. De was sitting in a corner reading a newspaper, and by the time we got there, Carolyn had returned to sit next to him. Neither saw us until we were upon them, and I barely got out a "Good morning" before Carolyn leaned over and asked me, "How did your comedy routine go?" (She asked far faster than my own parents did when I got back home.) I said it went okay except for one part where I completely forgot a vital line and couldn't go on without it. The pause had lasted only five seconds, but it seemed like five decades. Kat assured them that by the time the audience noticed that I wasn't just taking a dramatic pause, I was off and running again, so it wasn't the major gaffe I felt it was. Carolyn was disappointed that she hadn't been able to see the routine, since it was scheduled so much later in the day than De had been. We thanked them again for dinner and talked briefly, then headed back to my gate.

HUMOR – A DIFFICULT CONCEPT

After a convention the mood at home is somewhat ho-hum—think of post-holiday blues and you'll have the general idea—so I generally started imagining the next event, which was a De con scheduled for August in Oakland. I had seen De in a blue and white striped shirt in photos taken during a Trek cruise and at other cons, and had swooned over how attractive he looked in it. I joked that he'd never better show up wearing it around me, because I might ravage his body. That led into a couple of tamely ribald skits that led into DKFC history so it's only fair that I share them here with you.

INFAMOUS STRIPED SHIRT SKIT #1
De is onstage in Oakland on Saturday.

De: (to Kat)	Hi, Kat!
Kat:	Hello, you handsome devil!
De:	Well, thank you!
Kat:	I call 'em as I see 'em.
De:	I know you do. Glad you could make it. (To audience.) She's from Florida. She follows me everywhere. She's crazy about me.
Kat: (joking)	No, I'm not. I just want to be in the audience the day you slip up.
De:	Slip up? And do what?
Kat:	The day you slip up and wear that blue and white striped shirt in front of Kris
Kris:	Shut up, Kat.
De:	I don't get it.
Kris: (nervous)	Shut up, Kat.
Kat:	If I don't warn him, he might actually wear the darned thing sometime.
Kris:	You're right. And then I'd chew my knuckles to the bone. Maybe we should tell him. But how, without making me look like a fool?
Kat:	Don't worry. Let me handle it. Trust me. (To De.) She likes that blue and white striped shirt you wore to dinner on the cruise. And you've worn it a few times at other conventions since then—cons Kris wasn't at.
De:	Oh, I see. Well, I'll be sure and wear it tomorrow so you can see it in person, Kris.

Kris and Kat:	NO!
Kris:	Oh, God, no. Anything but that!
De:	Now, that doesn't make any sense at all: Tell me you like something particularly well, and then tell me not to wear it.
Kris:	Drop it, Kat. Forget it. Please.
Kat: (to Kris)	Don't worry. I can handle it. (To De.) It makes perfect sense. Kris likes you, and she loves that striped shirt. Combine the two and she can't be held responsible for her actions—and I sure as hell can't hold her down.
De:	You can't be serious. Are you telling me that my lack of a striped shirt is all that's keeping me safe from Kris?
Kris: (sweating bullets; jumping to her own defense)	
	Well, I wouldn't go that far. Kat, please.
Kat:	That shirt acts as a sort of visual stimulant to her, I guess. Sort of like an aphroDEsiac... (everybody in the audience laughs like crazy)
Kris:	Gee, Kat, thanks for explaining it so I wouldn't be embarrassed! Next time I'll handle my own explanations, thank you!
De:(also laughing)	Well, that's crazy!
Carolyn:	CONSIDER THE SOURCE! AND THROW AWAY THAT SHIRT!

INFAMOUS STRIPED SHIRT SKIT #2

De arrives on stage on Sunday wearing the blue and white striped shirt! He's grinning like a Cheshire cat and looking straight at Kris.

De:	Good morning, Kris.
Kris:	I don't believe it. You little (shit)
De:	Do you like my shirt?
Kris:	I love your shirt.
Kat:	Kris, would you like my help in beating him to a pulp?
Kris:	No...Let him have his fun. We'll see who gets the last laugh. (To De) Okay, smarty pants, you want to live dangerously...(she gets up and heads for the stage)
De: (laughing)	What are you going to do to me?

Kris:	I don't give away the ending of a story any more often than you do.
De:	You're not going to do anything you'll regret later, are you?
Kris:	Why, De….There's nothing I could do to you that I would regret later…
De: (his smile fades)	Kris—are you going to do anything to me that I would regret later?
Kris:	Gee, I don't know. I guess we'll find out!
De:	Kris….Kat? Help?
Kat:	Sorry, De. You were warned. You made your bed. Now you're going to have to lie in it. (Kat gets up, looking as if she'll assist Kris)
De:	OK, you two. Enough is enough. Just wait a minute! (Kris arrives.)
Kris: (fondling the material on De's sleeve.) Nice material, De…
De:	OK ,I surrender. You win. Let's call it even!
Kris:	Even? I haven't even begun to get even!
De:	CAROLYN! HELP ME!
Carolyn:	Sorry, De. You have it coming. I told you not to wear that shirt!
De:	CAROLYN! (Carolyn shakes her head and crosses her arms, showing no mercy or sympathy.) (To the girls.) OK, I'm taking this shirt off. Right now. OK?
Kat:	Great idea. That'll get KRIS off your back, at least.
Kris:	Of course, then you'll have Kat to contend with. She just loves hairy chests—especially yours.
De:	Oh, dear. Look, ladies…I'm sorry. I was just trying to add a little levity to these proceedings.
Kris:	Well, I'm entertained.
Kat:	Me, too. I don't think I've ever had a better time.
De:	Uh… perhaps I'll read my second poem now.
Kris:	Well, if you think you can, despite the interference.
De: (clears his throat) "Twenty years ago in a galaxy far far away…"
(Kris starts unbuttoning his shirt) Oh, dear… Where was I?
Kris:	Beats me!
Kat:	Frankly, my dear, we don't give a damn!
De:	CAROLYN! IF YOU LOVE ME, YOU WILL COME UP HERE RIGHT THIS MINUTE AND TELL THESE TWO WOMEN TO LEAVE ME ALONE!
Carolyn: (to Sue) I think he's had enough. He's about ready to cry.

Sue:	I agree. Poor guy.
Carolyn:	All right, girls. At ease.
Kat: (to Carolyn)	Thanks for the forewarning about the shirt, Carolyn. We worked on this skit half the night —and it went even better than planned!
De:	You…you had this planned? (glaring at Carolyn, completely flabbergasted)
Carolyn:	Well, of course, dear. You don't think I'd have let it go on this long if I wasn't in on it, do you?
De:	I am going to burn this shirt! And if I didn't like the three of you so much, I'd…
C,K. and K:	You'd what?
De:	I don't know. There's nothing I can come up with that's just punishment! I'd like to turn you all over my knee.
Kat:	Ooh, sounds like FUN!
De:	Oh, no! Here we go, again!

I sent the skits to the Kelleys and sat back in anticipation, figuring they would certainly put them on the floor (my usual aim in writing to them). So certain was I of their hilarious effect that I decided to share the skits with my parents. They listened to them as I proceeded along. Their faces grew more pale and their eyes grew wider the farther along I got. When I finished, Mom asked, "You didn't send these skits to the Kelleys, did you?"

"Yeah. Sure! Why not?"

Mom and Dad looked at each other.

"Oh, my God." Dad said, "I can't believe it. The Kelleys will never speak to you again."

Their horrified reaction and prediction put ice water into my veins like you wouldn't believe. I re-read the skits and decided that maybe on paper they weren't as funny as they'd been in my head. If the Kelleys took them as a true representation of my attraction to De, I was doomed.

Of course, I panicked. I kept telling myself, *Be rational, Kris. Don't let your folks panic you! The Kelleys know that if these skits were a true representation of your feelings, you would never have sent them in the first place! Calm down! The Kelleys are not going to assign any validity to those off-the-wall skits!*

But my folks' concern kept returning and their words kept reverberating in the corridors of my mind: **The Kelleys will never speak to you again!** I began to contemplate the odds of that happening. The Kelleys were of the same generation as Mom and Dad…they grew up under some of the same influences…and oh my God…De was a preacher's kid, for

God's sake! They *were* going to look upon these skits exactly as Mom and Dad had feared and I would be drummed out of the DKFC and out of the Kelleys' lives forever, amen!

I called Kat. She told me to calm down! The Kelleys would love the skits.

Mom and Dad were hardly talking to me. I later learned that Dad was really frightened that the Kelleys might take the skits wrong and distance themselves from me, which he knew would devastate me. He didn't want me to suffer through something like that.

Well, I was so torn by this time, I thought, *Well, it won't do me any good to sit here and fall apart. I'll write them a letter of apology just in case the skits weren't well received.* It was the only thing I could think to do in the event I had overstepped any boundaries and humiliated or angered De or Carolyn.

I don't think my letter of apology was even completely read by Carolyn and De before Carolyn fired back a note to me saying, in part, "Don't worry about the shirt skits you sent. We are glad you can have such a lot of fun with all that nonsense."

That was the scariest envelope I ever opened–and I was so relieved when I got to that part of the message.

Right after this major crisis, Kat came up with a skit based on the old I Love Lucy series. In it, the two of US (instead of Lucy and Ethel) go to the Kelleys home disguised as lawn care attendants, hoping not to be recognized–and of course, we are recognized instantly. I thought the skit was really cute and suggested she send it to De and Carolyn the next time she had occasion to write. She did.

The only problem was that she mistyped the word **skits**, and within days she got a response from Carolyn in which she wrote: "De feels you two have a long way to go on your 'shits.'" Kat vowed then and there to get even with the proofreader of her embarrassing misprint, and called me a couple of days later and said, "I want to short-sheet his bed."

I laughed so hard I cried at the impertinence of that remark. After I regained my composure, I said, "That's awful. Let's do it!"

She said, "There's no way!"

I said, "Did I hear that? From a Trekker? Kat, 'There are always possibilities!' Remember?"

The light went on and Kat said, "Carolyn!"

I said, "Bingo!"

Kat said, "Naw….She'd never go with us on this one."

I said, "Well, at least we can ask. If she says no, at least he'll find out he was very close to being in Deep Skit with that comment!"

Kat told me I should write the short-sheeting request.

That gave me pause! "Why me? It was your idea!" (Cold feet!)

Kat insisted, "You're the writer. You can sell the idea better."

I countered, "Carolyn is not going to buy the idea, no matter who sells it!"

Kat said, "I know...but at least you can keep us from being disowned for asking!" So, I sat down and wrote the letter:

Dear Carolyn,

Now you've REALLY got Kat going! Ever since that "shits" note, she has been thinking of a way to "get even."

Her best idea is to short sheet De's bed at the upcoming Oakland convention. If there was any way we could think to do this without your help, we would. But then YOU would get short-sheeted, too – since we have a strange predilection ever since Denver to short-sheet beds of people we like. (I think I may have fallen in with the wrong crowd, here. Before I met Kat, I never even knew what short-sheeting WAS! Then she educated me. It's ALL Sue's fault! If she hadn't put me with Kat in the first place, I would still be the sweet, respectful, reverent person I've ALWAYS been!)

ANYWAY -- Sue loved being short-sheeted in Denver. (She even cried when we left. Of course, she may have been crying with RELIEF, but it didn't look that way to US!) We are also planning to short-sheet Jackie's bed in Oakland. And we've had two T-shirts made up that say, "SHE DID IT!" with arrows pointing to each other. So Jackie won't know who to blame! There's no reason why we couldn't wear them AGAIN – and FOREVER – if we got permission from YOU to short-sheet De. This is exactly the kind of thing a legend in his own time would never expect or imagine (especially since we'd need an inside accomplice). And you would get to see his reaction firsthand! (We sure would appreciate a full report later! We'll even wait in the lobby to re-make the bed, if you want, so you won't have to do it! (OR we'll run and hide until De has had enough time to see the humor in it before he catches sight of us again. Whatever you think it best!)

If you say yes, you will be helping to forge CONVENTION HISTORY. Possibly to get us put away for good, too – so just think of the contribution to SOCIETY you would be making RIGHT THERE!) IF De decided to tell the convention-goers about it, everyone would be in stitches (and we'd probably be lynched! TWO opportunities to be rid of us!) Sue would wet her pants (just before barring us from the DKFC forever) and Jackie would not be far behind!

If you don't agree that it's a great idea (true inspiration) we withdraw the request! If you DO think it'll be a howl, we need your help (obviously) to accomplish the dastardly deed: a key, a word left with hotel management to let us sneak in some time when you're out to dinner... or, if your hotel is close to ours, we can get together for a drink and excuse ourselves to go "to the ladies room" and run over and perpetrate the crime in a couple of minutes. WHEE! What fun!

What'cha think? Huh? It's your last convention for a long, long time – THINK of the great MEMORIES you'll have! (?) (De remembers Rory Calhoun for some pretty dastardly pranks. In fact, if he wasn't so fond of those stories, we would never have thought of THIS! It's all DE'S fault!)

Now that I've placed the blame on everyone except myself (Kat, Sue, even De), I feel a lot better signing this. But I'm not taking the rap alone!

Kat and Kris
The DE-mentos
(Double Yolkers in Need of a Third Good Egg!)

While we awaited the response to this letter (which we weren't sure we'd ever get) we entertained ourselves devising skits relating to What Might Happen if Carolyn actually said yes and we were faced with having to face De again after the Incident. They were pretty hilarious.

A week or so after we sent the Official Short-Sheeting Request, I got a letter from Carolyn:

Dear Kris:

We were amused no end by your letter today. You and Kat are certainly having a good time – it was a lucky day when you were introduced as "roomies" – and I'm sure you'll have a wonderful vacation together in the Great Northwest after the Oakland convention.

I hesitate having to place a damper on your short-sheeting plan for De, but having some idea as to his reaction, I wouldn't advise it.

Enjoyed your article in GRIT ("Getting Down to Earth With The Reel McCoy") and the Dave Barry piece on sharks. You're as good as he is, right now. You just haven't had the breaks yet... but you will.

Best always,

Carolyn

Notice that even when Carolyn has to tell you, no way she does it in such a pleasant way as to make you feel blessed. I love her deeply.

So it was no go with short-sheeting De, but we had expected that... so we were just as excited as ever about the upcoming Oakland convention. We planned a few other outrageous "got'chas" (primarily against our beloved DKFC prez) and counted the days until we would be together again to perpetrate them. (Keep Kat and me separated by an entire continent and you have two reasonably well-adjusted De Kelley fans. Put us together in the same room and you have TNT.)

The Creation Convention folks had heard (via my "agent" Kat) that I had done a great job in Denver with my comedy routine, so Adam Malin said he'd like to see it presented at his Oakland con just before De would appear on Sunday. All right! This meant that Carolyn would be able to come over a bit early if she really wanted to see it. That excited and scared the stuffing out of me all at once. I kept thinking, I must do well because if I don't, Carolyn will see it and I will want to shoot myself and if I do that I will never see De or Carolyn again—so I must not blow it, must not blow it, must not blow it.

I rehearsed the routine until I knew it better than my own name, better than the Pledge of Allegiance, better than the Lord's Prayer. I practiced it until I was so sick of it that I couldn't see anything at all funny in it! Then, I decided that I had over-prepared and backed off and just imagined presenting it in front of (oh, my God) Carolyn Kelley. The other fans were a real concern, too—particularly my friends, who I had promised myself I wouldn't embarrass by falling to pieces on stage—but it was Carolyn who was the ultimate person I didn't want to disappoint.

I landed in Oakland and waited for Kat's plane to land, then we went to the hotel and wreaked havoc – and had havoc wrought upon us! (It was get-even time, apparently.)

On Saturday we were all in the front row in various locations, standing up and applauding like mad when De strode in wearing the infamous blue and white striped shirt! I couldn't believe it. I sat down and leaned waaay back in my chair, hoping he wouldn't spot me...because I was hysterical, embarrassed, mortified–all the good stuff. The DKFC members knew exactly what was going on with that shirt prank (the skits had been re-printed in the club's newsletter) although no one else did. The club members were all looking at me and laughing hysterically. I don't remember a blasted thing he said that day; I had to see the videotape later to recall that appearance because I was too busy dodging De's glances toward the audience in my direction to pay much attention to details.

The next day just before De's appearance I presented "Husband Hunting on the Enterprise," while seriously quaking in boots. Carolyn was in the audience, so I figured De was probably standing backstage listening -- and there I stood, lusting after Dr. McCoy! Could Judgment Day be any less traumatic during the "life review" part, I pondered briefly. (Thankfully, I had previously sent the text to the Kelleys, and received their approval to present it!) Here it is:

HUSBAND HUNTING ON THE ENTERPRISE Stand Up Routine

I just love being among STAR TREK fans. It's better than being anywhere else–on Earth. The only place BETTER would be the to be on the Starship Enterprise–NCC-1701. I'd go find me a husband! And who would I pick, out of all those eligible hunks?

Captain Kirk? Not on your life! I could trust him about as far as I could throw him. He has a lady behind every bulkhead! I'd always be wondering why he wasn't HOME yet. I mean, it's his JOB, isn't it? Up here, running this ship? But NO, he's down on some planet, with the most beautiful women in the galaxy! He has NEVER landed on an ugly woman planet YET! He gets one in his sights and says, "No WAY! Prime Directive! No interference! Blast off!"

Mister Spock? UNnlike Captain Kirk, Mr. Spock is only in the mood once every seven years, and THEN it is not exactly moonlight and roses. Can you imagine living with a man for nearly a decade running, "Not tonight, dear–I have other priorities"? A human woman would go stark raving mad living under those conditions. "Check back in 3.7 years." Poor Chris Chapel: SHE was so gone over Spock I'm amazed she didn't jump off a bridge railing and KILL herself. Spock would have looked up from his console and gone, "Unfortunate." Oh! And what about Vulcan foreplay? (Show the intertwining of hands held in the Vulcan salute.) I WAITED SEVEN YEARS FOR THIS?

Mr. Sulu? Cute little devil, isn't he? But he has a tendency to want to play Lancelot at unpredictable intervals. When he isn't doing that, he's jogging, or doing karate, or cutting up in Botany. And I don't know how long I could take that crazy laugh.

Mr. Chekov? Vell, he vouldn't be bad–but your kids would all talk funny, and if you ever said or did anything to anger or upset him, you could be deafened or given cardiac arrest by that blood-curdling SCREAM of his. I'd have to give him a 10 for his Gleem smile, though.

Mr. Scott? Aye, he's a darlin' of a man–but he has a bit of a self-image problem. He's forever tellin' the Captain he canna possibly to what needs to be done to save the ship from imminent and total destruction. You'd be up half of every night giving HIM self-esteem lessons!

Well, I guess you know who I'm after. Uh-Huh. Ol' Blue Eyes. Leonard H McCoy. The H stands for Hallmark, because Starfleet cared enough to send the very best.

Now, I may be prejudiced, but McCoy is handsome, gallant, fun, charming, the perfect gentleman, and his ethics are beyond refute–plus he has a nice little tush and the sexiest lower lip in the galaxy. I realize these last two items are non-essentials, but they DO add up. So, if I was beaming aboard the Enterprise, hoping to find somebody's boots underneath MY bed, they'd have to be McCoy's. Just imagine it: free physicals–as any times a week as you wanted them! Be still, my heart!

Since I am so crazy about McCoy, I have a major gripe with the writers of STAR TREK. They gave KIRK about every eligible female that came along! Even the celibate, cerebral Mr. Spock had somebody who wanted HIM every time he turned around. Unless he was approaching ponn farr, he'd react like, "I presume she TYPES, or does something else useful?" His ladies had to go through life unrequited.

But McCoy…Now here was a decent, good-looking man with normal "needs," shall we say?–unattached–who would probably have requited the unrequited and left the rest to Kirk! He was gentle, ethical, charming–and what did McCoy Get? ZIP! ZILCH! NADA! Oh, right–he did get Natira. Now, when THAT show finally came on, in the THIRD season, I thought we really had something. I was standing up and CHEERING, "HURRAY! Bones finally got the girl!" But how come the writers only give him a girl when he can't sit up? He has xenopolycethemia in this one, and in THE EMPATH he's all beat up the moment that you know Gem is crazy about him. I'm not making this up! Think about it! In SHORE LEAVE, instead of getting the girl, he gets a lance through the gizzard! In FRIDAY'S CHILD– you know, the one where Eleyan decides that only Mac Coy can touch her?––she names her child after him eventually, too–but not before she spatters him with a rock, layin' him out cold! And in the most recent example, STAR TREK III: The Search for Spock, McCoy walks into a bar and asks the waitress, "Anybody been lookin' for me?" and she says, "I have–but what's the use?" WHAM! Within two minutes, he's flat on his back in DETENTION! I tell you, I don't know what the writers have against McCoy and women, but it's detrimental to his health!

Anyway, back to my gripe about the Natira story. He finally gets this beautiful woman, and I'm thinking, "All right!" They get married. They exchange these lovely vows. I'm dabbing at my eyes and thinking, "Oh, how perfect! At long last, LOVE. At long last, HONEYMOON!!!"

But is Natira thinking "honeymoon" with this handsome devil she's been kissing since she got her first chance? NO! Natira wants to show him The Book! I'm screaming at her, "Wake up and smell the coffee! You have a great evening in the offing, and you want to talk about a book you haven't even READ yet?" I mean! Where are this woman's priorities? And McCoy seems just as happy to discuss the damn' book as SHE is! He has 365 days before he kicks off, right? So what's the rush?

Well, then I got mad at the writers again. I thought, "Who WROTE this blasted thing?" Someone with hormones well in check, I can tell you THAT much! If it had been ME, it would have been called, "GEE! JUMPIN' BONES!"–and it would have had a happier ending. And a sequel. And a spin-off.

Of course, in THOSE days STAR TREK couldn't get away with what The Next Generation gets away with THESE days. But I have news: For MY money, the sexiest guy on the ship is STILL McCoy–at 137 years old. And if they ever let ME beam up, he won't live to be 138–but he'll die with a really big grin on his face!"

After I left the stage, three nutty women fans—yours truly included— quickly donned our blue and white striped "got'cha" shirts, purchased just that morning in a lobby gift shop, for De's impending appearance. De came on, spotted us in those shirts, laughed and shook his head, and then settled down to read his poem, "The Dream Goes On." Sue, Kat and I hot-footed it back to where Carolyn sat. Carolyn laughed, delighted, when she saw us in those striped shirts, and told us, "I made him wear that shirt yesterday. He didn't want to, but I insisted!" We cracked up. Since I hadn't attacked him, I reckon I passed her test! Carolyn got serious then and put her hand on mine. She said of my appearance a few minutes earlier, "Kris, you looked like you have been doing stand-up for ten years."

Oh, sigh – Oh, Lord…Oh, Carolyn, thank you!

A man from a cable station approached me later about staying over one day following the convention and going to his studio to videotape the routine for his audience. Alas, I had a super saver fare and it would have cost several hundred dollars for an extra night and flight change fees…plus Kat was flying with me to Washington for a vacation at con's end, so I felt I had to decline. He gave me his business card and asked me to get in touch with him whenever I was back in the Oakland area. But that cable rep's nice comment and request still didn't outshine Carolyn's comment in my mind; rather, it added verification inside me that Carolyn wasn't "just being kind" and saying what she knew I'd love to hear!

That afternoon during De's appearance, I raised my hand and he picked me, smiling. I said, "On September 7th you will be celebrating 43 years of marriage."

De said happily, "That's right." There was resounding applause and then he added: "43 years in the valley with the very same wife."

I continued: "Can you share some of the ingredients of a successful relationship?"

De paused only a moment, and then said eloquently, "Well, the first thing you've got to do is pick the right girl. That's number one."

I grabbed Kat on the knee to get her attention and joked, "I'm not looking for a girl!"–but to De, it looked as if I'd tapped Kat, indicating that I'd found my girl! A silly grin lit up his face and he almost laughed, so I quickly pulled my hand back, in surprise, realizing what his interpretation had been. He quickly got serious again and continued, "And naturally you fall in love, and then, when you fall into life, you've got to sustain the love. And the love has to grow into a deeper thing: it becomes a friendship that is intense and becomes like two people living together and loving each other deeply about it. It's a kind of a thing that nobody can really put into words and in this business you have got to be awful lucky to *stay* married. If you don't go hide, they'll kill you!" He finished with, "Thank you very much for asking. I don't know that I'm the easiest guy in the world to put up with, and I've never asked her…"

That night we heard that De and Carolyn were in the restaurant in our hotel, rather than in their own, so Sue decided we should go up and see if we were still "alive" after the prank we had pulled on him during his appearance that day. We were happy to discover that we were not disowned.

While visiting with them then, De said that it was probably time to retire the striped shirt now, since he had worn it so many times recently that "pretty soon people will be asking, 'Doesn't that poor man have anything else to wear?'"

I boo hooed and hissed that idea, but then suggested, "If you're serious, why don't you give it to Sue and she can auction it off to benefit the North Shore Animal League?"

De laughed at such an outrageous notion, but Sue and Kat both joined in and said it would earn hundreds of dollars for the dogs and cats at North Shore. De pondered that for a short time, and then said, "Do you really think anyone would bid on it?"

I held up my hand immediately, of course, and said, "Sure! I know for a fact someone would bid on it!"

Shaking his head in befuddlement, he said, "Well, okay. We'll get it laundered and send it to Sue."

Then Carolyn mentioned to Kat that she hoped her vacation with me in Washington State would be a lot of fun "despite the rain." Carolyn and I have a running argument about rain in Washington—she grew up during a very rainy era, and we didn't get the amount of rain she remembers when I was growing up forty years later. In fact, in 1988 (the year of the Oakland convention) Washington had been in a drought for the past several years during the summer. I couldn't convince her that things had changed in Washington. I reiterated mock-pointedly that Kat would see no rain while on vacation there. Carolyn grinned and polluted Kat's mind some more by saying, "Just keep your rain gear ready…in case!"

When we got to Washington, it was ninety degrees outside, and not one drop of water fell the entire week Kat visited. The first day, I joked to Kat, "Weather forecasting ability: Kris: 1 Carolyn : 0". Kat cracked up at that and said, "We have to keep score and let her know every day that it doesn't rain."

I said, "She'll hate us by the end of the week, because it is not going to rain!"

Kat said, "Perfect! Then it'll be even funnier!" So we went to Hallmark cards and bought a handful of little one-line cards…pleasant, thoughtful little love cards and we altered them as necessary to suit our purpose and accommodate our "rude" remark for each day.

The first card was a lovely thing that said, "I love seeing the love in your smile, and knowing the smile is for me." Kat signed it and then added: Here four hours already, and still no rain!" I scrawled a P.S. on it: "Kris: 1 Carolyn 0"

The next day, I wrote the card: Roses are red, violets are blue I'm sweating like crazy and Kat is, too Temp: 90 degrees NO RAIN

Kris: 2 Carolyn: 0

Kat added the P.S. "The only water I've seen so far is from the sprinklers!"

The next day we sent a card that read "You are wonderful!" and then Kat added: "except as a weather forecaster!" I added, "I'm NOT the type to rub it in, but Kris: 3 Carolyn: 0"

The fourth day we had a photo of the two of us during our horseback ride the previous day. I wrote on that: Did it rain today? NEIGH!" and Kat added: "The horses got sunburned and went inside, and we learned the true meaning of the word rawhide!"

On Friday, we decided to let Carolyn win, despite the weather. So we sent her two Polaroid snapshots. The first one was of Kat holding an umbrella in a downpour of immense proportions, and the writing on the border of the print read: GOOD NEWS, CAROLYN! It RAINED TODAY….On the next photo the words in the border read: ".… In New York, New Mexico, the Mojave Desert–but NOT in Washington!" We had obtained the "rainy day" photo with a hose, squirting the water over the umbrella Kat held. Kat added: "I drought very much you are going to win this rain bet, Carolyn!"

Within a matter of days Kat and I both received notes of appreciation for that series of cards and photos–along with an admission that she was glad she lost the rain bet.

DE'S FIRST ILLNESS

A mere eleven days after Kat and I had returned from the Oakland convention, De underwent surgery for a collapsed colon. Kat was still at my place when the letter arrived. I pulled it out of the mailbox and asked Kat to open and read it as I drove down the half-mile road to my house. I nearly hit a tree when she got to the part about the unexpected surgery.

"I've been busy recently, playing nurse to the good doctor. Of course by now you've heard that De had surgery September 1st – and all is well. He is recuperating beautifully–no problems. All's well that ends well. Sue sent him a box of silly fun things that gave us both lots of laughs. She's sum'pin', that Sue. Fancy is staring at me and stomping her feet – it's her dinnertime– so must go. Take care, you two, and keep smiling. My patient sends hellos– and of course chin-tickles to handsome Deke. Love, Carolyn."

Luckily, Sue, Kat and I had just recently inscribed a hilarious photo to De. Jackie Edwards had taken a great photo of us three girls in our blue-and-white striped sweatshirts–the "got'cha" shirts we wore the day after De wore his "sexy" shirt, and each of us had inscribed a humorous little note. My note read: Somebody asked me what color pants you wore with your striped shirt. Did you wear pants? Kris." Kat wrote: "So…why wasn't it unbuttoned to the navel? Love, Kat") Sue ended with: "Some people like to live dangerously…don't you? Next time I'll join them instead of sitting on them! Love, Sue, Your Semi-Sane Prez."

We had sent the photo to De – having had no idea he was in a hospital – and Carolyn had taken it to him on September 7th – their 43rd wedding anniversary. De got such a kick out of it that Carolyn took a photo of him lying in his hospital bed, grinning broadly, holding the photo in his lap. She sent each of us a 4x6 of the photo and with mine was a note which read, in part: "De is doing just beautifully. Hope you like this picture as much as we liked the one of y'all -- take care -- keep smiling! Love, Carolyn. P.S. Chin tickles for YOUR De."

I was, by this point in my evolution, the manager of a continuing education school for real estate, insurance and securities agents and brokers in Tacoma, Washington. On the wall in my office, I had mounted an 8x10 photo of DeForest which was a great conversation piece and an immense help in building good will. (It seemed everyone was as crazy about DeForest as I was; they were just more closeted about it). Of course, I also had a photo of Deaken (Little De, or DeDe, or Tri-pawed, but usually just plain "De"), my serval, on my desk.

My boss, Eric Schram, came into the office one day, down from Seattle, to see how things were going. He was sitting at my desk, and I was facing away from him, doing some filing. Eric asked me, "How's De?" Presuming he was referring to my serval son—since he was sitting at my desk where the cat's picture was—I responded, "Oh, bless his heart, he's just fine, thanks. But I've had to start putting him in his cage at night, because he won't let me sleep!"

There was dead silence from Eric. That was strange! I turned back to him, and his jaw was open.

I immediately realized what had gone wrong, and I laughed. "Oh, you mean DeForest!"

Eric nodded.

I laughed, "Oh, my God! He's just fine, too."

Eric said, "This is how rumors get started, you know." We both cracked up.

Several months before filming began on Star Trek V, the Kelleys' Lhasa Apso, by now fourteen years old, began to fail. She was blind in one eye and her coordination was off. De took her to the vet for a check-up and was told that it was simply old age, and that little could be done. Both De and Carolyn knew that it was only a matter of time before she would become so incapacitated that her life would become a burden to her. She had already had accidents in the house, which seemed to upset her very much. Knowing how terribly attached they were to their pets, I wrote them a letter of consolation, hoping to clarify their choices. Their own serenity and stress levels were being affected by Fancy's declining health and abilities; they weren't sleeping well.

Knowing that, I advised them that perhaps it was time to consider having Fancy put to sleep. I told them that I had worked in a veterinary hospital and assured them that her death would be serene and peaceful, especially if De or Carolyn could bring themselves to be with her until she passed, so she would be with a loved one and feel safe. I told them that if that seemed too difficult a task, I would be willing to take Fancy in for them. I had done it for my sister's pet and for other friends' pets, and I would be willing to do it for them, "If the time comes and you think it would be too hard on you to do it. Speak with your vet about it and see what she can suggest or offer."

It wasn't long after that when I received a note from De:

"Dear Kris, Just a note of thanks for your thoughtful letter of 6/5. It was informative as well as heartfelt. We put Fancy down yesterday. I stayed with her and she went peacefully...I felt a deep sense of relief for her. She had lost her hearing and her eyesight and was beginning to lose her dignity. It was time – and we miss her terribly, but we are convinced it was the right thing to do. Our vet agreed. We thank you again for your lovely letter and Carolyn joins me with warm wishes. DeForest"

STAR "WARS" – 1988

When it seemed possible that Star Trek V might proceed without DeForest, due to a salary dispute, I wrote the following poem to try and convince the studio heads that the picture could not possibly fly without De. I didn't tell the Kelleys I was "causing trouble" at the studio, but word got back to them via Richard Arnold. Richard was so tickled with my poem that he called De (not knowing I was the author) and read it to him. De liked it so much that he called Richard back and had him read it again so Carolyn could hear it; then he asked for two copies of it to be sent to him.

FOR FRANK MANCUSO, WILLIAM SHATNER, HARVE BENNETT AND WHOMEVER ELSE IT MAY CONCERN....

STAR TREK V: DEAD OR ALIVE?

You waited a whole YEAR So "Spock" could appear.
You didn't use another actor: It'd have killed the Success Factor.

And we know you wouldn't swap Kirks
We don't believe we're addressing jerks!
So what makes you think you can do without Kelley?
What are you using for brains- sand or jelly?

You want our support and hard-earned money?
You'd better be bringing us DE, then, honey!
You'll ruin our joy and the bottom line
If you don't wake up and pay him to sign.

No one wants STAR TREK to die;
we ALL want to help it fly,
But we have this God-Awful premonition:
Without DeForest Kelley, who will pay the admission???

This is not an idle threat
If Kelley's out, you can take bets:
The show WILL fold, and the only long lines
Will be irate FORMER fans carrying signs!

K.M. Smith

Carolyn dropped me a note that read in part: "Richard called and read us your poem to the studio…very clever. Give handsome Deaken a chin-tickle. I've about worn out his pics, showing them around. 'Bye for now, Carolyn."

THE MOVIE

Not long after De's release from the hospital, the filming for Star Trek V began in Yosemite National Forest. I had written them early on, urging De to back out if he wasn't feeling up to the stress and strain of a motion picture. I was very relieved that De's doctor had given him a clean bill of health and had released him to do the work. I was still nervous, though; it seemed awfully soon to be making action-adventure movies.

I remembered how thin De had looked at the Oakland convention only two months previously, and figured he probably wasn't much better off after surviving a stint in a hospital. I took on a campaign to pack on some pounds, and sent him a huge gift box filled with cheese, candy, and his favorite chocolate. He wrote me a note back: "Cheese, candies and chocolates! You sure know how to make a skinny actor gain weight. (Happily!)"

A day or so later I wrote an Rx: "Carolyn, put a HUGE plate of mashed potatoes in front of that boy—and slap him upside the head if he don't eat every bite!"

While the Kelleys were on location in Yosemite and at Ridgecrest, Carolyn conscientiously sent post cards every few days, updating me on De's whereabouts and health. She was reassuring me that he was just fine. "All's well here – De never felt better, since his surgery, I'm happy to say. He's looking better, too. And all's going well with ST V. Hope you and Deaken are keeping dry. We hear there's rain in the Pacific North-Wet recently. Many, many chin tickles to Deaken!"

When production moved back to Paramount, the letters and notes from Carolyn continued: "De took my collection of Deaken's pictures to the studio this week, to show to a cat-lover there. He nor others who saw them had not even heard of a serval – so they were quite fascinated with his story."

"Our mailbox runneth over! I'm only glad you don't expect answers (except every six months)!"

"You guessed right about De's weight. He hit 135 this week and feels like a million, I'm happy to say."

HOPES AND DREAMS

I had long wanted to work in the entertainment industry as a writer or in some other production capacity. I mentioned this to the Kelleys in mid-summer of 1988 and from then on, Carolyn wrote back, sending newspaper articles touting the salaries that entertainment secretaries were getting at that time, along with other material touting the splendors of Southern California life. Compared with Washington State salaries, the sums seemed truly gargantuan. I hadn't factored in the much higher cost of living in California. Carolyn encouraged me to try and land a job at Paramount and other studios, feeling that once I had my foot in the door I could work up into a creative position if I had the talent, which she and De both felt I had.

Finally, after much thought and encouragement, in the summer of 1989 I took a deep breath and mailed out six résumés and samples of published articles to all the major studios. De had told me to go ahead and use his name as a personal or professional reference. I waited a couple of weeks, and then made a few phone calls, to be sure the material had been received, and to see if there was any interest. Paramount encouraged me to come down and take their typing and other tests, after reviewing the résumé. I quickly called Sue and asked if I could stay at her place. She agreed.

Just before I flew down to take Paramount's battery of pre-employment tests, Carolyn wrote me a long letter. It began: "Is my year up, yet? I wouldn't want to cause you to fall over in a faint by getting too many letters from me…"

It went on at length, chatting about our pets: "I hope Deaken had a wonderful 10th birthday and his fill of lobster. He and we have the same tastes! When we were in Australia (publicizing the last movie) I think we cleaned them out of lobster tails." She continued on about De's busy publicity schedule, and then began to wrap up the two pages: "Kris, we want to wish you much luck on your job-search while here. Know you will have a good time – that seems to be a sure thing for guests of the Keenan Hilton."

I flew to California and Sue drove me to Paramount. I filled out the paperwork, took their battery of tests, and then had a short interview with a personnel representative. By some miracle, I had scored 89 words per minute with zero errors, which I never had before and never will be able to do again. The representative told me that there would be no problem landing a job there. She explained that there were eleven new television pilots being prepared for the upcoming fall season, and felt certain that I would be able to land a spot on any of them. I was elated! I went back to the car with Sue, giving her the good news. I called Mom and Dad and gave them the good news. They were happy for me, but also warned. "Hollywood is a cut-throat, tawdry place. It's unsafe for a single woman."

I dropped the Kelleys a mailgram letting them know about Paramount's interest in me, then flew back home to get ready. Within days, I got a note from Carolyn which read, in part, "We are glad to hear your job-hunt was so successful. We feel the one who gets you will be the lucky one! De says thanks for all your mailgrams and letters. We can't keep up with you! 'Bye for now–Carolyn." She drew a heart next to her name.

Sue Keenan had offered me a place to land when I got there until I scored a job, which I figured would take maybe a week, tops. That left the problem of where to place Deaken while I landed the job. I called a long-time fellow animal crusader, Peter Rasmussen, and told him my tale. He said he knew someone who might be able to board Deaken temporarily. He said he'd call her and get back to me.

A few days later Peter called again and said the lady had agreed to board Deaken. Then he told me who the lady was: actress Tippi Hedren! "She has a wonderful preserve called Shambala. Deaken will be very happy there until you can get him back with you. I can't imagine a better place in all of California for him." Then he told me Tippi would be calling to confirm and get more information from me.

Of course, I knew of Tippi. She had been the star of The Birds and several other notable motion pictures. I was on top of Deaken's 7' high cage removing the roof one afternoon when Mom came out and reported, "You're wanted on the phone."

I said, "I don't want to have to jump down if it isn't important. Can you find out who it is?"

"Sure," she said. Ten seconds later she said, "It's Tippi Hedren."

I leaped off that seven foot roof and ran to the house.

Tippi said she was happy to offer "dear little Deaken" a home until I could land a job and find a land owner in the San Fernando Valley who would allow me to have Deaken there with me. She cautioned me: "That may take a little while, you know. But Deaken will have a home here as long as he needs us. There's no rush, here."

I thanked her profoundly, and then told her I had self-published a book of animal poetry that I would show her. "If you like it, and think it will sell there at Shambala to benefit the animals, I will give you all the copies I have left and you can sell them there for whatever you feel they're worth."

I also promised I'd give her a monthly boarding sum—which was paltry, but all I could truly commit to giving—and that I'd pay for Deaken's food and any veterinary services or inspections he might need. With that verbal agreement, it seemed the way had opened.

I wrote the Kelleys letting them know about Paramount's reaction and their assurances that I could get a job when I got there. Within days, a large package arrived for "D. Smith." I mistakenly thought it was for Mom

(Dorothea) and tossed it into a corner, since she and Dad had taken a trip to Alaska.

A few days later, I spotted the box again and thought, "Mom never orders anything. Maybe she ordered some bulbs for her garden. I'd better check it out; perhaps I should open it." That's when I noticed that the return address read Sherman Oaks, California. We knew no one in Sherman Oaks except the Kelleys. Sure enough, it was their address. With a start, I realized that the package was meant for Deaken Smith!

I raced to the store and bought some film; I'd already made it a habit to document everything about Deaken for the Kelleys. When I got back, I released Deaken from his enclosure and showed him the package. He sniffed it; I took a picture. For some reason he seemed to realize it was for him. Instead of walking away, he began to paw at it; then to drool on the packaging. I documented that. Then I tore off the soggy butcher wrap and pulled the box apart. Inside was something wrapped in tissue paper—something large. I showed Deaken the opened box, and he probed beneath the tissue with a long forepaw, then again rubbed his chin on the gift. I documented that. Finally, I opened the tissue and uncovered an African-print tote bag. Atop the tote bag was a letter.

"Dear Kris,

We hope Deaken will enjoy having his very own travel bag to accommodate all his gear on his trip here. We saw this bag the other day and decided it was just made to be Deaken's luggage.

"Sue sent us the tapes of your Pacific Outdoors show [a program on which I had been interviewed during my stint as an animal welfare activist]. We thought you came across just great, very un-self-conscious camera-wise. Are you sure you don't want to be an actress? I can't remember if I ever told you that we enjoyed the tapes you sent us long ago, with your stand-up routine. Very good! And the shots of Deaken are terrific. Thanks even tho' it's late." "My days lately are taken up with physical therapy visits, all this month, relative to my hip problems, but all will be well one of these days.

"Between you and me, want to tell you that De called _____at Paramount and gave you a boost – but told her, truthfully, that you had no knowledge of the call. Maybe it will help…De says hello and don't forget the chin tickles for dear Deaken. 'Bye – love, Carolyn."

I sent Carolyn a box of pine cones, to give her a little "aromatherapy" during her recuperation. Her response: "The cones are fragrant. You are going to miss all those lovely Northwest smells when you get down here in Smogville, I just wrote Kat a note (she'll faint!) and now I have to get going on an appointment. Love, Carolyn. P.S. Hello from the "other De.""

THE MOVE

My parents, Jack and Dorothea, helped me drive down. I drove my compact car towing a small U-Haul trailer; Mom and Dad drove their pick-up truck and a larger trailer rig that carried Deaken's spacious pen and all his "Deke-cor." As we drove out of the grapevine down the long hill into the Los Angeles basin, smog and an endless landscape of monolithic buildings dotted the far horizon. Mom said, "Are you absolutely sure you want to do this, now?" I reflected on the blue skies and the view from our home in Tacoma. It was suddenly a rather tough decision. I didn't wait long to make it though, because I'm convinced that had I taken more than ten seconds, the folks would have taken the next overpass and turned around, headed for the Northwest.

I told Mom, "Yeah, I'm sure. Mom, it's all I've ever dreamed of doing." I looked again at the smog, and added, "If it takes more than five years, I'll come back."

She said, "Okay. I hope you can hold your breath that long." That's the last we ever spoke of my returning home, until Mom fell ill seven years later.

All the way down from Washington, I had let Deaken out of the car every two or three hours to stretch and relieve himself. Each time, when the rest stop was over, and it was time to put him back into the car, he had balked. He was very, very tired of being confined to a cat carrier for hours on end. He was used to having the complete run of the house. So when we finally reached Shambala, I was as happy as I thought he would be. Finally, a place he could stay with others like himself, for the first time in his life. I thought he'd think he'd died and gone to heaven.

I was wrong.

I had raised Deaken from infancy in a human environment with domestic house cats. I had socialized him and prepared him for a life with raucous, crazy, unpredictable people. I had always prided myself on having raised a completely happy, completely normal, remarkably un-neurotic "serval son." So when I opened the car door and carried him out at Shambala, he took one sniff of the air, heard several lions roaring simultaneously, and pulled me back to the car door, where he banged on it feverishly with his front paw, telling me in no uncertain terms to let him get back in! With a pang, I suddenly realized he probably had no idea he was a cat, let alone a wild cat!

I fell apart. Talk about separation anxiety—I was afraid I had doomed my "baby boy" to a period of distress and anxiety second only to being set loose on the plains of Africa. Deaken knew by instinct that those lions were on the lookout for "serval snacks" and he had no interest whatsoever in remaining within a hundred miles of this place.

When I saw Tippi approaching, I quickly dried my tears and greeted her with a smile.

She said, "Hello, Kris. Welcome. And here's that darling little Deaken." He was, after all, the smallest cat on the place. The others were lions, tigers, leopards, cougars and cheetahs. He looked like a "pocket panther" in comparison.

I confessed, "Darling little Deaken is scared to death."

She said, "Oh, we have a big enclosure for him, blocked off from sight of the other cats. He'll settle in fine."

Reassured, I said, "Okay." Tippi took us to the enclosure. It was six times the size of the one I had brought down, and it was housed mostly inside a shed, with only a few feet of one end sticking out where Deaken could get a glimpse of the other cats.

Tippi said, "When he's all settled in, come up to the house and I'll get his Fish and Game paperwork from you and we'll chat."

I pulled out his rugs, toys, chairs, and other paraphernalia. I wanted to make the new enclosure as much like his old one as possible, so that his own scents would reassure him that he was in the right place.

Tippi told me to feel free to come up as often as I wanted, days, nights, weekends, to reassure Deaken and to do as much for him as I could. She told me I could take him outside the compound on long walks. She told me I could stay there weekends if I so desired, so Deaken would know he was not abandoned. She reassured me he'd settle in quickly.

I said, "I think he already has, pretty much. I put all his familiar stuff in the cage with him. He seems happy now."

Later that day, after I had gone, volunteer Leo Lobsenz went out to see the new serval addition. "Frankly, dear girl," he confessed to me later, "I nearly fell over laughing when I saw his over-stuffed chair, his rug, and his mousy. Where were his television and his refrigerator, I wondered!"

Mom and Dad drove me the rest of the way to LA, fifty miles distant.

Sue greeted us. Later that evening, the phone rang. De and Carolyn were on the line, wanting to know how the trip went. I told them it went fine. Then Carolyn asked what Deaken thought of Shambala.

I started to tell her of his first reaction to hearing the lions roar: "He slapped the car door, wanting to get the hell out of there as fast as we could!"

She burst into tears, crying and crying. I panicked and said, "Oh, but he's okay now, Carolyn! He's fine! Please don't worry!"

She apologized, "Oh, I'm sorry. I just could imagine, that poor sweet cat scared to death!"

I said, "It made me cry, too, but he's okay now, I can assure you, or I wouldn't have left him there!" (As if I had some other choice!)

PARAMOUNT PROBLEMO

I settled in with Sue and then called the studio to report that I had arrived. Ouch! Not one of the eleven pilots had been picked up as a series. The studio had no openings for me! I'd tell you my reaction after I hung up the receiver, but it's unprintable. Then I got scared.

Sue suggested that I call the temporary employment agencies with whose services the studios contracted. I did so and made appointments to take their admissions tests. Passing those, I began to get temporary assignments at Disney, MGM, the Disney Channel, Fox, and other places. But the work wasn't steady. I worked only two or three days most weeks. It was nowhere near enough. My attempts to find a steady job were thwarted. I was temping as much as I could. Jackie Edwards had willed me her job on Bay Watch in order to work on Midnight Caller, since it looked as though Bay Watch would be canceled at the end of the first season (which it was), and she wanted a show on her résumé that would be a step up. I was petrified. I had zero experience in the industry and didn't even know the software they used in their computer systems.

She said, "Don't worry about that; I can teach you in one weekend." She recommended me; her bosses interviewed me, and offered me the spot then and there, asking, "What are your salary requirements?"

I didn't even know what to say!

Jackie said, "What I was getting, of course!"

And so it was. I learned XYWRITE and SCRIPTOR over the weekend and started work the following Monday morning, shaking in my boots.

Bay Watch was canceled a few months later, but not before I managed to make a good impression on the bosses. Both wrote glowing letters of recommendation. I walked across the street with the letters and a résumé in hand to apply at Columbia-Tri-Star Pictures. I interviewed there at Human Resources. Once again, I made a good impression and began working shortly thereafter as a floater. I worked days or weeks at a time in different positions as the needs arose on the lot for the skills I possessed.

Sue assured me I could stay longer than we had originally agreed upon, which gave me a degree of relief, but my chief anxiety was not simply having a place to stay and steady work. My chief concern was getting Deaken off the hill and back with me, where he belonged. In order to accomplish that, I had to have steady work for a period of time so I'd know I was secure and could begin looking for a place in the valley to live, with a landlord who would allow me to keep a wild animal in the back yard. I had all the permits to have him legally, but that was only the first hurdle.

Landlords worry about liability—and how many landlords are going to say "Oh, sure!" to a serval cat?

When I wasn't working steadily, I would drive up to Shambala—a 100 mile journey round trip—to see Deaken and reassure him that he hadn't been abandoned. Every time I drove into the driveway, he'd hear my car with the "satellite dish" ears he sported and he'd cry at the top of his considerable lungs! I've heard that human mothers will leak milk when their babies cry with hunger. I nearly leaked tears every time I heard his plaintive wails for my immediate attention. I couldn't get from the car to his side fast enough! Tippi told me the only time she ever heard him make a sound at all was when he heard my car coming in. I was happy to know he wasn't crying from the time I left until the next time I came. Whenever I'd leave at the end of the visit, Deaken would cry out to me. That's when I'd cry, having to leave him. After several visits, I figured out that if I fed him just as I left, he'd be busy with his meal as I drove off, and then neither he nor I would experience the pain of separation. It worked, thank God.

We existed in this state of limbo for fourteen months. I spent every weekend driving to and from Shambala, and every night hoping that God's divine plan would very soon include the reunion of my unorthodox "family".

During this time, De and Carolyn continued to console me, encourage me, and tell me that I was just one step away from having it made. Each time I got a job, even a long-term temporary one lasting a few months, they would send a card or a plant, congratulating me and the new employer on our mutual good luck. Without their encouragement and help, I would probably not have stayed long enough for anything else to happen.

In April 1990 Carolyn called to tell me that De had called and spoken with Rick Berman, the executive producer of Star Trek: The Next Generation, and had told him about my skills and that I was a friend of his and was looking for a job at Paramount. "Rick told De to have you call him sometime this week and set up an appointment for an interview at Trek." I was beside myself with excitement and trepidation. Nearly unable to speak, I listened as Carolyn coached me: "Be sure you tell Rick you're a friend, not a fan; tell him that you're a friend and that De says you're just the greatest and that you can do everything well!" Then she said to ask for $600 a week. I just about croaked! She said, "If you don't ask, you don't get!"

That weekend, I wrote the Kelleys a note, not totally tongue in cheek and delivered it into their mailbox. In it, I mentioned that if I repudiated the fact that I was a DeForest Kelley fan, Berman would know I was lying, because "there isn't a person on the planet who isn't a DeForest Kelley fan!"

Carolyn responded, apologetic, saying, "I just want to tell you not to worry so much about that interview on Monday, and don't pay any attention to what I said about not saying you're a fan of De's. I shouldn't even have mentioned it."

I said, "A lot of people have mentioned the same thing, about not saying I'm a fan. They're kind of leery about fans working there from what I hear. They're afraid they'll get ———"

"Flakes?" she offered, laughing, quoting my letter.

"Yeah," I said.

"Well, we all know you're not flaky!" she said, and laughed.

I said, "Right!"

She said, "So you just go in there and be yourself and tell 'em you're De's biggest fan! It'll be all right. Everybody's a fan of De's!"

I finally said, "I'm just more nervous over this interview than is normal. I really want to land this job!"

She said, "Then just be yourself. And ask for $600/week!" Then she laughed again.

I said, "That all depends on what the job is. I don't even know that, yet!"

After covering several more, unrelated topics, she finished with, "Well, I just wanted to call and let you know we have our fingers crossed. We'll be thinkin' of you on Monday. Don't worry about a thing. Just treat it as you have all the others and you'll have good luck."

I said, "Thank you so much."

On Monday, I drove to Paramount and entered the Star Trek offices. Berman was busy—a meeting was running overtime—so the receptionist seated me in the hall and I waited 90 minutes. When at last I was ushered into Berman's office, I was flabbergasted when the first thing out of his mouth was, "De Kelley says you're the greatest thing on earth!" I thought, *Well, so much for trying to sell myself!* I blushed, embarrassed, and finally responded, "Well, allowing for a little hyperbole, I hope to prove him right!"

Rick asked me what I wanted to do and I said I'd had experience as a writer's assistant and as a producer's assistant. He said, "Well, I can't hire for my writers or for my other associates, but I'll let them know you're interested, and if they give you a call, come on in and interview with them." I said, "OK. That sounds good." I left the Star Trek offices with high hopes. I felt it was just a matter of time before I'd be helping in some small way to perpetuate the legacy started by Gene Roddenberry and his cast and crew so many years before. Alas! When I did get an offer, the money wasn't adequate to meet my needs.

WALK OF FAME GAMES

In 1989, the Chamber of Commerce had voted to give De a star on the Hollywood Walk of Fame. Paramount Pictures had nominated De for the honor. We were thrilled. Then we waited for what seemed an eternity, and still no announcement as to when the star would be presented.

During this interminable waiting period, De became concerned that perhaps Paramount or the Chamber had dropped the ball. Over the phone he asked me, "Do you think they have forgotten about me?" He sounded serious, so I assured him that couldn't be the case, and called Paramount to find out what the hold-up was. That's when I learned that Paramount was planning to present De's star when the next Star Trek motion picture came out – to help publicize the movie's release! So I called De back and let him know the scoop. He said, with gallows humor, "Lord God Almighty, I hope I live that long!"

I assured him that his longevity shouldn't be a problem, here!

Sue, Kat and I were in Hollywood one day and found a store that would put anyone's name on a Walk of Fame star in their shop and then take a photo of it. We shelled out the money for a DeForest Kelley star and then bought several prints of it. We mailed one in an envelope to De, c/o Carolyn (with a note to Carolyn that read, "You'd better stand behind De when he opens the envelope, in case he faints!").

De opened the envelope, saw the star, and then the attached note: "WE WERE THERE. WHERE WERE YOU?!"

De called us and asked us how we managed the illusion. We explained what we had done, but then Kat took the phone and said, "Actually, De, what we did is we jack-hammered Arnold Schwarzenegger's name out of his star and replaced it with yours! I hope he doesn't get pissed when he finds out, or you could be in big trouble!"

De guffawed at that!

The Christmas following the announcement as to when and where De would receive his star (December 18, 1991, 7021 Hollywood Blvd, in front of the new Galaxy Theatre), Kat's son made both of us jackets to wear to the event. The jackets had marvelous painted portraits of De on the backs, along with the date of De's star ceremony. Kat wrapped mine in a box as a Christmas present and then told De and Carolyn all about it.

That Christmas, I opened the box and flipped when I saw the jacket. I put it on and wore it all day and into the evening. That evening, the Kelleys called to ask how our Christmas had gone; they also, of course, wanted to know what I thought of the De jacket. Carolyn said to me, "I understand you got a rather special gift from Kat this year."

I said, "Oh, yeah! You know about that?"

She said, "We know about it, but you can tell us again."

I said, "It is the most fantastic, beautiful DeForest Kelley Walk of Fame jacket in the universe! I haven't had it off all day! I wear it all the time! Oh….I suppose Sue will make me take it off when I go to bed tonight, though."

Out of the blue, Carolyn chimed in, joking, "Oh – so you want to sleep with my old man, eh?" I could hear both of them (De was on another extension line at their house) guffaw! De's laugh sounded very surprised and a little embarrassed, and I became speechless with embarrassment. But only for a moment, thank God!

Inspiration struck, and as they came down from their laughs, I retorted: "Well, safe sex IS best, you know!"

From that moment on, my Walk of Fame jacket became The Safe Sex Jacket to everyone who knew about the conversation!

I sent De and Carolyn star paperweights. One had "Carolyn" on it; the other had "DeForest." Carolyn opened hers early and then wouldn't allow De to open his until Thanksgiving. When he saw it, he called to thank me and then said, "Good! Now that I have this star, I don't have to worry about that f——n' star in Hollywood!" It was the first time he had ever "talked dirty" within earshot of me and I laughed!

HOUSE HUNTING – KELLEY STYLE

As a temporary, I was gaining recognition and a good reputation and feeling that almost any time now I could consider myself permanently employed and start looking for an understanding, wildlife-loving landlord who would allow me to move in with an African serval cat. As soon as I reported to the Kelleys that I was feeling pretty secure and that I'd be able to get a rental now and bring Deaken home off the hill, they pitched in. They reviewed classified ads and called me often to report on places they had found that looked like good candidates. They suggested areas of the valley to search. They even called a Realtor friend and asked her to lend a hand.

Before long, another call came in from Carolyn. She just had to tell me a story: De had found a place where I could have Deaken. She told me that he had been driving around and had spotted this nice house not far from them.

She continued, "So he stopped in there. The landlord happened to be there at the time, painting, so De stopped in. The landlord recognized De right away, and De told him he had a lady friend who needed to rent a home with a nice, high wall fence, and this place seemed to be a good candidate. So then De told him, 'The only problem is that she has a cat.' The fellow said, 'Oh, Mr. Kelley, a cat is fine; a cat is no problem.' So then De said, 'Well, it's a rather large cat,' and the fellow joked to him, 'As long as it's no bigger than a lion, I have no problem with it,' and De said, 'Oh, no! It's no bigger than a lion!'"

"So here's the address; you go on over there and introduce yourself and tell him that you're the girl De told him about."

She gave me the address and then I asked what the rental price was. She said, "$1350 a month."

I just about croaked. "Oh, Lord! That's way out of my league, Carolyn!"

"It is?"

"Heavens, yes."

"What do you want to spend?"

"550-600 a month, unless I find a co-renter."

That didn't end their search. I'd be sitting at work and the phone would ring, and it would be Carolyn:

"We drove around a little bit this afternoon, looking at rentals in your price range." I was speechless.

"My hip is hurting me, so I couldn't get out of the car, but De knocked on a few doors and we have a few addresses we think you should look at!"

I could just imagine the looks on the faces of the people who had opened the doors after hearing De's knock. I wondered if any of them had passed out.

I confessed to the Kelleys that I felt I should wait until I had such an established record in the industry that there was no way I would ever lose my job.

De advised me, "The entertainment industry is probably the most insecure place there is to work. You'll never be able to count on it absolutely. You just have to proceed on faith. And we want you to get Deaken back home where he belongs."

So did I. So did I.

I found three possible roommate candidates, but one by one, they didn't pan out. I was becoming morose. I was feeling like a rotten Mom-cat. I was even considering giving up the dream and returning home to Washington, but the Kelleys wouldn't hear of it. They just knew I'd be a big success as soon as I'd had my break. But waiting for my break was breaking my heart...

THE KELLEYS MEET DEAKEN

After seven months of waiting for me to get Deaken off the hill and into their valley without success, the Kelleys could wait no more. Carolyn called and said she and De would like to take a drive up to Shambala and meet Deaken. She asked if Sue and I would drive them there. I said, "Certainly!"

She said, "Oh, good!" We decided on a day. Then Carolyn said, "So, we'll see you here at the house at—oh, how about 9:30?"

I said, "Sure. You'll have to give us directions."

She was astonished by that. "You have our address!" she exclaimed.

"Yes, I know," I said, "But neither of us has ever been by there."

She said, "You're joking!"

"No, I'm not." She couldn't believe that we hadn't driven by to sneak a peek at their home.

I said, "We're not voyeurs, Carolyn!"

"Oh!"

Excited and a bit rattled, Sue and I wondered which car to use. To us, my ten year old compact car didn't seem adequate for the occasion, while Sue was concerned that her larger, classic beauty might not have the gumption to get up the mountain. Sue called Jackie Edwards and asked if we could use her new Hyundai for the occasion. Jackie was more than happy to oblige.

So, on the Big Day, Sue and I drove to the Kelley's house. We had no sooner pulled up than De and Carolyn came out the door, grinning, looking like two kids on their way to a candy store! Sue was in the driver's seat, and I figured De would join her in the front seat, and that Carolyn would join me in the back. I was wrong. De suggested that Carolyn ride up front with Sue, which she did. De climbed in the back with me. My favorite actor in the rear seat with me in a small vehicle.

We put our seat belts on, and Sue started to back out of the driveway. De surprised me by grabbing my knee and grinning, "Hi, Kris! How ya doin'?" I nearly jumped out of my skin—and he could tell! I was so embarrassed—and so was he.

I stuttered, "Aw…fine. I guess! Thanks!"

Almost as soon as we got on the freeway, an inattentive driver came over into our lane without looking and just about wiped us out. Carolyn and I both saw the impending crash. Carolyn raised one leg to cushion the impact and I yelled, "Oh, God! Look out!" Fortunately, Sue quickly got us out of harm's way, with only inches to spare. The driver continued on, blithely unaware that he had come *this close* to taking out one of the Big Three of Star Trek! No sooner had Sue avoided the collision when De commended her, saying, "Great driving, Sue! Sure am glad we didn't dent Jackie's new car." Of course, the thought running through our minds, Sue's and mine, was, "Thank God the world wouldn't be reading about a very tragic accident on the highway!"

The rest of the trip was happy. De told us about revisiting his boyhood home in Conyers, Georgia about twenty years previously, trying to locate a black woman whose son he had grown up with. "He was one of my closest chums," he told us. "I found the family's home. They had lived on a street, I'll never forget it: the street name was Needmore Street, and was it aptly named. These people were so poor. I found the home, and knocked on the door, and an old woman came out. I asked her if she had any idea where Emma Banks might be. She told me, 'I saw her only a few years ago...Three or four, I think. She was very old, was in a rollin' chair...'" De said he had done several interviews in the area at the time touting Star Trek. At the conclusion of each interview he had asked anyone with knowledge of Emma Banks' whereabouts to call the radio or television station and provide an address or a phone number where he could reach her.

"Unfortunately, nothing came of it. I would have liked to do a little something for her." What a thoughtful man.

When we arrived at Shambala, we got out of the car and De noticed the back of my DeForest Kelley Hollywood Walk of Fame jacket, which I planned to wear at his star ceremony. This was his first opportunity to see it since I had received it from a fellow Kelley fan. De queried humorously, "Who's that handsome fellow on your back?"

I said, "Oh, some guy...I forget his name."

I directed everyone to remain very quiet outside Deaken's enclosure while I went inside to greet him, so they could see how we responded to each other without his being aware there would soon be other people entering his domain. I stepped inside the cage and greeted him, leaving the cage door open. He was sitting high atop his 5' tall den box, and when I hopped up to sit beside him, he greeted me with the customary mew and purrs and enthusiastic head rubs, then started watching the cage door, knowing that something was up. He continued to purr and head-rub, so I invited Carolyn in first. She was halfway in already: I thought that to delay her long-awaited meeting any longer might be detrimental to her health!

Carolyn came in, grinning ear to ear, and approached him. I told Deke, "This is Car'wyn, sweetness...the lady who sends you all those chin-tickles." I'm sure Deaken didn't understand a word, but he instinctively understood the love she was telegraphing to him and the fearlessness with which she approached him. He continued to purr as she came right up to him. He kissed her hand several times, and then rubbed his chin on the back of her fingers. She was in seventh heaven.

I jumped down from the den box and had Carolyn stand next to him so I could get a few photos of them together. After the photos, Deaken started looking outside the open door for other visitors, and saw Sue and De standing there. A little growl rose in his throat, but nothing outrageous; he continued to purr in between little growls. Carolyn and I patted him and tickled him some more, and then Carolyn said, "De, come on in and meet him."

Deaken let De come near, but hissed and mumbled, so De stepped back and said, "He's nervous, and I don't want to push him to do anything he doesn't want to do."

I said, "Let me carry him out of his own territory so he won't be so protective of it." I wasn't sure that was the problem.

I leashed Deaken and walked him outside the compound gates, to areas where we often played, turning him loose in the elephant straw pile. He immediately settled in to roll and play in the stuff, which everyone enjoyed watching. He still wasn't amenable to having so many people near him all at once—one of whom was male, tall, and undoubtedly "a veterinarian with a big needle" in Deke's mind—so we just watched him play for a time from a relative distance.

After a while, I positioned everyone near Deaken and took a few group shots of the occasion. Deaken kept facing away from the camera, so occasionally I'd call, "De!" in a high-pitched, serval-like chirp, which was my way of getting his attention. Well, it surprised me when DeForest stopped watching Deaken and looked in my direction.

I laughed heartily and then clarified, "When I chirp 'De', that's for Deaken. When I say—and here I assumed as masculine a voice as I could— 'De', that's your cue."

De grinned and nodded, but forgot the next time I chirped, "De!" I laughed and faux scowled. De said, "OK, I'll try to forget that I've always been De, too!"

I said, "It should be easier for you than for a cat!" It wasn't.

I was delighted that Deaken was being civil and loving to the Kelley who most wanted to meet him "up close and purrsonal"—Carolyn—or this entire first visit would have been a fiasco. Deaken just wasn't into being a celebrity that day. But he did cope.

After the photo session in the straw pile, I put Deke away and said I'd take the gang on a trip through the compound. I directed Sue to drive to the first compound gate. "I'll be the gatekeeper all the way through," I told her. "Any time we come to a gate, I'll jump out and open it." Sue drove to the first gate and as soon as I opened it, she drove through and kept going!

65

I called out, "Hey! Wait for me!" and ran after it and thumped on the trunk to get Sue to brake so I could get back into the car. I opened the back door to get in; De was grinning ear to ear.

Sue said, "It was his idea. He told me to drive away and leave you wondering!"

I threw a scowl at him. We proceeded to the next gate—and it happened again! De thought it was great sport. Now I knew why Rory Calhoun called him "a little shit"—what a prankster!

We finally got a complete tour, although I was quite out of breath from chasing the car down that was supposed to be transporting all of us. I told them I'd go get Deaken again and we could sit by the lake for a spell and relax.

I walked to Deaken's cage and picked him up, then carried him back to the lake area. When De saw me packing a 35 pound serval over my shoulder, he joked, "Is that how Deke gets his exercise? No wonder he's having a tough time losing weight!"

I explained to De that Deke didn't enjoy walking around in "lion country" because the king of beasts views serval as snacks, "and Deaken knows that somehow." Carolyn was completely enamored of Deke and stayed right near him while Sue and De walked around to view the lions, tigers, and cougars. She couldn't keep her eyes off him.

Shortly after we settled at the lake to take some photos of De with Deaken, Tippi came out to greet us. I introduced everyone and they had a pleasant conversation. Tippi invited them back on a Shambala weekend, a weekend that would be open to the public. When the morning was over I put Deaken away and we headed back to Los Angeles. As Sue drove back, De said he and Carolyn would take us to Hamburger Hamlet in Van Nuys for lunch.

The meal was wonderful. I was famished after having chased the car and carried big boy three-legged Deaken around half of the morning. I'm embarrassed to say I wolfed down the food in such short order that I was finished almost before the rest of the party had buttered their toast.

Carolyn looked over and spotted my empty plate and exclaimed, in true amazement, "Goodness!"

De noticed too, grinned, and then joked, "Well, carryin' around a serval cat all morning makes a girl hungry!"

Since I couldn't melt and fall underneath the table, I just turned beet red and endured the razzing.

De said he'd like us to meet Myrtle, the Kelleys' octogenarian desert tortoise, when we got back to their house. Sue and I were tickled pink to be invited to do that.

As we got out of the car at their home De—behaving like a gentleman—picked up my jacket and Sue's purse, hidden within the jacket—from the back seat. Sue headed to the rear seat to fetch her purse. No purse. I opened my mouth to reassure Sue but De gave me a look that could kill which indicated, "Keep your mouth shut." I hated to do that, knowing what a trauma it is for a lady to lose her purse, but complied. Sue looked on the back seat, then on the floorboards—I was agonizing for her—while De looked on, oh so sympathetically. Sue began to get a little nervous, then stepped backward and noticed that De had my jacket in his hand. She regarded his face for a moment; he was innocent as a lamb, and concerned for her loss. Finally, Sue looked at me. I wasn't concealing the joke very well, I'm afraid, so she figured it out and grabbed at De's handful of goods, saying, "You tacky actor!" The gig was up, he was busted but delighted that he had pulled one over on Sue, too.

We went inside the house and then out to the back yard. De found Myrtle in the shrubbery and carried her back to a spot on the lawn; Carolyn arrived with an already-prepared "Waldorf" for Myrtle. Sue and I got on the ground to meet Myrtle face to face and to watch her eat. De decided to join us on the ground, so I quickly grabbed my camera and took some shots of Myrtle, Sue and De. When Sue saw what I was doing, she muttered, "I hate having my picture taken." De dead- panned, "So do I." I laughed and got Sue's reaction shot; it became one of her favorites.

Carolyn gave us a tour of the house and then Sue and I took turns having our pictures taken with De and Carolyn. Sue wasn't certain how to operate my camera, so I gave her a little instruction while tucked arm-in-arm with De.

I held up a forefinger vertically and told Sue, "Just focus on my finger. When it looks like a clear shot, we'll be clear, too."

She focused and then said, "I think I'm ready."

Then I said, "Oh, what am I saying?! Don't focus on this (my finger), focus on this!"—and I pointed to De! De grinned at me with such love and pleasure that Sue said, "I snapped the shot. I wasn't going to lose that look on his face!" The photo turned out beautifully.

De then said he wanted to pick a few lemons from their lemon tree for us, so he proceeded to do that. He picked an entire large grocery sack full and then said he'd carry it to the car for us. Good thing. It could have given Sue a hernia. It weighed in at nearly twice Deaken's weight!
Carolyn was radiant at visit's end. She had been the one drooled over by Deaken that day and I'm not sure I ever saw her as overjoyed again in all the years I knew her after that—except when she was with Deaken on a few more occasions.

Seattle Convention - 1990

In September 1990, I flew back to Seattle for a visit with some of my family and a few friends, whom I hadn't seen in nearly a year, at the same time De was scheduled to appear at a convention there. I contacted my friends and family and let them know I'd be arriving and said I hoped they'd all want to take advantage of this opportunity to see De on stage.

My sister, Jackie, and her son, "little" Philip, now age 15, 6' tall and nearly 200 pounds jumped at the chance; Mom and Dad were out of the area on their way down to Southern California to see me at the tail-end of their trip, and couldn't be there.

Melody Adams, with whom I'd worked in Tacoma at the continuing education school, and her daughter and son-in-law, Johnni and Gerald White, were also eager to see De and me. All three were big Trek fans and had never seen De in person before. Also in attendance was Edward Smith (no relation), with whom I had worked at a wildcat sanctuary several years before. He shared his life with a lion so we were still in touch and exchanging "lion son/serval son adventures," the way two doting parents often do.

Just about the first thing out of De's mouth when he got on stage the first day of the convention was the story about how he had met me in Wenatchee. He said that since that day I had become a successful freelance writer and that I had recently moved from Tacoma to Hollywood "with all the animals" to see if I could carry my writing career even further. The audience applauded and roared their approval. Then he motioned to me to come onto the stage. I was speechless and became almost weak-kneed. I gave him a kiss and wrapped my arm around him, mostly to keep myself upright in front of all those fans, who continued to clap and make a big to-do over someone most didn't even know.

As the crowd quieted, De asked me, "You were just in Los Angeles a few weeks ago at a con I was at, weren't you?"

I nodded my head.

"And now you're here."

I nodded again. The crowd started to clap and cheer again, so I said to De quietly, "I'm still following you around [meaning 'since 1968']."

When the crowd was quiet again, De repeated, "She's still following me around! I can't shake her!" Then he insinuated, "She has something on me; that's why I have to introduce her." My mouth flew open with shock and surprise as he uttered this spectacular verbal intrigue, because it was utter nonsense and he grinned broadly.

I knew I had the perfect opportunity to say something nice about De to the people gathered there, but I was profoundly speechless and couldn't say a blasted thing. It was a thrilling moment for me, but also embarrassing.

While he read one of his Trek poems that day, I went to the back of the room to sit with Carolyn. She said, "I want you to know we called Deaken just before we left there and he said to tell you it was all right for you to be up here this weekend, instead of with him." That was so sweet, because they knew I was feeling real guilt over being away from him for eight straight days, which was unheard of and unforgivable in my own personal Book of Sins.

I told her, "Thank you. I'm sure glad you asked him. If I had been the one to ask, he would have told me no."

Carolyn noticed that the convention's owners and promoters were hanging out at the registration table, and asked if I knew them. I said I knew them a little—knew them by sight, mainly. So Carolyn introduced me to the woman first, asking her if she knew me. The woman smiled and said that she'd seen me at a few of their conventions—any convention De was at.

Then Carolyn asked the fellow if he knew me, and he said, "Oh, yes! Of course I know Kris! I've known her for years!"

That was news to me! Either I was known in fandom before I was aware of it, or exaggeration ran rampant for that moment. I'm not sure which.

Carolyn asked when Sue and I would be flying home after OktoberTrek, the next convention, and I told her. I also told her that Kerstin Dartsch, from the former East Germany, would be coming to L.A. with us from the Oktobertrek function. Kerstin had been writing to the Kelleys for about six years, and since the Berlin Wall had finally come down, this was her first opportunity to see De in the flesh, and she was looking forward to it. Carolyn was happy to hear that Kerstin would be able to get to the Baltimore convention and then to L.A. afterwards.

At that point, De was finishing his poem, so Carolyn turned to head back to her seat. She said, "Let's get back in there and sit down," indicating that she expected me to go in and sit with her.

I stopped and said, "Uh...Carolyn?"

She turned back.

I said, "I think I'd better go back and sit with my friends and family from here—if that's okay with you."

She nodded; she understood.

The next day when I got to the con, the convention owner came over and said, "Carolyn told me to take good care of you."

I joked, "What does she mean by that? Hire a hit man?"

Very sincerely, the woman responded, "Oh, no! The Kelleys are very fond of you. Don't you know that?"

I didn't know how to respond to that, so said nothing.

She added, "We had dinner with them last night and we all talked about you. The Kelleys think you're going to be famous."

I flushed bright red and said, "Well…wow…I hope I don't disappoint them."

She said, "Oh, you won't. We feel the same way."

I was shaken by her information—in a good way, of course—but still it seemed a leap of faith to truly believe she had heard all of that from the Kelleys. I wondered how I had become so lucky.

After a while, Carolyn came up and stood in the doorway until I spotted her, which didn't take long. She motioned to me to come over. As I reached her, she was responding to a question I hadn't heard, from a young fan. She was saying, "I married him before he became a movie star."

She looked at me after answering the fan and as he walked off; I just shrugged and gave her a big hug. Then she hugged me and said, "OK, now skedaddle back to your seat!"

She could tell I was amidst lots of friends and family that day. I said, "I love you!"

She said, "I love you, too, Kris."

OKTOBERTREK SHENANIGANS

OktoberTrek in 1990 was long anticipated. Anticipated with a certain degree of trepidation, it's true, because Sue Keenan and Sandy Zier had conspired with the Kelleys over Something Evil. Kat and I didn't know just what it was; all we knew was that it had arrived in a box from De and Carolyn to Sue. And Sue had told us it was alive. There were holes in it. It was for Kat and me, but was kept carefully secured by Sue "until OktoberTrek". She would let us gently (because it was "alive") shake and rattle the box, but not a word slipped from her lips as to what it was. Kat and I were nervous – with a Capital N!

Sue was Getting Even for all the grief our shenanigans had caused her in the past. She had even led a Boy Scout (De) astray (not to mention the hotel staff itself, as we later found out). This did not bode well for our reputations.

Upon arriving at the Hunt Marriot Valley Inn convention hotel, Kat and I checked in. Kat had been waiting for seven hours to check in, but the staff kept apologizing and telling her that the room wasn't ready yet.

We finally got up to the room and found that Sandy and Sue had DE-corated (more like DE-stroyed) our room with more than 700 balloons and Disaster Area streamers. We were in shock! Kat kiddingly slammed the hotel staff man up against the wall and shrieked, "So, this is why you kept me waiting for seven hours?" The fellow apologized profusely and got a hug and an "It's okay," in response.

After we "sorta" cleaned up the room (shoved all the balloons into one corner so we could find the beds), we went to Sue's room and found her hiding beside her bed. She thought we had already seen it (the long-anticipated "got'cha"). No, the balloons and the streamers were not it. There was more. We decided we'd better go back and check things out more thoroughly.

Short-sheeted? No.

More balloons in the closet? No.

Cellophaned toilet? No.

What we eventually found was "Bones" (an inflatable skeleton) luxuriating in a bathtub that was more than half-filled with shaving cream (30+ cans of shaving cream!)

The shaving cream was the '**it**' on which Sue and De had done their research. She had written him of her plans for our bathtub, but had said that she didn't know how long shaving cream would last after it was out of the can, so De had taken it upon himself to test its durability in a dish near his bathroom sink at home. That's why he had told her "it's still alive," and what Kat and I had been scratching our heads over for 3 ½ months! The box Carolyn had sent to Sue was actually a decoy: It was empty except for some excelsior shavings; she had sent it just to add additional mystery and intrigue to Sue's plan.

Well! We took many photos of "Bones" enjoying his bath – and many more photos of Kat and I enjoying "Bones" -- and we had the photos developed the next day at a mall across the street. While we waited for the photos, we took a walk in the mall and discovered an insulation display with two, two-foot-tall mounds of what looked exactly like shaving cream! We wanted them, needless to say, for a get even got'cha in response to Sue's got'cha. Kat called the insulation firm (since no one was manning the booth) and explained why we needed the cone insulation so desperately. The owner of the firm chuckled and gave us permission to take them.

We took one of them to Sue's room in a black plastic garbage bag. Jackie Edwards (Sue's roommate for the weekend) gave us the key to the room after we cleared the joke with her, so we broke in – only to find Sue sitting there! Yikes!

Sue looked at the large garbage bag and asked, "What's that? And how did you get in here?"

"Oh, this?" I said, lifting the bag. "It's nothing, really. Just a little token of our affection for you. See you later!" I turned to leave, bag still in hand.

"Get back in here."

"Yes, ma'am," I said, and returned. Kat was still standing in the hallway, not knowing whether to flee or support me.

"What's in the bag?"

"You wanna know what's in the bag."

"Yes."

"OK. Go into the bathroom for about 30 seconds and we'll show you."

Sue looked dubious.

"Who gave you the keys to this room?"

"Jackie."

"Jackie?"

"Yeah. So you know that what's in the bag isn't harmful or trashy. You'll like it."

"O.K.," she finally decided, and stepped into the bathroom.

I closed the bathroom door and put the "shaving cream" insulation cone near it, then made a sound as if I was spraying something out of a can. I "sprayed and sprayed" for a good thirty seconds. Sue could hear me.

"Kris? Kris! What are you doing? Is that silly string? You'd better not be doing anything to the room that will damage it!"

I continued to "spray." Finally, she couldn't stand it any longer and burst out of the bathroom. The look on her face indicated that she was -- livid. If looks could kill….

She looked at the pile of "shaving cream" and hissed, "I hope you put something underneath that."

"No," I said breezily. "Shaving cream can't hurt the rug – can it?"

I could see her thinking, "They've really done it this time. They've damaged hotel property. They've gone over the edge and betrayed good sense and common courtesy." She was speechless, but it was evident that we had crossed the line as far as she was concerned.

I couldn't take it anymore. I smiled and said, "Sue – relax." I leaned over and lightly kicked the cone of insulation; it moved over about two inches.

Sue cracked up. The relief on her face was evident. She loved it!

She said, "I should've known it was fake. It would've taken three or four cans of shaving cream to make that big a mess!" (She'd had experience in that area. Her thumb still hurt from filling our tub with the stuff.)

We hugged her and left, then went to our room with Reggie Holloway from Turlock, California and began to prepare for out next got'cha for De and Carolyn. We prepared a ransom note by cutting out words from a newspaper. We took one of the "Bones-the-inflatable-skeleton in Bed with Kris" photos (from Sue's got'cha in the bathtub) and attached it to the ransom note which read, "SEND US $50,000 IN UNMARKED BILLS OR THESE INCRIMINATING PHOTOS WILL BE TURNED OVER TO THE NATIONAL ENQUIRER!" Another "Bones and Kat" photo showed "Bones" sitting up in bed and smoking a cigarette with Kat in the background on the bed looking exhausted, exhilarated and ecstatic. The caption on that one read, "WAS IT AS GOOD FOR YOU AND IT WAS FOR ME?" Other photos showed "Bones" dancing with Kat, sitting on a table near the balloon pile, etc. We put 'em all in a manila envelope and asked Sandy to deliver them to the Kelleys the next time she drove over to their hotel.

She also had our "Pachyderm Poo Plaque" to deliver. Kat and I had made two shellacked plaques – one for Sue, one for the Kelleys (whom we considered partners in crime over the 3 ½ month long nervous mystery). Both had an enormous elephant dropping on them, borrowed from the dung pile up at Shambala, and both had an engraved brass metal plate, as well, which read, "THANK YOU FOR PUTTING UP WITH ALL OUR SHIT." Atop the pachyderm poo we cemented two little love bugs, and they had little placards, containing songs:

De's and Carolyn's Song

We love you, D&C
Oh yes we "doo"
We don't love anyone
As much as you
Sometimes it's hard to tell
That's true –
But D&C we love you!

Sue's Song

We love you Sue Keenan
Oh yes we "doo"
We try so hard to prove
This fact to you
But we are sure you know
It's true
Oh Sue Keenan we love you!

UNDERNEATH the plaque, we affixed a "contents" label:
Contents: 100% Pure Pachyderm Poop
Compliments of Shambala Preserve(d)

Sue received her "award" Thursday night. The Kelleys' was delivered to them on Friday. The "ransom note" and photos were delivered on Saturday.

Friday night I presented my comedy routine once again. It went well.

We spent Saturday waiting all day for De to appear on stage at 5:30 P.M. We did a lot of laughing and visiting with DKFC members and friends and also visited the Dealer's Room.

By this time, we had met Kerstin Dartsch (from what was formerly East Germany), and I had become family to Kat's friends, Ruth and Cosby, so we were all hanging out together in front row seats: Kerstin, Reggie, Ruth, Cosby, Marcia Coates…(We'd earned the front row seats by lining up for them as early as 3:30 A.M.)

As the time approached for De's appearance, those members who had not seen De live before were fit to be tied. Ruth and Kerstin were beside themselves with anticipation. Ruth had a chocolate cowboy that she wanted to present to him, and wasn't sure she'd have the guts. (She did, eventually.)

De came on-stage to thunderous applause and a standing ovation – which was typical of his fans' reaction. He was in a fantastic mood – for some reason, even more fantastic than usual. (That should have been a tip-off, but we're naïve.) He didn't seem at all nervous, and he razzed Kat and me unmercifully from the stage.

His introduction of us actually started out very sweetly – but quickly DE-evolved. An unknown fan raised her hand and told De, "I have something for you." De responded: "You have something for me? Come on up here." As she delivered the wrapped package into his hands, he smiled at her and said, "Thank you very much. I'll open it later, if that's all right with you?" The girl nodded her consent.

Then De went on: "I hope your gift is as interesting as what a couple of people that really deserve mention…Kris Smith…and another one is Kat Lane…They have been assisting Sue Keenan, my fan club president here, and contributing to their fan book which comes out periodically…and Kris and Kat presented me with a lovely gift this afternoon before I came. Kris has a very beautiful animal that she keeps at Shambala, which is a lion preserve. She has a beautiful serval and we were out there to see Deke…that's the serval's name. And animals are strange. Deke loves to roll in elephant dung. I know there is some joking going on in this group, and I opened this present today and here was a petrified pile, elephant dung, mounted on a lovely plaque with two weird shellacked love bugs, and it said, 'We love you…we doo doo doo.' Thanks, girls! I really appreciated it!"

De brought Kerstin Dartsch up on the stage and introduced her as his little East German friend who had recently "been set free from her cage." Kerstin got a rousing ovation and lots of cheering. De told her he enjoyed her letters and the pictures of her pets. He asked her a question, but she was so stunned by the focus on her, and so afraid to try to speak English (which she had taught herself) that she wasn't able to say much, beyond, "Thank you so much!"

Later the same day, there was a bit of confusion about the speaker that had been placed on the stage so that the entire audience could hear the questions that were being asked before they heard De's response. De took full advantage of the weird set-up by pretending he didn't know what the heck was going on long after he had figured it out. (He pretended he didn't know where the questioner was standing, and kept talking to the sound system speaker.) As it got crazier and funnier, De turned in mock exasperation and said, "Boy, this is a crazy bunch. Kris, you certainly have found the right crowd!"

After De's Saturday appearance, Kat and I had to escort two happily tearful fans to their rooms: Ruth and Kerstin. It was wonderful.

Following that, the DKFC auction began, with all proceeds to benefit De's favorite charity, the North Shore Animal League. We were into the 15th or 16th item up for bid when Sandy opened the door and asked Sue,

"Is it all right if I bring two members with me who aren't pre-registered?" Sue said, "Sure…" and in walked De and Carolyn. Everybody gasped and stood up but, out of respect, no one stepped forward; they just all applauded and then sat down again. Two DKFC members relinquished their chairs to the Kelleys and sat on the floor at their feet. De said he wanted to stop by for a moment to thank Sue and everyone for their support and love all through the years.

After a short time, De suggested that all of the members introduce themselves and say from whence they came. The members did so, and if De had been in their areas of the country or world, he remembered and mentioned the specifics. He had a great memory for detail as everyone found out, even recalling who had asked which questions during his appearance earlier in the evening.

After the Kelleys left, folks swooned for a while, saying how nice the Kelleys were. Then the auction resumed, and $2,500 was raised for North Shore. The party lasted to the wee hours of the morning, so I got only two hours of sleep.

During the party, Sandy left to take De and Carolyn back to their hotel. Then, unbeknownst to me, she got back into our room and trashed it again! She put a little "Bones" on the bed wrapped around a shaving cream can and left shaving cream footprints leading from the bathtub to the bed. In the bathtub, she had sprayed the words "IT WAS HERE." She put more streamers – and toilet paper – all over the room. I invited the party guests in to see the old trashed room, and walked in on the new trashed room. Sue and Sandy were hysterical over that!

The next day we got in line for De's final OktoberTrek appearance, claimed front row seats, and then took turns having breakfast in the hotel restaurant while others saved our seats.

De appeared at 4:30 PM and once again had to bring up the pachyderm poop plaques! (Kat and I were afraid some reverent Trekker might take us out behind the hotel and lynch us afterward, so we really wished he hadn't brought that particular got'cha to public attention!)

We had carried huge yellow fans to the convention, which Kat had designed to read DE KELLEY FAN when opened. When De saw those fans, he got a big kick out of them and had us turn around to show the rest of the audience what was on them. Then he said, "That's some bunch of fans I've got. You all see that? That's the same smart ass group that presented me with that petrified…I told you about that yesterday. Elephant dung. It's an inside joke, but now that it's outside, I was thinking about it and I know why they did that. They know the story. A number of years ago I was doing a Western with Rory Calhoun, and Rory is a prankster. He's always doing devilish things like pretending to sneeze behind your back while dipping his fingers in a cup of coffee and then flinging it on the back of your neck…that sort of thing. So one day we were sitting outside and it was very cold. It was in the winter. We were shooting on location and we all had these little canvas dressing rooms that they had thrown up…put electric heaters in all of them for us. But, I was sitting outside on my chair, and Rory is walking by with Chill Wills…so he feigns tripping over my legs and spills coffee all over me 'accidentally.' I thought I'd had just about enough of that, and I noticed that one of the men, who took care of the horses, was walking around cleaning up the horse manure. So I asked him if he would do me a favor and take a shovel of that fresh manure and put it in Rory's dressing room. So he did – and I went with him, of course, you know…He put it in Rory's dressing room and I had him place it inside this little bitty closet. I turned the electric heater on it. True story!" The audience was in stitches by now. "Rory had to appear that night on the Art Linkletter Show and had this beautiful sport coat and flannel slacks hanging in that closet. So, I checked first with the Assistant Director, and asked him, 'Am I still getting off early this afternoon?' He said, 'Yes,' so I left!"

"The next morning I was doing a fight scene in a corral and Rory came in. He was a big strapping guy, ya know? He came in and he jumped over that corral and he grabbed me…and he shook me, and he said, 'You little shit!'

"But he never played another trick on me!

"So I know the reason for that little joke you gals played on me!"

Later during De's appearance, a fan asked him to describe a typical week in his life, and he said, "Well, the first thing every single morning is I sit down and read my daily letters from two of my fans sitting here in this room…" He indicated Kat and me. We blushed over his slight exaggeration.

Following De's appearance, Kat and I were invited up to Sue's room for drinks and conversation with De and Carolyn and Sandy. We talked for what seemed like an hour and then Kerstin, from Germany, came in to thank Sue for such a wonderful weekend. She was stunned to find the Kelleys there, and apologized for her intrusion, then attempted to leave. De and Carolyn both said, "No, don't go!" The Kelleys discussed with Kerstin the positive changes in her life she would experience now that the Berlin Wall was down and Germany was reunited once more. It was poignant. I nearly cried.

Not long after, the entire gang went to our room to show the Kelleys our balloon corner. On the way down the hall to our room, De told Kat that now that I was back in the motion picture industry (working at Columbia Tri-Star, later Sony Pictures Entertainment) and "on my way" there would be a lot of changes. Kat responded that she worried that I wouldn't have time for her anymore. I turned around and said, "You don't have to worry about that." De continued: "In a few years, Kris will probably be the head of a studio." I turned around again. "Oh, right!" Unfortunately, De looked very serious about that! I again noticed how his dreams for me were much grander than mine were for myself.

We had our pictures taken at our room, visited a bit more, and then the Kelleys departed.

Not long after the convention, Carolyn sent to me (at the studio) a congratulatory note and a photo of De in a large manila envelope telling me how lucky the studio was to have me. Attached to the back of the envelope was a sticker showing a character running wildly, as though frantic. The sticker read, "You gonna write -- or shall I sell my mailbox?" Apparently I had dropped the ball and hadn't written them in three or four days!

MORE HOUSE-HUNTING – KELLEY-STYLE

After having met Deaken and seeing the relationship he and I had—which was wonderful and trusting beyond belief—the Kelleys decided that he and I just had to get back together under the same roof as soon as possible. I had by this time established a good reputation at the motion picture and television studio, but I did not by any means feel completely secure in it. It was again in a position as a floater, and I didn't work steadily. I was getting great reviews from every person I worked for, though, and the Kelleys felt certain that I would have a job at that studio just as long as I wanted one.

They again began to look for places to rent. They found one in the newspaper in Encino, drove by it, and then called to tell me about it. I checked it out and fell instantly in love with it. It was perfect! I met with the landlord, and miracle of miracles: he even knew what a serval cat was, having seen one on a camera safari in Africa a few years previously. The landlord was happy to allow me to have Deaken there. I was on Cloud 9. I had located a roommate—presently living in Pennsylvania, but planning to move to the San Fernando Valley—and proceeded to let Fish and Game and the City Animal Regulation Department know the address and the other particulars, so they could inspect the area and okay the permits for Deaken. It was only a matter of a few weeks, now, I thought…

Two days before the move-in fees and security deposit were due my friend in Pennsylvania called to back out on the deal, saying she couldn't leave her mother, who was in failing health. I was beyond devastated. If I didn't get those fees to the landlord right away, not only would I lose my earnest deposit, I'd have to start all over again, from scratch, with permits and landlords.

I called the Kelleys from work, nearly in tears, and told them what had happened. They were easily as upset by the news as I was. Then Carolyn said, "Kris, will you let us help?"

I said, "Oh, Carolyn, I can't. I can't get this place without a roommate. The monthly rent is $925 plus utilities. There is no way I can afford it by myself."

She said, "Suppose a little fairy helps with the rent."

I said, "Oh, gosh, thanks, but I could never live with myself if I did that."

She said, "OK, then, let us loan you the money for the move-in fees and the security deposit. You can pay us back whenever you can."

I repeated, "I can't afford that place by myself. I have to find a roommate."

She said, "You will. Now, you get that house and worry about a roommate later. It won't take long."

De got on the phone and said, "Get that house. Don't worry about it."

I moaned, "This is scaring the s— out of me." I had never spoken in colorful metaphors like that to them, ever.

He said, "I know it is, but do it anyway."

Carolyn got on the phone with me again and said, "De will get in the car right now and go get a certified check for the security deposit and the move-in fees. What's your new landlord's address? I'll have him drive it over to him right now for you." I gave her the landlord's address and then I started to cry, "Oh, Carolyn! You guys are so good to me! I'm crying!" She said, "So am I! See you later!"

I hung up the phone and called the landlord's wife to tell her that someone would be coming by to deliver the move-in fees and the security deposit. She was happy. Then I felt obliged to forewarn her, "Uh, don't faint when he gets there."

She asked, "Why would I faint?"

I said, "Well, did you ever watch the original Star Trek?"

She said, hesitantly, "Yes."

I said, "Well, the fellow who's bringing the money is DeForest Kelley."

She said, "Which one was he?"

I said, "Dr. McCoy."

She said, "Oh, my God!"

I said, "He'll be by real soon."

She said, "OK."

Later, she told me that she felt great trepidation waiting for De. She was under the impression that he would be as irascible and quick-tempered as McCoy was in his tiffs with Spock. Then she said, "But, Kris, when he walked in the door, he was just the sweetest, gentlest man I have ever met! And do you know what? He is your biggest fan! He says you're going to be famous some day!"

I thought, *From De's mouth to God's ears.*

So, the place was mine, at long last. On December 22 1990, I moved in. I was certain that it would be just a matter of days before my serval son would join me there. I couldn't wait! But there was a glitch. Although the inspections for Deke's facility had been made and approved, and the permits had been issued and were tacked on the facility door, the Fish and Game inspector hadn't been by for the final inspection. I called two or three times but didn't receive a call back. Finally, I called and said I'd hold until someone could speak to me and let me know how soon I could expect the final inspection. A lady came on after a while and reported that the final inspection wouldn't take place for another "six weeks or so." I just about flipped. I begged, I cajoled, I told the long, long story of how long Deaken had already been up at Shambala, waiting to re-join me. It fell on deaf ears.

Deflated, dejected, and utterly beaten, I hung up and cried.

I finally recovered and called the Kelleys, who had told me to call them the moment Deaken got home with me. I told them the sad story, and De again offered his help; he said he would call Sacramento for me. I said, "Thanks, De, but I don't think even you can perform a miracle with a state agency. You can't fight City Hall. If what I told them didn't work, nothing will."

De consoled me with, "Well, I know it's hard to wait, but six weeks is certainly better than six months." I agreed.

Then I hung up and cried again.

In early January, Desert Storm broke out. The newspapers reported that, depending on the length of the war, gas rationing might become necessary. I was living 35 miles away from Shambala. "If we get gas rationing," I told the Kelleys, "Deaken may as well be in Siberia! We'll only be rationed enough gas to get to work and back." A day or so later, the Sacramento-based Fish and Game agent called me and said, "With Desert Storm underway, you'd better get up to Shambala right away and bring your cat home. I'll take the responsibility for any flack you get when our inspector finally gets there." I thanked her, and Deaken was underneath my new roof within four hours.

I will never know if De made the phone call to Fish and Game, but it is not outside the realm of possibility that he did fight City Hall and win yet another battle for Deke and me. I suspect this, because not long after Deke came home I got a very nice letter from Fish and Game apologizing for any inconvenience or extra trauma their delays may have caused me or my loved ones. How many times does a state agency write such a letter?

Within days, the Kelleys arrived for a tour of my new digs and to see how well (and how immediately) Deaken had settled in. I found a roommate, and all was family bliss again.

MICHAEL LANDON'S BATTLE WITH CANCER

I was working at the Columbia Tri-Star switchboard when word got out that actor Michael Landon had been diagnosed with terminal cancer. Like everyone else who had grown up watching Bonanza, Little House on the Prairie, and various other productions in which he starred, I was enormously saddened to learn the news. Landon was a Columbia Tri-Star man at the time, and a huge gray cloud descended across the lot.

Sitting at the switchboard, I was one of six others. Our supervisor let us know that the switchboard would likely be inundated with calls from thousands of people seeking to speak to Michael and to fax him cures, clinical trials, prayers, and anything else they thought might help. "Now, I want you to remember—as hard as it will be to do it—we are not working for Michael Landon here. I want you to spend no longer than 30 seconds on each call that comes in for him." I understood the supervisor's concern that the six operators could easily become tied up with tearful and insistent fans, doctors, and the like. On the other hand, I realized the public's immense feeling for Michael.

The calls came in a flood. It seemed that eight or nine of every ten calls were for or about Michael. His voicemail capacity soon reached its limit; there was nowhere else to route the callers. Tearful, long-time devotees poured out their hearts to me and to the others. We had to "cut them off at the pass" in as short a time as possible, although it broke our hearts to do it. I devised a short statement for myself, sharing the caller's sorrow and hope for his recovery, thanks for prayers, and I gave out his fax number to any doctor or researcher who seemed to have anything of significant value to offer him. I was on their side; I wanted what every caller wanted: reassurance that Michael would learn—in case he didn't already know—how much he was loved, and that prayers and hopes and medical information would be sure and get to him. Grown men were sobbing on the phone; doctors from Russia were insisting that they had a treatment that would cure him. It was a trying time for everyone, and we were Michael's ears, trying to decide who to allow through and who to handle personally, briefly, compassionately ourselves.

After a couple weeks of this, I realized that callers were personally asking me to do what they couldn't do: reach him with their love. This was one thing I could do: to let him know that the calls he was receiving were only the tip of the iceberg and that many callers were leaving it to the switchboard operators to let him know the depth of their love and devotion to him. So, I bought a hopeful, humorous little card, and enclosed a brief note letting Michael know how many thousands of people had been calling that we at the switchboard hadn't put through—this was to protect his remaining time and to allow him to use it in the ways he needed to use it—and then I enclosed a few photographs. One of them was a photograph of DeForest and myself. On the back of this photo, I had inscribed, "I'm the girl in this picture. You know who the fellow is: You doubled for him in an A.C. Lyles movie during your Bonanza days!" I drew a smiley face next to the inscription, put it into an interoffice routing envelope, addressed it to him, and sent it off.

It was after Michael passed away that I received a sweet, thoughtful response from his personal secretary telling me how deeply moved Michael was by my reaching out to him with love and hope. She especially mentioned that the photo of DeForest had brought back many happy memories. Needless to say, I was thrilled to know that something I had instigated had touched Michael so deeply and had given him smiles during what was surely the toughest time in his life. Yet little did I know, until De's star ceremony reception at Paramount years later, how truly impressed Michael had been.

Not long after Michael Landon passed away, the studio began cutting back the hours of temporary secretaries and floaters (I fit both categories). I went from being requested 40 or more hours a week to fewer than twelve to fifteen hours.

SECURITY GUARDS & MISTAKEN NOTIONS

At the end of March I called Carolyn to see if she and De would be attending the annual Equestrian Celebrity Horse Show's Star Trek Night, hosted by William Shatner. Carolyn told me that she wouldn't be attending, but that De would. Her bunions were killing her and she was going to stay home and soak her feet. Then she said, "But you go ahead and look for De. You can give him a hug!"

I drove to the horse show with a friend. We wandered around, star-gazing, until the event began. It seemed that every star from the original series was in attendance, as were several of the stars from The Next Generation including Brent Spiner and Marina Sirtis. My friend and I walked over to the area where the Trek stars were all sequestered in celebrity boxes. I had purchased a stuffed bunny and had written a little note on it for Carolyn. The note read, "Some bunny loves you and missed you tonight at the horse show—ME!" I was planning to give it to De when I saw him so he could transport it home to Carolyn.

Problem was, I was unaware that where Shatner and Nimoy are, there is something known as heavy security. I was wearing my Walk of Fame DeForest Kelley jacket, so I was immediately a suspect. Not knowing this, I approached the celebrity box, and four or five security guards, men and women, blocked my way. I said hello and asked them if I could say a word to Mr. Kelley. "No." I then asked if they would give him a note from me, or if they'd relieve me of the bunny and deliver it to Mr. Kelley for me. "No." I was getting nowhere, fast. Worst of all, it was freezing in the arena that year. My feet were frozen, my nose was cold, and I wasn't looking forward to staying around for very much longer. Still, Carolyn had said to go say hello to De, and I had the bunny, so I stuck around a bit longer.

At various times, I could see De twisting around in his seat, looking for someone. I figured it might be me, so I'd lean in his direction, but always there would be a maximum security guard watching my every move, and whenever I'd lean to catch De's eye, he or she would lean to cut me off! I contemplated pitching the bunny rabbit in a high-flying arch, hoping the trajectory would put it somewhere near De in the celebrity box. But then I thought, *If I do something that outrageous, the security guards will take me out of here, for sure.* So I waited some more. My feet felt like ice cubes. I began to think that perhaps it wasn't worth it; I could mail the bunny to Carolyn...

That's when De decided it was time to leave the celebrity box for a break. As he stood up, my security guards crowded together in a tight configuration, right in front of me. They had my number, and I was not getting anywhere near Mr. Kelley. Knowing I was defeated, I signaled my surrender and stepped back. At that moment, De spotted me as he climbed the steps toward me. His face lit up in a big grin and he called out, "Kris! There you are! I've been looking for you!"

You should have seen the looks on the faces of those security guards. Like the parting of the Red Sea, they stepped aside so I could approach De. He gave me a big hug and quick kiss and I handed him the rabbit. We walked to a safe area and visited for a short time before he excused himself to use the bathroom. I went home and saved my feet from frostbite!

SO CLOSE...AND YET SO FAR...

The phone rang one day and I picked it up with a cheery, "Hello! This is Kris!" and the voice on the other end responded with an equally cheery, "Hello! This is DeForest!" I laughed, delighted, and said, "Hi, De!" He joked, "Are you fired yet?" I said, "Fired?" Then I realized he was pulling my leg and said, "Nope. Not yet. Wednesday is my last day on this temp job."

He said, "Well, I have some news for you. I was at the studio today for some fittings, and as I was leaving, I ran into Martin Hornstein, the Production Manager for Star Trek VI. He asked me, 'Is there anything I can do for you, De?' and I said, 'No...' and then I got back to my car and thought about you, and I turned back to him and said, 'Yes...there is.' And Marty said, 'Anything.' So I said, 'I want to tell you about this girl I know...' and I told him about you, and he said, 'Gee, I wish I'd known about her three weeks ago. I'd have her working right now! We're pretty well staffed, but have her give me a call and if anyone drops out or I can think of another job, I'll give her a call.'"

I was struck dumb. I finally managed to say, "De...thanks!"

He said, "Now, it's nothing at all certain. He said he doesn't have any openings, and that it's a matter of someone dropping out...but it's a start anyway." I called Mr. Hornstein and he gave me an appointment to meet with him the following week. I quickly mailed off my résumé and a few letters of recommendation, along with a brief cover letter stating, "I'm the race horse DeForest Kelley is backing." I thought that was kind of cute—and who knew, perhaps Mr. Hornstein was a racetrack aficionado! I decided "it couldn't hoit" to be a little avant garde!

On the day of the appointment I walked into Mr. Hornstein's office and he greeted me warmly with, "Well, you must be Kris Smith, the race horse De Kelley is backing!" I smiled, acknowledging that he had received my résumé package. He pointed to a memo on his bulletin board. "As you can see, I already have issued a memo stating that if there are any drop-outs in the production, I want to be notified. That way, if it's anything you're qualified to do, you will get it." There was no way to respond to that verbally.

I looked at the floor, and said, "Gee, I feel...overwhelmed by all this! Thank you."

He said, "If I had known about you a month ago, you'd be here now. I don't even have a spot for you on camera in a scene." I just about dropped dead! "We like to do that with good fans of the show, to show our appreciation." I shook my head and said, "That's okay. Just knowing I'm under consideration to work with you is fantastic." He didn't say anything more, and I realized he was busy, so I excused myself and floated out of there. It didn't even matter that I hadn't landed A Job. I had landed something far greater: a sense of adequacy, of belonging, of validation.

It seemed I was in a strike-out pattern with all things Trek. I had to call and let the Kelleys know about it. They were supportive and said that things usually happen for the best, and that perhaps something better was coming along, and that's why this hadn't panned out. I hoped they were right.

VISIT TO THE SET OF STAR TREK VI

Sue, Kat and I drove to Paramount to watch a bit of Trek VI being filmed. I was a little anxious, as De had told me that the drive-on and the stage visit passes were listed under my name, "so you're responsible for the behavior of your party." I mock-panicked and asked him, "Even Kat?" He said, "Even Kat."

We got onto the Paramount lot and eventually made our way to one of the stages where Trek VI was filming. Ralph Winter's secretary had told us it was the stage where De would next be working. She said we should plan to stay no longer than about 40 minutes; I nodded my agreement, and we went over and entered.

Jimmy Doohan (Scotty) and Walter Koenig (Chekov) were standing around shooting the breeze. De was nowhere to be found at the moment, so we struck up a conversation with the other actors, exchanging jokes and other comments.

After a short time, Shatner and Nimoy entered the sound stage, but passed us by and went to a corner where they could run their lines. Still no De, so Doohan and Koenig and we continued to chat.

After about fifty minutes, De ambled into the sound stage. He was dressed in a Starfleet uniform that was draped with deer hide and his feet were covered with animal skins as well. His blue eyes shone so brilliantly, even from thirty feet away, and he looked so handsome that I caught myself nearly gasping.

I had never seen him in person as McCoy before, and it almost took my breath away. At the time, I was sitting in De's director's chair, and before he could come over and claim it, I asked Jimmy Doohan "to act like you've known me for decades." Taking up the little improvisation, Jimmy got behind me and draped his arms and hands over the top of my shoulders, almost grabbing my breasts! I quickly vetoed his assertion regarding that much knowledge of me! He snuggled his face next to mine and looked to be crooning into my ear.

De came around, spotted us, and—perplexed—asked, "Do you two know each other?"

"No, we've just met!"

"I see!"

I peeled Jimmy off me and asked De, "Do you want your chair back?"

De said, "No. I've been sitting all morning." So I stayed put for a time. But then I got up, again noticing his deerskin wrap, and accosted him.

"Mr. Kelley, I guess you know what Deaken will think when I tell him Uncle De was dressed up in animal skins."

De's eyes became real wide, and he said, sounding slightly panicked, "Don't tell him! I'm not responsible! It's what they gave me in wardrobe!"

I laughed then and said, "Okay, then. I won't tell him. It's our secret."

Soon thereafter, the director, Nicholas Meyer, came into the sound stage and De introduced him to us. De said, "I'd like you to meet Sue Keenan, my fan club president." They shook hands. Then De said, "And this is Kris Smith, who's working on becoming a screenplay writer." We shook hands. Then De continued: "and – this one (indicating Kat) -- this one…" He wondered how to introduce Kat (the lustful one), so after he hesitated too long, Kat blurted, "Aw, the hell with it. I'm Kat, and I do hugs, not handshakes!" She enfolded Meyer in a bear-hug, and since she's a tall gal and he is not a tall man, he found his face practically in her bosom.

As he parted from her, he turned toward me and mumbled (to no one on particular), "I have to meet a lot more of De's fans!"

Not long after that, Meyer called "Action!" to the cast and the rest of us watched while the actors exited a turbo-lift and headed down a corridor of "the Enterprise" talking about assassins…

De called later that night to ask me, "Why did you leave? The next scene was mine!" I apologized and told him we didn't know what to expect, and that we had already overstayed our time limit by more than an hour. "I didn't want to have the crew thinking you had fans who didn't follow instructions." He agreed that I was right in leaving, but we were both sorry that we had missed his scene.

CAPTURING 50 YEARS OF LOVE ON FILM

Although De had been photographed from every angle thousands of times during his career, I wondered if he and Carolyn had ever sat down for a photo session together, so I asked them. They had never had it done, they said, because they had no children and didn't know of anyone else who would want something like that. I quickly assured them that their friends and a number of relatives would undoubtedly love to have a photo of them together. They had been married 46 years by this time and I thought a photo session was long overdue. I told them I knew a professional photographer, Bill Dow, who would photograph them for free at my house in my back yard, even with Deaken if they wanted. Carolyn said, "Let me think about it." A few days later, she called back and said they would like to take us up on the offer. I called Bill Dow and decided on a date and time, and then let the Kelleys know.

Bill hadn't met the Kelleys before, so there were a few minutes of chatting and getting to know each other before the photo session began. They chatted while Bill erected the umbrellas, lighting and other paraphernalia. De gave me his crew cap from Star Trek VI, which I immediately planted on my head for a moment.

While Bill finished setting up, De and Carolyn went out into the yard to visit with Deaken who was friendly but not overly so. He was on steroids for an ear problem, so after a little while he "checked out," closing his eyes— his way of indicating that while he still appreciated petting, he didn't want to have to react personably. He wanted to relax and enjoy it without reciprocating. The perfect guests, they understood and didn't force the issue.

When it was time to shoot the photos, Bill got several of De and Carolyn together. While they sat for those, we chatted and laughed—a lot! At one point, Bill apologized to them, saying that he was more accustomed to photographing wild animals up at Shambala or dogs and cats—at which time De assured him, "Oh, that's all right!" and he began to bark! Carolyn jumped right in and began to meow! I took my cue from their silliness and grabbed a few squeaky toys and began to squeak them and call to "doggie" De and to "kitty" Carolyn, in the way a pet photographer would in order to get an animal's proper attention for the camera. De and Carolyn cracked up; so did Bill and I, and Bill caught the hilarity in a couple of photos. Bill then asked Carolyn if she'd like a few photos alone with the newly-acquired Poppy (a black and white kitten, whom Deaken had promptly adopted). Deaken was still in the yard, not amenable to having his nap spoiled by the goings on beneath the patio roof. Carolyn said yes, eagerly, so Bill took several photos of her with Poppy. Then Bill asked De if he'd like to sit for a few pictures. When De said he would, Bill asked him, "Which is your good side?" (knowing that some actors have a preference). De responded, "I don't have a good side!"

I objected, telling Bill, "De doesn't have a bad side!"

Just as the photo session appeared to be over, De motioned to me and said, "Get over here, Kris. We want our picture taken with you."

I was flabbergasted! I sputtered, "But, I'm dressed for Deaken. I'm not dressed for a photo session!" I looked real frumpy.

De wouldn't take no for an answer. "Well, go change, then!"

I said, "Good heavens! Why? Are you serious?"

He was.

Then Carolyn directed me, "Go get changed!"

I quickly bolted inside the house, threw on a blue turtleneck shirt, and then returned. Bill sat me on a chair between De and Carolyn, and one of my favorite photos of all time was snapped at that moment. I'll always be grateful De thought of that, and insisted.

After the photo session under the eaves of the patio, we sat in the back yard hoping Deaken would eventually decide to have his picture taken with the Kelleys against the lovely background Bill had provided. It was not to be. Deke just wasn't in the mood that day to have his serenity botched by flashing cameras. I cajoled, begged, and petitioned mightily, carrying Deke into position for the photos, but he got grumpy, growled unhappily and slapped me with a forepaw.

De said, "Don't force him. We'll do it another time."

I suggested that they could just sit with Deaken on the lawn, under his own terms, and have their pictures taken with him there. They smiled and agreed with that.

As the afternoon wore down we visited more, talking about many different topics. De mentioned that security on the set of Trek VI was so tight that "You'd think we had something to do with National Security! It's to the point where they almost ask to look in your trunk as you exit the lot!" De told me he got everyone to sign his script so Sue could auction it off and get the best possible price for it to benefit the North Shore Animal League.

After De sat with Deaken on the lawn for a few photos of just him and me with Deke, I explained how a cat on steroids is more unpredictable than a cat with all its senses intact. De put his arm around me and hugged me playfully, then shoved me away—equally playfully—and said, "Now you tell me—now that I've put my life in jeopardy with a drugged cat!"

I responded, "That's why I was sitting so close to you and watching Deke's every move—so I could intervene if he decided to do anything uncivilized!"

De said, "I know. I'm just joking. I didn't really feel in any danger!"

91

Bill intoned, "The serene confidence of sheer ignorance." They both laughed.

As we parted company that day, De and Carolyn spotted Bill's car, which had a bumper sticker attached that proclaimed, "ONLY ELEPHANTS SHOULD WEAR IVORY." De agreed with the sentiment and mentioned that it was hard for him to watch circuses on television because of the exploitation of the animals.

STAR TREK CEREMONIES — 1991

Sue had asked her club members to send De cards and notes of congratulations for his upcoming star ceremony on the Walk of Fame scheduled for December 18 that year, so she could send them to him and Carolyn as part of their anniversary package. Carolyn called to tell me how choked up De was by the sentiments expressed therein, from all the fans who had responded to Sue's request.

The card that I had sent De read: "Great men may be among us…but none compare to you." I had taped a few small photos of De, De and me, and De and Carolyn inside the card and then written, "Congratulations on your STAR and for remaining the wonderful person you are! Love, Kris." On the empty, inside facing page, I had quoted the trailer from Trek VI: "They have been our guides, our protectors, and our friends." Beneath that, I had written, "How very fortunate I feel! Most fans have had only the reel McCoy as their guide, protector and friend—and are grateful. I have had DeForest Kelley as 'all of the above.' Your caring has transformed me into someone worthy of being cared about. Thank you. God Bless you. I love you." For the accompanying letter, I created a special letterhead on my PC. The heading was respectfully engraved, "YOU DESERVE ALL OF LIFE'S GOOD THINGS. YOU ARE ONE OF LIFE'S GOOD THINGS."

The letter read:

Dear, Dear De,

Where do I begin?
Your star ceremony affords me the opportunity to get really serious (for once) and to pour out to you all the love, pride and respect you're engendered – seemingly FOREVER.

So where are the proper words to adequately express any of it?! sigh I'll try…

Your skill as an actor is exceeded only by your skill as a wonderful human being. In a way, I wish I had met you first in the way that I met Tippi – without knowing much, or caring much, about "who" you were as an artist. Why? Because it took me so long to get OVER seeing you primarily/chiefly as "my FAVORITE actor" with all the accompanying jitters and shyness and paranoia that that "awesome" perspective entails. It took a long time before I could genuinely relax in your presence and appreciate you as a real, flesh and blood human being who is special despite what you do for a living (instead of because of it).

That's what I first responded to in Wenatchee in '68 upon scrutinizing you from the sidewalk (before introducing myself): your genuine niceness. I stood fidgeting on the sidewalk, gauging whether or not you were going to disappoint me if I approached you for an autograph and a smile. (My initial fear was, "Do I really want to risk being turned off by an actor I'd really love to keep on liking?" It had happened before!)

Well! After studying the situation for several long minutes, it became abundantly apparent that you and Carolyn were very nice people. So that's when I gathered the courage to step forward and open my mouth—and hope my heart wouldn't leap out of it and land on the floorboard of your convertible!

You deserve the star—and I mean this in the "old-fashioned" way: You deserve the honor to the degree for which stars were originally bestowed, not in the way they are too-often awarded nowadays (as a publicity gimmick). Your career has spanned (don't say "Ouch!") nearly five decades. You're genuinely one of Hollywood's decent, honorable guys (there might be four or five others, but their names escape me at the moment ☺). You do good deeds (quietly, which makes them even "gooder," 'cause they're not done for the sake of publicity). You're a gentlemen star (who's an accomplished and convincing "bad-ass" only in the movies). You meet, exceed and annihilate the criteria for being awarded an "old-fashioned" star. In fact, I can easily envision you being named MAN OF THE YEAR, no problem…no exaggeration…no stretch of the imagination. I think the Creator (the real "Big Bird of the Galaxy") delights in you and sees you in the same way He sees Yosemite or a healthy new bud on a rose bush: as a damn' fine piece of workmanship, if He does say so Himself…

I don't know what else to say…how else to express how proud I am of you… how lucky I feel to have "fallen" for you…how blessed I am to know you well enough to know I'm right about all of the above!

You are an inspiration to me. "When I grow up" — I want to be just like you.

I love you, De.
Kris

There was one other important ceremony that year, thirteen days before De's star ceremony. On December fifth Mann's Chinese Theatre in Hollywood honored the entire original Star Trek cast by having them place their signatures and handprints in the forecourt of that world-renowned place. Hundreds of fans gathered hours ahead of time to get good spots from which to observe the proceedings. We arrived at around seven a.m., and we were among the first, so we were positioned against the restraining rope. It wasn't long before the entire boulevard was crowded with fans. Bleachers had been erected across the street to accommodate as many as possible; crowds of fans also extended down the boulevard for a block or more in each direction. Fortunately, microphones were set up so that those in attendance farthest away could still hear the event, if they couldn't actually see it. At about 11 o'clock, a local band approached Mann's from the east, playing the Star Trek theme. Behind them, in three separate cars, was the cast. The crowd went wild.

Before the ceremony took place, there was a photo op for the media.

The cast gathered on the sidewalk and milled around as the cement was prepared for their signatures and prints. While there, they engaged in some private banter that no one else was privy to. There were lots of smiles; there were also some somber faces.

De looked ready to cry a time or two as he apparently considered the honor that would soon be bestowed on the cast. When the time came to write their names in cement, Shatner and Nimoy went first. Their names appear side by side at the top of the large cement slab. Then it was De's turn.

The space provided to him was immense, as he was writing alone, so he took advantage of it and signed his name twice as large as the other two had. During the signing, a photographer called out to him, "DeForest, look up here! Look up and wave!" so De obliged him, then went back to his signature – but left the 's" out of DeForest! The emcee for the event, Johnny Grant, who had previously mentioned that sometimes people were so nervous that they misspelled their names, jumped right on the situation, and announced, "I told you! It has happened again! DeForest Kelley has misspelled his name!"

De, still on his knees, assumed his gruff McCoy persona, then threw his hands outward in mock exasperation, and groused, "Damn it, Jim, I'm a doctor, not a bricklayer!" Everyone cracked up; De quickly added "s" to his name, and then stood up, laughing and shaking his head. Following the cement-signing, someone on the stage asked Shatner if the rumor was true that Star Trek VI would be the last feature film for the cast. Boos emanated from the crowd the moment the question was posed. Shatner responded, "Star Trek VI, without question, is the last of the Star Trek movies." Boos and catcalls met his comment. He continued, "The heads of Paramount, who are wise men, told us this was so, and we never go against the heads of studios."

Shatner handed the microphone to Leonard who confessed, to many laughs, that he was emotional. He mentioned that Gene Roddenberry had been the first writer honored with a star on the Walk of Fame. Then he thanked the many craftspeople responsible for the show. He said the cast was receiving an honor which could not have happened were it not for the thousands of writers, directors, producers and other behind-the-scenes folks who had made it all possible. He handed the microphone off to De, who at

95

first joked, "Damn it, Jim, you didn't say it was gonna be big!" Then he thanked the late Gene Roddenberry for his creation and vision, and then he thanked Mann's Chinese Theater for the honor; and then the audience. "If it wasn't for you, the fans, none of us would be standing here today." The crowd cheered wildly. De handed the mike to Jimmy Doohan, who disagreed vehemently that this would be the last Star Trek.

Walter Koenig respectfully and sincerely thanked the behind-the-scenes folks (especially the writers) who made Star Trek possible. Then regaling the crowd with a humorous account of the last time he had played in wet cement: "I was a 9 year old boy in New York and what I wrote in wet cement at that time is unprintable in a family newspaper." He then handed off to the ebullient Nichelle Nichols, who looked heavenward and said, "Mom, daddy said I'd be here someday, and here I am!" George Takei said, "On the future of Star Trek: I agree with Bill Shatner. We do go by what our bosses tell us, and I think our bosses don't reside in the executive corridors of Paramount. My bosses are all out there!"—indicating the fans—"and frankly, I think we will keep on Trekking!"

On December 18th, hundreds of fans gathered again to honor De when he received his star on the Hollywood Walk of Fame, only a block and a half west of Mann's Chinese Theater. Once again, Kat, Sue and I were there, along with Sandy Zier (later Zier-Teitler) from Maryland, Ann Johnson from Texas, the Gerald White's and their new-born daughter Amber from Washington State, and many others. Kat and I wore our DeForest Kelley jackets. It was a glorious morning, perfect for a star ceremony. Some of us silently thanked God or Gene Roddenberry, up in heaven, for the weather, as a terrible storm had been forecast, and here it was, sunny and warm!

Sue, Kat, Sandy and I were honored guests of De's, and were afforded the opportunity to stand with the celebrities during the ceremony. After consideration, we elected to stay with the crowd for two strategic reasons. The celebrities and honored guests were positioned behind De and the podium, which would have prevented us from seeing De's reactions to what was being said. Also, Kat and I planned to document the event on still cameras, so we could give the Kelleys an album of photos afterward with which to remember the day.

The event began in a spectacular manner. De's star is located at 7021 Hollywood Boulevard, directly in front of the Galaxy Theater, a two-story complex with two escalators leading up to the theater. The powers that be had decided De should make his entrance down the west end escalator, so Johnny Grant announced, after a few preliminaries, "Today we have the pleasure of honoring the man who brings to mind the qualities of a self-confident, mature actor who has honed his skills with deliberate care and success. Today in front of the Hollywood Galaxy, we honor DeForest Kelley…And now—I know that you all know the characters, I know that you all know the stories better than I do—but I must tell you a little more about this gentleman. I want to remind you this morning and the historians who will be looking at these tapes years and years from now. As you know, DeForest is known worldwide for his popular role as Dr. Leonard 'Bones' McCoy, Chief Medical Officer of the USS Enterprise in the highly successful Star Trek television and motion picture series. DeForest was born and raised in Atlanta, where he first used his talents in the church choir. Later, a radio performance on stage at WSB earned him an engagement with Lew Forbes and his orchestra at the Atlanta Paramount Theater. After moving to California, he joined the Long Beach Theater Group. During WW II, a Paramount talent scout noticed him in a Navy training film. This resulted in a screen test and a contract. DeForest remained with Paramount for 2 ½ years, making his motion picture debut in Fear in the Night. Let me tell you just a few of the other films he has appeared in: Gunfight at the OK Corral, Raintree County, Warlock, Where Love Has Gone, The Law and Jake Wade, and a myriad of television appearances include Schlitz Theatre, Playhouse 90, Zane Grey Theater, Rawhide, Bonanza. DeForest made his debut in the Star Trek television series in 1966, and needless to say, the rest is history. DeForest has given freely of his time and talents to many humanitarian efforts, including his many hospital visits to children and veterans. DeForest is currently reprising his role as Dr. McCoy in Star Trek VI: The Undiscovered Country, which I have a feeling all of you have seen at least six times." Cheers. "Ladies and gentlemen, please join me in welcoming DeForest Kelley as he receives his star on the Hollywood Walk of Fame! And here he is, beaming down from the Enterprise: DeForest Kelley!"

De suddenly appeared at the top of the Galaxy escalator, as the Star Trek theme played. He stepped onto the escalator and rode it down to the thunderous cheers and applause of the crowd gathered there. De told me later that it was the longest escalator ride he had ever taken. "I felt like a Ziegfeld Girl! After I threw the Vulcan salute, I didn't know what else to do!" To the crowd assembled there, he looked calm, collected and radiant.

Upon reaching the elevated staging area, at least two feet above the level of the sidewalk, De vaulted right up next to Grant, who marveled, "My God, you're nimble!" De shook Grant's hand, then stepped back while Grant introduced the many celebrities and other guests who had come to say a few words about De. Grant first welcomed and introduced legendary Paramount producer A.C. Lyles, a long- time friend of De's, who spoke of his affection for De and of their long association. A.C. bounded up on the stage and joked, indicating De's entrance on the escalator,

"We at Paramount love DeForest Kelley so much that we spared no expense; we built him this escalator just for this occasion!" The crowd and De laughed, and AC added, "If that isn't an entrance, I don't know what is! As Johnny Grant mentioned, I have been with Paramount 54 years, and De has been with us 45 years, but the best thing is that Carolyn, here, has been with De for 46 years." There were cheers and applause. "And I tell you, I look over there and I see some of De's fans, like Kris Smith and Sue Keenan, and I know that when they say Star Trek, the word STAR means DeForest Kelley." More applause, as other fans agreed with the statement. "And now De has his name and his prints at Mann's Chinese Theater, and he's going to have his name here on Hollywood Boulevard, but the main thing is that DeForest Kelley has his name in all of our hearts."

De was overcome by A.C.'s statement, and lifted his glasses to wipe away some tears. The fans whistled and cheered and applauded. "Our arms are around him, our hearts are with him, and we at Paramount love De as much as he loves us. Thank you."

Then A.C. said, "You will see all the stars of Star Trek here today to honor De, but Bill Shatner couldn't be here, so he sent me a letter to read for him. It says: 'DeForest Kelley has long deserved a star on the Hollywood Walk of Fame. I'm just a little apprehensive that all this excitement might be too much for him, so everybody put your arms around him and make sure he knows he's loved. I'm very sorry I can't be there with you, but I'm in the tropics trying to get you a coconut! Love, Bill." A.C stepped down and Grant introduced Leonard Nimoy.

Nimoy jumped onto the stage, shook hands with and hugged De, and then grinned into the microphone, "I wouldn't miss this for anything. This is really great. I hope that one time, during this ceremony, we will hear him say one more time, 'He's dead, Jim.'"

Then he got serious. "In the great tradition of people like Gary Cooper, this is the man who stands there beside you and says the lines, and plays the drama when it's drama and gets the laughs when it's funny – and don't turn your back on him, because he really knows what he's doing. He is great. He's a friend, he's a colleague; he is a rock on which much of Star Trek stands. De, may you live very, very long and prosper. God bless you."

Next Johnny Grant introduced George Takei. George was eloquent. "This is a very, very happy day for all of us. It's great sharing this wonderful day with De. Two weeks ago, we shared another happy day, just a block down, at Mann's Chinese Theater, and De announced that he was a doctor, not a bricklayer. After he finished, he didn't have to tell us that; we knew. But one thing that doesn't need to be said, he is most definitely an actor, and he certainly most appropriately belongs right here in the Galaxy – Dr. McCoy right here in front of the Galaxy...It's appropriate that he be here, because he has friends all over the galaxy. He's beloved by everyone, and De…it's wonderful to be able to say: Friend – we're really happy to be here to share this happy day with you."

Walter Koenig stepped up next. After hugging De, Walter recounted a tale. "Several years ago, DeForest was at Madison Square Garden as part of a celebration honoring Dr. J, and they asked various doctors—fictional and factual—to come down during half time and to be saluted by the crowd. When DeForest was introduced as Dr. McCoy, there resulted an unprecedented eight-minute standing ovation, which no one else was accorded. Dr. Ruth was there, and she asked DeForest, "What is it? What do you do?" Dr. Ruth was not only the only person in Madison Square Garden, but in the entire world, who doesn't know that DeForest Kelley is Dr. McCoy."

Producer Harve Bennett bounded to the podium with great enthusiasm, after hugging De, and said, "Well, I didn't expect to say anything, but since I'm here…I'll tell you a short story about the only time I've ever seen De Kelley thrown for a loop…It's my first picture, it's my first—and almost last—Star Trek convention, in Houston. It's come to be known, in Star Trek annals, as The Con of Wrath. And the story simply is, I'm fresh off the airplane, I walk into the hotel, and Dr. Bones McCoy – ACTION! – greets me and says, 'A thousand people are in the streets! Nobody has rooms! You've got to do something!' We did something, and in the bargain, became friends for what I know is life. This is a really great guy."

Nichelle Nichols was last. She said, "I am so thrilled and excited to be here. It is also an honor. It's an honor because DeForest Kelley is such a special, special kind of guy. He is always exactly who he is. He is so down to earth." Then she recited a poem she had written especially for the occasion. "I love you, De, and you deserve every moment of people walking all over you!"

Johnny Grant then brought his part of the ceremony to a close by reading a proclamation from the LA Board of Supervisors, which congratulated De on his honor. The document also proclaimed December 18, 1991 as DeForest Kelley Day in Hollywood!

At that point, De stepped up to the podium to accept the document and to speak a few words. "I want to thank all of you wonderful people for coming out here and helping me celebrate this very special, special day. I am particularly proud that Paramount Pictures happens to be sponsoring my star, because in 1946, as AC Lyles pointed out, as a young man, I started my career at Paramount. There are so many people to thank: from Bill Meikeljohn all the way through to Gene Roddenberry. My career has also encompassed a great number of people who perhaps you never heard about, but there are the directors Don McDougall, Bill Witney, the guys that make fast and hot television shows; and there's AC Lyles, who kept bringing me back to Paramount, and eventually John Sturgis brought me back for Gunfight at OK Corral; and then Eddie Dmytryk, who finally got me out of those bad guy roles by bringing me back to Paramount again to do a picture called Where Love Has Gone. So, all of those people and too many more to name here, the people who have worked so hard on this event, Allison Jackson and Hank Ehrlich, all of these people that have worked to bring me to this position that I'm finally going to be in. I'm particularly proud that all of my roommates" indicating the Star Trek cast, "are still here, and I'm proud that I can look at Leonard, and that I don't have to say, 'He's dead, Jim.' This has been a very exciting year for us, as you know. Everyone has mentioned dates: December 5th at Mann's Chinese Theater; December the 18th for this event; September the 8th, which was the celebration of our 25th year of Star Trek. A very important date just preceded that: September 7th, when I celebrated my 46th wedding anniversary with this lady sitting here. And speaking of support, I can assure you I would never be here without her. I have often said, and I say it again, I make the living, but she makes the living worthwhile."

STAR CEREMONY RECEPTION AT PARAMOUNT

After the media-driven "grip-and-grin" photo opportunity pictures were finished at the site, four ecstatic women—Sue, Sandy, Kat and I—headed for our cars in the Galaxy garage for the trip to Paramount, where a reception for De was scheduled in the studio commissary. In the garage, we crossed paths with De, Carolyn and AC Lyles, who were traveling to the reception together in a studio limousine. We hugged them. De was all grins, and said, "It's times like these when I need to remind myself that I still have to go home and take out the trash!" We laughed, knowing that the humble De was still alive and well.

Kat and I got into my humble, "Lifestyles of the Poor and Unknown" car – the "accordion" – and drove to the main gate at Paramount. As we pulled up at the guard station, I couldn't help feeling embarrassed and out-of-place. Here we were at a fancy function, and our chariot looked like something that belonged in a wrecking yard—well, to me, it did.

Just then, the white limo carrying the Kelleys and AC pulled up beside us on its way through the employee gate. The driver honked—which is what alerted me to their presence. I looked over my right shoulder and melted when I saw that the rear limo window had been lowered a little—just enough for De's fingers to reach out and give us a wave! I thought, *What a guy! Most actors in this situation would drive by and not even acknowledge they knew the people in a car like this!*

We walked to the commissary, reconnected with Sue and Sandy, and chose a table near the door, just inside the commissary. The Kelleys, AC and a few others were seated across the room from us.

Sandy, Sue and Kat chose seats that were more-or-less facing the action. I took the seat that was facing our wall, being more hearing-oriented than sight-oriented. I was just happy to be there; it didn't matter that I couldn't scan the crowd of well-wishers or the Kelleys during the luncheon. I knew I'd be able to turn around and view any toasts that were given, or anything else, when something noteworthy began to happen.

Lunch was delivered and we ate while chatting happily. Afterward, a few people stood and offered toasts, and then AC stood and said some very kind and true words about the honoree. "On the logo here at Paramount, as you know, there are a series of stars spanning across above the mountain. DeForest Kelley is definitely one of the stars represented in that logo. He means so much to us here, as he does to fans around the world. Not long before Michael Landon died, I called him in the hospital. I think most of you know that Michael doubled for De in a fight scene here on the lot when Bonanza was being filmed and De was doing a movie here for me. Well, when I called Michael shortly before he died, I told him, 'Michael! You

101

don't sound sick at all!' and he said, 'AC, it isn't my voice that's sick.' Anyway, we chatted for a short time and then he told me, "You know, AC, I just have one concern left.' I asked him, 'What's that, Michael?' and he joked, "I don't know who's going to double for DeForest Kelley now!'" The audience chuckled. I just about fell out of my chair! The remembrance of my note to Landon at De's reception felt like a miracle.

AC continued: "But I want to tell you something. Michael Landon may have been able to double for De in a western, but nobody—nobody—can double for De in real life. De, you are unrepeatable. Our arms are around you and we are so proud to be able to claim you as our own. Congratulations, you rascal!"

After people finished eating and the plates were cleared, De stood and made his way slowly around the room. As he got very near, breathing at our table became shallow and hearts beat faster. I could tell by the gaze of my friends that De was practically behind me, but I didn't know his exact location until two warm, friendly hands caught both of my shoulders, and rubbed them, then patted them. They felt like the hands a dad would put on the shoulders of a daughter sitting at home in familiar surroundings—so comfortable and unabashed. I grinned and looked up into his eyes. He grinned back and patted me on one shoulder one more time. Then he proceeded to kiss one of the hands of each of my tablemates. We felt blessed.

Not long after De finished making the rounds of the tables, people began to leave. We waited until De and Carolyn were heading out the door, then approached them, thanking them for inviting us. He turned to me last. I smiled and whispered very discreetly into his ear, "Thank you so much for inviting me to your f———n' star ceremony!" His head came up and he grinned like a Cheshire cat.

A few days later De and Carolyn called to thank Kat and me for the photo album and the video of the star ceremony. De told us that he finally spotted us in the star ceremony crowd. "I was looking for you girls, but I mistakenly thought you were newswomen for the longest time, because you were all dressed up, for once."

I joked, "We clean up real nice, don't we?"

He said, "You sure do!"

De said he had been going over in his mind about the ceremony… what was said, stuff he should have said that he didn't. Carolyn interjected, "There are two dizzy people here right now!" I assured De it was a wonderful ceremony and couldn't have been better. "It was just perfect."

I told them about Sue's Rowdy Cowboy Celebration at the Holiday Inn in Hollywood the night De got his star. I mentioned that Kat and I had created what looked like a horse dung centerpiece for Sue's table, with fake flies buzzing around it, while everyone else got nicer ones. I added, "Before the centerpieces were put out, Richard Arnold showed up and announced that he wanted to sit at Sue's table. I tried to discourage him, but he insisted, so he got to sit at the horse dung table, too!" They both laughed and De commiserated, "Poor Sue."

I reported, "Then we had some games. We played Pin the Star On De – blindfolded everyone, spun them around, and then had them pin a star on a full-length photo of De. I can't tell you where some of those stars ended up!" They laughed.

"Then we had a game where we tried to guess the title of De's movies by pictorial clues. They were pretty decadent. The only two I'll tell you about are these: I took a map of the US and over the top I pinned a pair of under shorts. Know which motion picture that represented, De?" Total silence greeted my question, so I solved the puzzle: "The movie was 'The Undies-Covered Country'! No one else got it, either, De, so don't worry.

"They got APACHE UPRISING, though! That drawing showed an Indian with his loincloth sticking out at about a 45 degree angle!" Carolyn howled and De guffawed!

SHAMBALA REVISITED

The two hundred or more copies of the book I had donated to Tippi Hedren's Shambala Preserve had all been sold. Tippi expressed an interest in having her Shambala Press reprint it. The book, Let No Day Dawn that the Animals Cannot Share, had been self-published in Washington State, so I was thrilled to hear that Tippi felt it was worth reprinting. The copies I had given her had sold very well and the cats and elephants at Shambala had been the recipients of that boon. The preserve photographer, Bill Dow, had taken hundreds of fantastic photos of many of the animal residents there, and he said he'd choose his favorites and include them in the book. I thought that was a sensational idea, as my primitive drawings in the original book were not what I would have called stellar. ("Dammit, Jim! I'm a writer, not an artist!") They were passable, but hardly impressive.

I gave Tippi permission to proceed and then thought about rewriting the foreword, since it was ten years later and things had changed. Then I wondered if perhaps De might consider writing the foreword. I knew it would probably sell better, and get the critters more donations, if he would give it a boost. So, I asked him.

The request threw him for a loop. He said he wanted to think about it. I quickly assured him that if it was a stress or something he didn't want to do, it wasn't necessary. He said, "No, I want to do it. I just have to think whether or not I CAN do it." I said, "Oh, I'm sure you're capable!" He said, "I don't know. Let me kick it around for a while, and I'll let you know." I said, "Now, don't stress over this. If it's a pain in the butt, don't even worry about it." He said, "I won't."

About a week later, I got an envelope in the mail. Inside was De's foreword, in his own handwriting. It was beautiful. I knew it would be a big hit with Tippi and with the Shambala visitors. It read:

Foreword by DeForest Kelley
("Dammit, Kris, I'm an actor, not a writer!")

"My first meeting with Kris Smith was on a beautiful, clear, crisp day in May, 1968. I was serving as Grand Marshall of the Wenatchee Apple Blossom festival. My wife, Carolyn, and I were riding in an open convertible. The streets were lined with people. Suddenly I noticed the shining face of a teenager running alongside our slow-moving car waving a sign which proclaimed, "We Love DeForest Kelley." We managed to exchange some hurried dialogue with her as our driver kept pace with the other parade vehicles.

"Sometime later I received a letter from Kris, along with an essay which described her experience meeting us on that festival occasion. I was so impressed with her writing ability that I sent the essay to a national motion picture magazine – and they wanted to publish it. I wrote to inform her of this, and to express our hope that it might lead to something interesting for her future.

"At a later date, we learned that Kris has always had a great love for animals (a devotion we share) and we were delighted to find that she had put her writing talents to use to benefit animal welfare in various national publications. Today, while pursuing her goal to become a screenwriter in Hollywood, she continues this dedication at Shambala, which provided her gorgeous "serval son" Deaken, a much-needed place to stay during the lengthy transition from Washington to California. They rent a nice house now with a big back yard, and Carolyn and I have been privileged to meet Deaken, both at Shambala and at their home in Encino. Deaken must have known that "Mom-Cat" Kris approves of us, for he immediately greeted us with enthusiastic head rubs and licks, which Kris says she had never seen him do before to anyone but herself.

"I refer to Kris as "the best Mom-Cat I know" for she has a touch of magic with animals, wild and domestic. She is deeply concerned about their welfare in the wild and in captivity…and about our own environment and welfare on this planet.

"As you will see within these pages, Kris possesses a real talent for expressing her feelings regarding matters that tug at so many concerned hearts.

"But make no mistake about it. She has a "wild" sense of humor, as well. She is known among some of us as "Krazy Kris." She's crazy, all right – crazy like a fox!"

Needless to say, I was overwhelmed! I called to let him know he was a writer and to get busy on his autobiography! He laughed, "Give you an introduction and you want a book!"

Not long after this, my cat, Poppy, wound up in the back yard at the top of an electrical pole. I regaled the Kelleys with my courageous/foolish attempt to rescue her; told them I climbed the pole like a pro and brought her down, "with her sharp little claws imbedded in my face." De said, "Next time dial 9-1-1 – or call Bill (Shatner)!"

I asked, "What would he do? Send one of his Dobermans up the pole after her?"

On De's 72nd birthday in 1992 Kat and I called to wish him a happy birthday, which had become a tradition ever since I'd moved to California in '89. Carolyn answered the phone. I asked if the birthday boy was there. She said he was out in the back yard cleaning the bird bath. I mentioned that Kat and I wanted to call and sing him Happy Birthday sometime during the day. She said, "I'll get him." I said, "Wait! Before you do that, we have something we want to deliver for De's birthday, but it won't fit in the mailbox. Do you have something else out front where we can hang it?"

Carolyn said, "No, but I can come to the door and take it from you."

I said, "No, it's too heavy for you to lift. We'll try hanging it on the doorknob."

Carolyn called for De in the back yard.

About a minute later, De came on the line and said, "Happy birthday!" I laughed and said, "That's my line!" Kat and I sang Happy Birthday to him.

De said, "Thank you very much. I'm standing here with wet feet and dirty hands."

I said, "We be sure sorry, sir! We didn't mean to interrupt."

He said, "Well, it was certainly worth coming in for!"

Kat joked, "We'll get our recording contract right after you get yours for ***Row, Row, Row Your Boat***!"

De shot back: "You sing on your record and I'll sing on mine!" Then he said, "It's a shock being 137 years old (referring to his portrayal as the 137 year old Admiral McCoy in "Encounter At Farpoint," the pilot for The Next Generation five years earlier)."

I said, "137? No! It's 142 now!"

De said, "Oh, yes. Time sure flies." Then, referring to the fact that his birthday had fallen on Martin Luther King Jr. Day, he joked, "It's about time they made my birthday a national holiday, after 142 years!" Then he asked, "Will you be at home later today? Oh, yes, of course you will! It's a holiday! Good. I'll call you back later."

At about 5PM De called again to thank us for the gifts we had delivered to his front porch. De said, "Sweet Jesus! We're supposed to go to dinner tonight, and I won't be able to eat. Thank you for that wonderful food basket. And that's gonna be one sad lady (Carolyn) if I see her going out to her squirrels with my almonds. You'd better knock this off now, girls!"

Kat said, "We won't do it again – until next year!"

De said, "Next year? You girls were mis-cast. You should go into business together doing something like this (specialty baskets). It's wonderful!"

Kat asked, "Did you like the hat?"

De replied, "Oh! That hat! I won't go anywhere without that hat. I'll wear it to bed!" (The hat read, "MY NEXT FANS WILL BE NORMAL!") And those balloons. Wow! You made my day very memorable. Thank you!"

Kat and I flew to Sacramento in February to attend a Creation Convention that featured De. We stayed at the home of a long-time friend and former co-worker of mine, Nancy Graf, a school teacher and animal welfare worker. Reggie Holloway also stayed at Nancy's, as his home was 90 minutes away from the convention and he wanted to attend both days.

Almost as soon as De got on stage, he began razzing Kat and me. We sat there and took De's got'chas without getting even, mostly because we were enjoying the notoriety and because we really felt we should behave once in a while, even if De didn't.

As soon as De's appearance ended, Adam Malin (Creation's owner) came up the aisle to us and said, "You have to get even tomorrow, you know."

I laughed and said, "No, we don't."

Adam said, "Oh, yes, you do!" I looked at Kat. She looked at me. We were truly fresh out of ideas. This wasn't a convention with Sue or Sandy, so we hadn't planned any shenanigans whatsoever. Adam continued, "If you don't think of something to do to him, I'll think of something for you to do to him."

Well! We looked at Reggie and he gave us definite "no way" gestures with his hands. ("Don't involve ME in any way, shape or form!" he was indicating.) But he was our buddy this weekend, and that's what you get when you hang around with the two chief DE-mentoes at a convention.

We sat down and came up with a "got'cha" for De. It wasn't great. It wasn't even all that funny, but we felt it would satisfy Adam's desire to get De.

Reggie is a big guy. He resembles Mr. Clean. He looks like a Hell's Angel in a way, a real "don't mess wit' me" kind of guy. So we decided that Reggie would portray a Security Guard and that he would deliver us to De on stage with a report of our nefarious Southern California activities. Kat and I would be sorry, we'd ask for forgiveness, and then let the chips fall where they may.

Not long before De appeared the next day, we got a little nervous. I didn't think it was fair to spring something on De that he didn't know anything about, so I went to Carolyn and told her, "Adam Malin told us we have to get even with De for all the stuff he pulled on us yesterday. We don't want to do it if it will throw De for a loop. Do you think it will?"

Carolyn said, "Let me ask him."

I said, "Okay."

Carolyn left the auditorium and then returned a little later. "Kris, he says go ahead and do whatever Adam says. He's okay with it."

I said, "OK."

I went back to Kat and Reggie and let them know that the plan was a go.

When De came on stage, he chatted for a while and then read one of his poems. At about that point, Reggie grabbed both Kat and me by the scruff of our necks and pushed us halfway up the stairs leading to the stage. De saw us coming and employed a delaying tactic, to make us more scared than we already were. Finally, he pseudo-glared at us and asked, "What's this?"

Reggie pushed us onto the stage, folded his arms like the biggest bad-ass strong-arm man on the planet, and then said, "I found dese two women loitering around your star on Hollywood Boulevard. Dey looked suspicious. I thought you should know."

Kat said, "We were just polishing your star, kind sir ---!"

I added, "---for the fourth time this week, Mr. Kelley!" We both dropped to our knees and lifted our hands up, prayer-like, to De in a sort of "Have mercy!" gesture.

De looked around back stage and called out, "Security!" Pause. "Where's Security?" No response. "Where the hell is Security?" he repeated, sounding really serious.

We were getting a little bit nervous. He sounded awfully serious to us.

Finally, De smiled and held the microphone out in front of him, moving it in the sign of the cross, as though absolving us of our sins. Then he said, "Now, get outta here!"

We jumped up and ran off the stage. The audience loved it and applauded. As we stepped back to our seats, De said, "Those two women seem crazy, I know – but they're really two very sweet gals."

INSTANT GARDEN

In late February, I mentioned to the Kelleys during a phone call that I was thinking about starting a little garden in the back yard, even though I was just renting. They thought that was a terrific idea. De said he had been thinking about thinning out some of their plants and that he'd give me some of the cuttings, which I could plant in my yard. That was a terrific, money-saving idea. (I was still temping all over town, so I was pinching every penny until it shrieked.) I happily thanked him for the offer.

I arrived home one morning to find seven complete Lilies of the Nile plants and one orange blossom plant on my back porch! De had called Kat and asked her to come fetch them for my garden.

I quickly planted them and then dialed the Kelley house. De answered the phone, much to my surprise.

I said, "Hello. I have a very beautiful garden this morning, thanks to you."

De said, "Oh? How did that happen? Oh! Is this Kris?"

I said, "Yes."

He said, "I thought you were somebody else. You sound like somebody else. You sound like somebody else pretty often!"

"Only when I'm being 'bad'" (using various character voices and inflections, the way I sometimes do at conventions or at work to add variety to monotonous hours or tasks).

De said, "So! You got your garden put in – already?"

"Yep, and it is gorgeous. Deaken tried to help me – had to inspect every hole I dug."

De said, "That must have been fun."

"For him. Not for me."

De said, "I tried to pick plants that had good root systems for you."

I said, "You did. They're fantastic. I thought I was getting clippings, for heaven's sake. I wasn't expecting entire plants. Instant garden! Thanks!"

De said, "You're welcome. How's the job situation?"

"It's been pretty slow this month, but it's usually dead in February, with hiatuses all over town."

De noted, "Carolyn tells me you have some exciting job prospects."

"Yeah. At Disney and Warner Bros. Nothing is going to happen immediately, but somewhere down the road, I know it will."

De said, "I'm sure it will."

I said, "They asked me what I wanted to do, and I said it'd be faster to tell them what I don't want to do: accounting or finance!"

De added to that list: "Or filing!"

I said, "Filing wouldn't even be bad, if I don't have to do it eight hours a day."

De chuckled and then said, "Let's see if I can dig CC up."

"CC? Carolyn?"

"She's in the middle of making jalapeno jelly. She says she'll call you back."

"OK."

"Bye, doll." I groaned and then laughed, "You're bad, De."

Grrr! The doll reference was another "got'cha". For a week before this call, I had been working in an office for a female producer who kept referring to me – and to everyone else -- as "Doll" in the most annoying and impersonal manner. I had written and told the Kelleys I was about to drop kick this woman off the top of a building if she didn't learn my name or at least stop calling me "Doll"!

Carolyn called about a half hour later and I thanked her for the plants. She said, "I'll bet you were surprised when you got home!"

I said, "I sure was. I about flipped! I was expecting clippings, not full-blown plants!"

Carolyn said, "Well, we wanted to get you off to a good start."

I said, "You sure did that, all right. Deke had to help me plant them, you know. Deke put his face into all the holes I dug and rolled in the potting soil and steer manure as though he was luxuriating in the elephant dung up at Shambala."

Carolyn laughed and said, "He gets a bath, I'll bet!"

She wanted to know precisely where I planted them, and then had me relocate the orange blossom, saying that it didn't like full sun. I told her I had spread lawn seed and bird seed, hoping to keep the birds' beaks out of the lawn seed until it germinates and gets some roots. She said, "I hope it works."

I said, "Me, too."

She said, "De used to go over and slam the door to get the birds to stay off the lawn seed when he spread it every spring, but I told him to stop it."

I guessed, "You'd rather have the birds than the lawn, right?"

She said, "Right. I just tell him to put enough down so we can have both!"

I told her about befriending a baby fly in the back yard. "It came around looking for the steer manure, I guess. It was the cutest little thing." I went on for a while, with Carolyn laughing like crazy at my craziness. Then she said, "You should write that up for Sue's next newsletter. That's a very funny story!"

I laughed, "Oh, right! It will fit right in there with the rest of her DeForest Kelley news!"

Carolyn joked, "Well, you said she was wanting you to write the whole thing. That should discourage her!" We both laughed over that.

Then I said, "But she still wants us to do the entertainment at the next club party. Can you believe it? Won't she ever learn her lesson?"

Carolyn said, "Well, you make a lot of fun for everybody. That 'Pin the Star on De' was a real cute idea."

I said, "The Shatner club asked if they could use the idea!"

She said, "They did?"

I said, "Yeah. I told 'em, 'Sure! It isn't exactly copyrighted!'"

Carolyn said, "You should have told them, 'Sure – but it'll cost you!'" I laughed.

THE ENCINO WALK OF FAME

On June 20, 1992 Kat and I hosted a get-together in our back yard for De and Carolyn, AC and Martha Lyles, and Mary-Ann and Robert Dunlap, AC's secretary and her actor husband. De and Carolyn arrived at 3:20, in advance of the starting time for the party, because they wanted to cuddle Deaken before the rest of the pack arrived and Deaken folded into his self-protective breadbox position.

Kat and I had made "Walk of Fame" stars on our front sidewalk emblazoned with the names of each of our guests, plus one additional star: Dennis Morgan (Carolyn's favorite actor). Morgan's star was placed last on the sidewalk, in order of appearance, because it was a "got'cha" for Carolyn and would be a total surprise.

De and Carolyn arrived and headed up the sidewalk, tickled at the real look of the stars on our sidewalk. A little sign in the yard proclaimed, "ENCINO WALK OF FAME." De walked ahead of Carolyn, as he was packing a huge bag of home-grown lemons and oranges, but as soon as he saw Dennis Morgan's name, he stopped dead in his tracks, knowing something was up and waiting for Carolyn to spot it.

I was with Carolyn as we proceeded up the sidewalk with her carefully reading each name as we reached each star. I explained to her, "There's a star here for every person we invited to this get-together."

She said, 'Oh, isn't that nice? That's very thoughtful, Kris." That's when she saw Dennis Morgan's star. She stopped, studied it, then looked up, eyes wide and mouth agape, breath held!

I had heard the story: The few times Carolyn had chances to meet her favorite actor (thanks to De), she knew she would be so tongue-tied and nervous that she refused to meet him.

Carolyn looked again at the star and then at me and said, "Dennis isn't coming here, is he?!"

I smiled and said, "Well, Carolyn, he was going to, but then he said he didn't think he could handle three hours of your incessant chattering!" Carolyn and De cracked up at that, and Kat (hiding in the front room) captured the moment in a priceless photo.

We went inside and I sat the plant down Carolyn had carried in and presented to me. Carolyn gave us three magazines and an autographed LIVE LONG AND PROSPER ad.

De and I headed out the back door to see Deaken. Deaken took a couple sniffs of De and started to drool into his outstretched hand and face-rub him like crazy. About three or four minutes later, Carolyn came out and joined us. Deke continued to drool into Carolyn's hand and then rub his face in it. I groused at one point, "Deaken, I wish you wouldn't drool on my

112

special guests!" De laughed and Carolyn said, "Oh, don't tell him to stop. I love it!"

I said, "It's tacky, but it is a high compliment. He's marking you by making your skin wet and then face-rubbing the mess. That way he ends up smelling like you and you end up smelling like…" I hesitated, and De completed the sentence, "-- a serval!"

I joked, "I was going to say 'like cat spit,' but I like your version of it better!" We laughed.

After at least 20 minutes of that, we went back under the roof of the porch and I made De a drink. (He showed me how, so I wouldn't overdose him.) Carolyn had a wine cooler.

Pretty soon after that, Mary-Ann and Robert arrived, so I went out to greet them while De and Carolyn waited in the back yard. The Dunlaps were tickled by the stars.

When I got back into the backyard, Carolyn asked if she could go see Deaken alone, without me along, and I said I didn't think that was a wise idea. She said she wished she could. I said, "I wish you could, too. And you probably could -- but I sure wouldn't want to find out I was wrong, and neither would you!"

Mary-Ann and Robert then met Deaken. He was his usual noncommittal self with them; so De and Carolyn were able to see with their own eyes that Deaken definitely had the hots for them but not for many other people, other than his Mom-cat!

Shortly thereafter, AC and Martha Lyles arrived, so I dived back out the front door to greet them as they scrutinized our Walk of Fame, smiling.

They came inside and walked straight through the house and into the back yard to greet the Kelleys and the Dunlaps. Deaken was even less friendly with the Lyles. He had reached what he felt was the maximum number of occupants in his territory, and checked out for the rest of the day, lying in a breadbox position, napping (or perhaps just ignoring us!).

I don't recall the specifics of all the fun we had. We had made director's chair type banners for the guests' chairs. Both wives and Mary-Ann and Robert had their names respectfully emblazoned on their chairs. However, De's banner read, "WHAT'S HIS NAME" and AC's read "AWFULLY CUTE MAILROOM CLERK." (AC had started out at Paramount Pictures in the mailroom, and had gone on from there to become a producer. We had often asked him what the initials AC stood for and he wouldn't tell us, so we had decided they stood for "Awfully Cute," hence his banner.)

I got Martha and AC settled in. We all sat down and AC launched into a non-stop monologue that was insightful, delightful and wonderful. De and he talked about the disastrous Bel Air fire in '61 which almost destroyed the

Lyles home, and De mentioned that one of his childhood homes burned down around them, which is why he had only a few photos of himself as a small boy. They talked extensively about the retirement home for motion picture people. They talked about actors they had worked with or known. It was either funny or poignant, depending on which story they were telling.

The time flew by! The Kelleys were there for at least six hours (a record!) and everyone else was there for nearly five hours. They all left at around 9:40 PM and said they'd had a wonderful time. I said, "I guess we will have to make this an annual event, then!" and everyone seemed to be all for it!

THE LANDERS QUAKE

On June 28 1992 at about 4:58 a.m. eighty miles east of Los Angeles, the Landers earthquake struck with immense force: 7.4 on the Richter scale. Because the epicenter was in a less populated, more isolated area, it did not cause San Fernando Valley residents the grief or disruption that the subsequent Northridge quake did. However, it did rattle us awake -- and it caused nerves to be on edge for anyone who had experienced the 1972 Sylmar quake -- which De and Carolyn had. Because of that earlier quake, De always kept a flashlight and shoes and socks located next to the bed, just in case.

The Landers quake was the first major (albeit distant) quake I had ever experienced. Since I had been in a few lesser shakes, none of them serious, I had a more-or-less Spock-like view of the phenomenon. I thought it was fascinating that a house could rock and roll and sway and creak and gyrate so distinctly without windows breaking or the structure suffering some kind of permanent damage. Still, it was a "waterbed" kind of experience, and I was not unduly unsettled. The quake rekindled memories in the Kelleys, however, and they thought we might be rattled more than we were, so they called us at about 6:30. I picked up the phone and said, "Good morning!"

Carolyn asked, "Are you okay?"

I said, "Oh, yes. Are you?"

She said, "Yes."

I joked, "Did we wake up suddenly this morning?"

And she joked back, "Oh, yes, we did!" She asked if my folks had called yet to see if we were okay. I said, "No. They're probably out camping and haven't even heard the news yet." I told her about my reaction during the quake, as I stood in the doorway holding the door jams and studying the situation analytically. Carolyn asked if anything broke at our house. We said no and she reported that nothing had broken at their place, either. "It was amazing that nothing did break, as much as we rocked and rolled! That was quite a ride!"

She asked how the cats had responded. I reported that they all slept right through it. Then she said, "We'd better get off the line in case there are emergency calls out there to or from Landers. That's why I waited this long to call you, and didn't call right away. We just wanted to make sure you girls were all right."

We thanked her for calling. I wondered at that time why she had been so concerned about us over such a little (albeit interesting) quake. I thought it rather odd. That's because, unlike the Kelleys, I hadn't experienced a big quake at close proximity before. I would get my chance with the Northridge quake—two years later. Then I would understand!

DE ARTIST AND DE FARMER

I had told the Kelleys an unbelievable, but entirely true, story about Deaken's acute hearing in the distant past, when we were first becoming acquainted via letter. In the letter, I had written, "I read in an encyclopedia of mammals that a serval's hearing is so acute – with those satellite dishes of theirs that we call ears – that they can hear a rodent burrowing three feet underground. They wait there until it surfaces and then they nab it. But you know, that never really registered until I got Deaken.

"I was wrestling with him in a corner of our living room when he was a kitten – this was just after his ears had stood upright and everything caught his attention, before he learned to screen things out and ignore miscellaneous noises. Anyway, I was wrestling with him in a far corner of the living room, which was a good twenty feet across – and in the farthest corner from us was a wood stove, which was located on tile. All of a sudden, Deaken stopped tussling with me. He had heard something in the corner behind the stove. It was distracting enough that he had stopped playing with me. It was a big deal to him.

"Right away, I thought, 'Gosh, there must be a mouse or something behind the stove—or maybe Ivanhoe (my German Shepherd mix) is outside the wall there.' But no! Deaken got up from where we were, and—I swear to God on a stack of Bibles—he walked over behind the stove and started pawing and squeaking at something there. I thought, aha! A mouse!' So I went over there, and…you will not believe this, but it's true…what he had heard and responded to was an ant! An ant, walking across the tile behind that wood stove! I could not believe it—and I'll bet you don't either. Imagine all the stuff he had to learn to ignore in order to stay sane, at an early age!"

No one countered the claim I made, but one day I was shown, in no uncertain terms, what De had thought of that preposterous story. On July 8th, I received a large envelope from the Kelleys. Inside was De Artist's rendition of what he believed had to have happened the day Deaken heard the ant. He had drawn an elephant eating dog kibble from a metal pan outside the cabin Deaken and I shared as a dwelling!

Carolyn called me later that day. I told her I had received the cartoon from De and she laughed, delighted.

I said, "I can see he still doesn't believe that Deaken heard an ant!" Then I said, "I wouldn't believe it either, if I hadn't seen it with my own eyes, so I really can't blame him."

She laughed again and said, "I believe you!"

Reassured, I said, "Awww, Thank you, sweetie!"

Not long after that, she told me to come by the house and get something out of the mailbox. I did so, and found a medium sized paper sack with something very heavy inside. On the outside of the sack, De had written, "My latest experiment with growing organic lemons. De Farmer." I looked inside, expecting to find three of four lemons, since the sack weighed so much. Instead, I found one gigantic, enormous, colossal, elephantine, immense, unbelievably huge lemon. My chin hit my chest! I took the lemon home and took a photograph of it. Then I wrote a note, asking De what his secret was? I guessed, "Miracle Grow? Tortoise poop? De wee wee? What, man?" I'm sure he got a good laugh out of those off-the-wall final two guesses!

WHEW! STEADY WORK!

On Sept. 9, 1992, I began temping at Warner Bros. through an outside temporary agency. I worked in Consumer Products for Michelle Sucillon, a vivacious, raven-haired beauty whose enthusiasm for her work matched my own.

After just a few weeks there, I knew this was the place to begin my career with the studio. I applied for the position officially and, after a couple of months, got it. Before long I was working for four of the bosses there, practically running to keep up with all the tasks I was given to accomplish. I loved it – and the comments I got from my bosses!

During this time, De asked if I would computer-generate his poem The Dream Goes On and On and On. I readily agreed. The Kelleys were thrilled with the look of the book, so I printed about fifty copies for them and said, "Just let me know when you need more, and I will print more!" As a thank you, De personalized a copy of The Big Bird's Dream to me. He wrote, "Thank you for doing And On and On and On... DeForest."

In the department I served, we constantly received samples of products which outside companies would send, hoping WB's quality control people would approve the item and license them to sell it. I would occasionally spot an item that I knew Carolyn would like. I would get permission to have one to take to her. I was never denied the sample, and the few things I chose never failed to delight Carolyn.

One of the items I got for her was a book of cookie recipes. She was so taken with it that she asked if I could get another, for a friend of hers. I said, "Sure, I think so."

Then she said, "Do you have one on hand right now?"

I said, "Yes."

She said, "The recipe for you is on page 59."

That threw me. I thumbed through the book and found the page. "Awwwww, Sweetie Pie!" I read, smiling.

She said, "That's you! You're a sweetie pie!"

I quickly scanned the ingredients and then joked, "Wait a minute. This recipe has nuts in it!"

She joked back, "Well, you're a little nutty, too, you know!" We both laughed.

Rather late one evening in early October, just a few days before her birthday, Carolyn called me, in a happy tizzy, saying, "Oh, Kris! De and I were just getting into bed and De told me, 'Look outside!'" She asked me, "Guess what was out there!"

I guessed, "A possum?"

She said, "Right! No. Not a possum. You guessed wrong!"

118

I asked, "What was it?"

She said, "Oh, it was a—you know—it was an animal like the one you had in Washington the same time you were raising Deaken! That little orphan that someone brought you!"

"Oh!" I responded. "A raccoon!"

"Right! It was a raccoon. It was going away by the time I saw it, but De saw its whole face, right here at our screen door. I told him I wondered what they eat, and he said to call you. You know."

I told her that they're omnivorous. I let her know what sounds to make to make it feel welcome and safe, if they wanted to encourage it to stay around. Carolyn said, "I'm just so thrilled to have another wild one in our neighborhood."

De got on the line then and said, "I watched a Disney movie once and it related that raccoons can be destructive."

I said, "You bet they can."

He said, "In this movie, they peeled the roof off a miner's cabin so they could get inside to eat."

I said, "That's right, they can. I'm not encouraging you to tame the little guy – or girl; not at all. In fact, you might want to tell Carolyn it's illegal to feed wild animals."

De said, "I will. Not that she'll stop feeding the squirrels and birds, but I think this raccoon thing is a little over the line."

A few days later, when Carolyn saw what I had delivered to their front porch for her birthday, she called again. "I think I've stopped crying long enough to thank you for my lovely gifts – my stuffed raccoon and squirrel – and those beautiful cards! And those balloons!" – and she started crying again.

I just about fell to pieces with Carolyn and told her, "I'm glad you like the gifts, Carolyn, but don't cry. I gave 'em to you to make you happy!" Carolyn said, "I can't help it. I cry when I'm happy. I'm so emotional about it all!"

So I joked, "Well, I can tell you're having a wonderful day."

She laughed and said, "Oh, yes, I am."

I said, "I'm glad."

She said, "Everything is so terrific. Those cards are what got me. I'm very sentimental."

I said, "Well, they're how I feel about you. They had your name written all over them!"

At about that time, Carolyn said, "I just heard the phone click. I think De's on, so don't say anything you wouldn't want him to hear!"

I asked, "What wouldn't I want De to hear?"

De said, in a very McCoy-like manner, "Well, I want you to know you've screwed up my Sunday royally with that little delivery! I was enjoying a lovely, quiet, restful day until that arrived. Now all I've heard for the last two hours is Carolyn sobbing!"

I was at a loss as to what to say about that, so I said, "I'm sorry." – not truly meaning it. I knew he was only feigning being cranky. Then he said, "And I want that raccoon!"

I said, "You do? Well, you can't have it! That's Carolyn's. But I bet she'll share."

He joked, "I doubt it."

Carolyn reported, "It's sitting on a chair holding the balloons, just the way you placed it outside on our doorstep. I had De take a picture of it before he brought it in, too. It looks like he's giving me the balloons and basket. I just love it. And the squirrel is on the window ledge. The window ledge is exactly the right height and size for it. And the Tweety banner is taped on the window above that."

I told Carolyn she could put the raccoon by the window and it might attract the real one. Then I said, "Never mind. You really don't want to encourage it to get into your house. It might try, and wreck your screens."

De said, "I think its living in Myrtle's excavated condo."

I said, "That, or it might be living in a tree."

De said, "I think it's in Myrtle's condo. She hasn't gone in there for a while. I'll bet that's why."

They asked a lot about raccoon teeth and claws, and asked if they should attempt to touch or hold the (real) raccoon. I said, "Absolutely not. I know it's tempting as sin, but don't risk it. You could get a very nasty bite. It is a wild animal. Remember that."

A few days later, Carolyn called to report that her birthday balloons had lost their helium and were all on the floor now except for the vinyl ones. I joked, "If you were Deaken, the fun would just be beginning! You really should jump on them now and bite them!"

She laughed and then said, "Why don't you stop by here after work and get these for him!"

I protested, "No! They're your balloons. He'll get some on his next birthday."

She said, "I'd love for him to have them. Tell him they're from me!"
I protested again, but she insisted that I should drive by and get them for him, so I finally agreed, and Deaken enjoyed two birthday celebrations that year.

OKTOBERTREK 1992

Kat and I had just landed permanent positions at our respective jobs, really for the first time, so our finances were anemic. Carolyn kept asking us if we were going to make it to OctoberTrek in Baltimore, and we kept trying to reassure her that we wanted to and planned to but that we also had to be prudent and be sure we'd be able to do it and still eat. She had so enjoyed the report of our last OktoberTrek in Sue's Fan Communique newsletter that she said she felt it wouldn't be the same without us. I again said, "Carolyn, I promise you: If we can get there, we'll be there. We're as dedicated to getting there as we are to breathing in and out on a regular basis!"

A few days later, she again asked. I had the same answer. Finally, she said, "Look, I've made you reservations on US Air and at the hotel. You're going!"

I protested, "Carolyn!"

She said, "It's a gift; you're going, and that's the last word."

I sputtered and said, "We will pay you back somewhere down the road."

She said, "No, you won't. Now hush up."

I said, "Well, thank you."

She said, "You're welcome."

When I told Kat, she wept. Then she cheered, and we started making serious plans.

We wrote a humorous parody of Row Row Row Your Boat as an example of what we had in mind for the other fan club members to do with show tunes to honor De. As luck would have it, De called that day and we told him that there would be an audio tape in his mailbox in the next day or so for him to preview.

"What kind of audio tape?" he asked.

"Songs we wrote about you to sing at OktoberTrek," I responded.

"Oh…" he mused.

I said, "Do you want to hear one of them now, over the phone?"

He said, "Sure."

I sang,

SCRUB SCRUB SCRUB DE'S STAR
WE DO IT WITH SUCH JOY
MERRILY MERRILY MERRILY MERRILY
BUFFIN' UP McCOY

De queried, sounding a bit shocked, "What was that last line?"

121

I said, 'Buffin' up McCoy."

He said, "Whew! I thought you said something else!" He chuckled.

I said, "You'll get the audio tape soon. There will be a few other songs on it."

He smiled, "Okay. I'll look forward to it."

On October 16, I was on another floor at work when Michelle called me and told me to come right down. She said, "Your Trekkie friend is on the phone." My Trekkie friend? I answered the phone, "Hello! Kris speaking."

"DeForest speaking!"

I said, "Wow! Now, you're some Trekkie friend. Michelle called me down here saying my Trekkie friend was on the phone. I thought she meant Kat."

He said, "I want you to know we were out all day today, but I just got back and listened to your audio tape. I want to tell you how much I enjoyed it. The choir is very clever and I appreciate it very much." Then he said, "Now I'm waiting for you to write me a musical to appear in."

I said, "OK!"

He asked me how things were going "there at Warner Bros.," and I said, "Just fine." I added, "I've applied for this position permanently, officially, and if I get it, I will be off the temp agency payroll and on at WB – with benefits and the whole nine yards."

De said, "That's terrific, and you'll get it. I know it."

I said, "Thanks."

Oktobertrek was a blast. I wrote a convention report afterwards that Carolyn exclaimed over numerous times thereafter. The text follows.

HIGHLIGHTS AND LOWLIFES OF THE OKTOBERTREK CONVENTION

Reported by Krazy Kris Smith

Usually it's possible to provide a chronological rendition of happenings at a convention. In order to do that with OktoberTrek, though, it'd take up the entire newsletter, so…forget it. Here are the highlights, from my limited perspective. (I only witnessed the parts that I witnessed, so everyone else experienced a different set of circumstances unless they happened to be loitering with me…So be it. Here's what happened to me/us/you?)

US AIR…the official airline of OKTOBETREK…went on strike on the Monday before the convention. But what's a little "transporter malfunction" to a die-hard Trekkie? We all just hopped a red eye and still managed to reach our DE-stination!

Kat and I arrived on 6 AM flights on Thursday and were greeted by Sue and Sandy, who whisked us over to Sandy's place, where we loaded the rented Ryder truck with boxes and boxes (and boxes and boxes) of OktoberTrek paraphernalia. (We believe this was the first of Sue's and Sandy's got'chas. The second got'cha would introduce himself to us shortly…)

At about 2 PM we arrived at the convention hotel, where we deposited our baggage (the room was mercifully and pleasantly Unadorned, much to our relief: Sue and Sandy had been too busy – HOORAY! What? Watching us load boxes? -- to trash our rooms this time.) Then we took a nap…or tried to. We were zzzausted.

At about 7 PM we met Reggie Holloway in the hotel lobby, and then headed for FOOD. We were famished. We ordered a pizza from one of the hotel eateries and as we waited for it…

Right on cue, over came a good-looking, compact, hyperactive, genuine descendant of some bronzed Italian, who announced in a loud voice – while pointing a finger at us as if pronouncing sentence – "I KNOW YOU!!! You're the two crazy ladies! Sue has told me about YOU!!! I've got videotape of YOU!!!" That's how we met got'cha #2 – in the person of Daryl (Bones'-the-cat's doting daddy). Cute kid, we thought… until we remembered this "kid" is twenty years old and well on his way to becoming a veterinarian. (He only looks and acts 12!)

We knew Daryl was our Designated Sidekick, by order of Sue and Sandy. He was determined to be a companion. It was a calculated decision on his part. Proof follows shortly.

We connected with Ann Johnson, Susan Beasley and their friend Diane, all of whom are from Texas, and sound like it. ("How ya'all doin'?") We also spent a few minutes visiting with Jackie Edwards, who lives all of five miles from me, but we only see her at De cons. (Not because we're not crazy about her, but because our schedules seem to be mutually exclusive.) All of us were tired and looking forward to crashing shortly.

Friday morning we delayed getting up until it became mandatory and then went down for breakfast in the hotel's main restaurant. We registered for the convention after that and got our badges. While waiting in line, we reconnected with Marcia Coates from Michigan and others. Upon returning to our hotel room, we found – hanging over our shower spigot – a rubber snake and a sign which ominously forewarned: "IT'S COMING." The Nemeses had begun their assault. We gulped and decided it was time to launch our counteroffensive.

We pulled out some Dr. McCoy photos which we had embellished with original and bizarre "quotes" and Kat and Ruth Cordary (her good buddy from Florida) took them to Sue's and Sandy's rooms, "beamed in," and placed them intelligently in "appropriate" spots. For example, one photo of McCoy grinning broadly found its way into Sandy's bathroom, where he proclaimed, "Lookin' GOOD, Sandy!" Both of their pillows had a photo of a reclining McCoy holding his hand to his head, with the "quote": Not tonight, dear…I have a headache." They also short-sheeted Sandy's bed. (Not that anyone felt Sandy would ever get a chance to climb in and NOTICE she was short-sheeted, since she was running the convention day and night…but "just in case" she did…the bed was ready!)

Friday was spent visiting mostly. At about 7 PM, we decided we should go to our room and round up a dinner party by inviting all our friends… even Daryl. As we approached the door of our room, who should we spot at our door but DARYL HIMSELF, who was preoccupied at the moment and didn't spot US. We shouted, "Daryl!" He jumped up and yelled, "Oh, shit!" I said, "Don't go! We want to invite you to dinner!" "Oh, shit!" Daryl repeated, and fell onto the floor in a perfect imitation of a puppy's "I give up!" posture. (Fortunately, he DIDN'T pee, the way a puppy would have.)

Right away I knew something was not quite right. I grabbed his wrist and noticed that he held in his hand – a small can of shaving cream. "A-ha!" I said. "What's this?"

"NOTHING! I swear it!" he lied.

"Nothing?" I queried.

"NOTHING!" he cried.

"We'll see about that," I said. Kat and I dragged him through the doorway into our hotel room, and spotted a note which he had just written and placed underneath the door. It read: "Kat and Kris: the Italian Stud Puppy was here."

"The Italian Stud Puppy?" I repeated. "Well…the Italian Stud Puppy is going to get very, very wet right about now."

We dragged him into the bathroom and I turned on the water in the bathtub.

"NO!" he protested.

"Oh, YES!" I confirmed.

"My pockets are full of stuff I can't get wet!" he told us frantically.

"Then take your pants off," I suggested calmly.

"NO!!!!!!" he screamed. (So much for the "Italian Stud" proclamation)

"OK, then," I said, "We'll just unload your pockets." Which I did. Then we lowered him into the tub.

After we let him up, we made him sit on the rim of the tub and held up his "stud puppy" note as EVIDENCE that we had every right and obligation to defend ourselves. Then I took his can of shaving cream, which he had so generously provided, and wrote WE LOVE DARYL on his pants leg. Then we took pictures, which we assured him would find their way to the Kelleys and to Sue Keenan.

NO!!!" he yelled. "I'LL KILL YOU!!!" (We were scared. Ahem...)

Kat went to his hotel room and fetched him some dry clothes, and reported back to us the variety of styles she had to choose from out of his suitcase, including a pair of Garfield shorts. By this time, our room was filled with friends who had thus far been informed about the dinner. They were enjoying the wailings of Daryl-in-the-john, changing clothes and bemoaning his sorry existence under the thumb of these two crazy ladies. As soon as he emerged from the bathroom, we grabbed him again, threw him on the bed, and tied him up. There wasn't a dry eye in the house.

Saturday morning we were up early to be first in line to earn front row seats for De's appearance, along with other early birds with the same intention. We chatted until the doors opened and then claimed seats.

At about 1:15 that afternoon I spotted Sue and Sandy at the DKFC booth, together for the first time that I'd noticed, so I ran down to the main room and informed those involved that it was time for our SECOND got'cha for Sandy and Sue. Kat, Reggie, Ruth and the Italian Stud Puppy left the auditorium and raced for our banners, doodads and camcorders. Our "parade" gathered at the foot of the escalator; our "cameraperson" Ruth positioned herself at the top. At her, "ACTION!" signal, Kat, Reggie, Daryl and I started blowing horns, twisting noise makers, and ascended on the escalator to within sight of our two Nemeses. At the top of the escalator, we began yelling, "Speech! Speech!" and entered the DKFC booth, where they read the banners: SUE KEENAN FOR PRESIDENT – NINE MORE YEARS!" "SANDY ZIER FOR VICE PRESIDENT -- PRESIDENT IN CHARGE OF VICE!" The banners looked very political and polished. Sue and Sandy were mortified, which was our objective. As soon as they seemed to have recovered, we sincerely asked Sue if she would accept our nomination and remain our President. She said, very sincerely (while hugging me), "Of course..." Then she reconsidered and yelled, "NO!!!" (But we know she was just kidding about the second part.)

De appeared at 4:00 on Saturday, and he was a real hit with everyone. (This isn't news, but....He was FANTASTIC!) He must enjoy being at OktoberTrek in particular, it seems: He always seems to be just a little bit nuttier at Sandy's conventions!

He looked great (and very sexy), as the fan-written songs at the DKFC party/auction will attest. He read his latest poem, THE DREAM GOES ON AND ON AND ON, and then handed it to Ann Johnson, one of his "Texas gang," with a "Happy Birthday, Ann" greeting.

At the Question and Answer portion of his appearance, De made a big playful issue out of having his fans question him from a microphone placed in the middle of the auditorium. He pretended he didn't know where they were, due to the fact that the sound system – and the fans' voices – were on the stage with him and the fans were someplace else. When the first fan's disembodied voice addressed him with, "Mr. Kelley --" De looked heavenward and responded, "Yes, Lord?" and then proceeded to let the fan believe (for more than a minute) that he really DIDN'T know where he was! It was hysterical.

After his appearance, many of us headed to our rooms to rest or to prepare for the evening's DKFC party and auction. Kat and I were in charge of the Entertainment portion of the festivities, and so in advance we rehearsed our "musical numbers," which were songs about De, McCoy, and the Rowdy Cowboy sung to familiar tunes on a Karaoke machine. Satisfied that the new lyrics were firmly entrenched in our minds, we waited for the time to go downstairs and make complete fools of ourselves. (Neither of us can carry a tune in a bucket, but what the heck! MORE humor for the funny bones!)

On our way out the door, we noticed a pair of men's underwear hanging on our doorknob. The Italian Stud Puppy had struck again. We made a sign that advised: "ITALIAN STUD PUPPY UNDERWEAR" and took it and the BVDs down to the party suite with us. Figured it might embarrass the little shit. (Hope springs eternal.)

We arrived on time and hung the briefs and the sign in the branches of a decorative display the hotel had provided for the party suite. Then we helped ourselves to the sumptuous meal Sue had arranged.

We visited with most of the club members at the party until Sue officially gave us the floor. We explained the Italian Stud Puppy's antics and our (very understandable) responses, to everyone's amusement.

At that point, we broke the large group into five smaller groups to write their own songs to the tune of De's most popular hit, ROW ROW ROW YOUR BOAT…or to any OTHER tune they cared to attempt.

We were astounded at the creativity that flowed from the gathering in such a short time. With only ten minutes to write, five of the dandiest songs ever written were devised. Then we had the groups stand up and audio tape their songs into the Karaoke machine, so that we could deliver a copy of the audio tape to the Kelleys at a later time. Then we all learned a song that Kat and I had written, to be included on the audio tape (a kind of "Welcome Back to Baltimore" song to the tune of HELLO DOLLY.)

The auction to benefit the North Shore Animal League followed. A representative of the League, Mike Arms, detailed (with photographs) the North Shore's recent rescue of animals displaced or injured by the hurricane in Florida. He received a round of applause, and by the end of the evening, the club members had rounded up not only some nice mementos from the auction, but more than $2,5000 for the animals at North Shore.

Just as things were about to wrap up for the night Sue received word that Carolyn had found another star pin (a memento of De's star ceremony which attendees to that event had received), and that it would be sent over to auction off. Since we had one book of poetry without a star pin attached, and figured it would bring a dandy price, most of us decided to hang around and wait for it. Lucky thing!

The "messengers" were DE AND CAROLYN! The crowd fell silent, after a mighty roar of approval, and Sue quickly snatched the Italian Stud Puppy's underwear off the flora in the room. (Sorry you missed it, De and Carolyn!) (I'm especially sorry because Daryl would have been so completely mortified HAD you seen it!)

After Carolyn had taken her seat, and just before De took his, I asked the group if they'd like to sing, "HELLO DeFOREST" to him LIVE, and they all responded with great enthusiasm. So, we sang to De, in unison, up close and personal:

Hello DeForest
Well hello DeForest
It's so nice to have you back
In Baltimore.

You're lookin' swell, DeForest,
We can tell, DeForest
You're so sexy, you're so handsome
And a whole lot more

We feel the room swayin'
All your fans are sayin'
"You are our favorite guy,
Don't you forget

So take a bow DeForest
We'll love you forevermore, DeForest
You're our favorite actor –
You're the best!

At the words, "Take a bow," De did just that, graciously. It was terrific and touching. When the song ended, De thanked everyone in attendance for their support of his career and then asked if everyone would introduce themselves.

Wellll....Daryl had indulged quite heavily during the evening. (By this, I mean he had ONE drink, and inside his diminutive body, that's all it took.) I looked over at him at one point after the Kelleys had arrived, and he confessed to me, "Oh, great! Now they're here and I feel like puking!" He sat back and tried to look unobtrusive, but since he has been writing to them for eons, when it came time for him to introduce himself to them, De said, "Oh, I know you! Daryl. Come over here. I want to get a good look at you." Daryl stood up and said, incredulously, "You do?!" De said, "Yes, we do." So Daryl stepped over and shook hands. Carolyn's first question to Daryl was, "Where's your cat? Where's Bones?" Daryl answered, "He's in my room." To which De responded, "Well, go get him!" Daryl, obedient for the first time in anyone's memory, headed out the door at near-warp speed. De turned in his chair, studied the door that had closed behind Daryl, and proclaimed with great conviction, "That is the LITTLEST vet I have ever seen!" (Daryl was told, later, what De said about him, and now says that his veterinary practice will be named THE LITTLEST VET...and I believe him!)

After everyone finished introducing themselves (while Daryl fetched Bones), the final auction item was put up for bid: A copy of De's latest poem, the star ceremony pin...and a hug from De! Everyone who had already spent their money was mortified. Obviously Sue had not shaken every last dime out of everyone, because the bidding ended at $205.00 (only because Sue wouldn't take MasterCard or VISA). Sue didn't hear Carolyn match the "winning" bid, so an attractive blonde fan got the pin, the book of poetry and the hug. She generously offered the pin and the book to the bidder just below her. SHE WAS AFTER THAT HUG!

Soon after that, De and Carolyn excused themselves (they had been in attendance for a good hour) and Sue admitted it WAS time to call a halt to the festivities. (It was after midnight by this time.) Most of us headed for bed...the logical choice after eighteen or more hours of non-stop activities!

The next morning the die-hards were up and first in line again to claim good seats, including Vicki Potter from St. Louis, who we had met at OktoberTrek 1990. She was bemoaning having to spend the last night in the hotel alone (her roommates were flying out that night), so we invited her to join us in our room that night. (A Trekker should never be alone at a convention: it is an unwritten law!)

De appeared at 3 PM on Sunday and was just as full of mischief as he had been the first day. The questions were more sobering, though, so he was able to reflect on his career, his marriage, and other important matters to a greater degree than he was usually asked to address publicly. Someone asked him what it was like to be an international icon, and he said, "Well, it feels a little as if I've DIED already!" He expressed gratitude that he had met and worked with Gene Roddenberry closely for so many years. It wasn't all serious stuff, though. He said he'd vote for Sue Keenan for President of the United States, since she runs his fan club so well.

After De's appearance on Sunday, Shery Veltkamp gathered a gang of renegades together (15 of us) and we went down to the hotel restaurant for a farewell get-together. Kat abused the server mercilessly, which he loved, and says she became officially engaged to the Italian Stud Puppy simultaneously. (How Kat manages to flirt with a waiter and still become engaged to the guy sitting next to her is beyond me, but she manages, and Daryl didn't seem at all upset by the two-timing instinct Kat obviously possesses, so…what can I say?! Those two deserve each other! Hee hee hee)

After dinner, Daryl went into hysterics, saying he had been sent to dinner with us by Sue, so that she could "do" our room without interruption. When the rest of the dinner party heard this, they decided they HAD TO accompany us to the room to see what had happened. We walked less-than-eagerly to the room and opened the door.

All weekend long, every time we had left our room, we would find – upon returning – additional creepy-crawly creatures (rubber spiders, snakes, skeletons, etc.) and additional signs warning us: "It's Coming Real Soon!" So we were NOT eagerly anticipating anything even remotely PLEASANT. Not at all. And we were not disappointed.

We opened the door and found…a blow-up skeleton sitting under the covers of one bed. On his chest was the sign: "It was here. Where Were You?" We happily jumped into bed with "Bones" and lots of people took pictures. Because we had been going non-stop for days (weeks, even) our enjoyment of "Bones" did not go as far as it had at OktoberTrek 1990. We behaved ourselves and just hugged him. There was no dancing, no suggestive poses, nothin'. We did take him home in our suitcase, however. Now that Kat's "engaged" I don't guess Bones has a chance anymore… and I'm too respectful and reverent to even consider such things…

Oh, just one more thing. Sunday evening I was ready for bed…half dead would be more accurate…In fact, I WAS in bed…and Daryl walked in to tell us good-bye. Upon seeing me, he proclaimed with incredible conviction (and very loudly), "YOU LOOK LIKE HELL!"

I thanked him for noticing and I'm enormously glad he's engaged to Kat instead of to me. His is a type of honesty I can live without, thank you very much

LOVE (OR LUST) SONGS BY DE'S FANS
AT OKTOBERTREK 1992

To the tune of ROW YOUR BOAT

Sex, sex, sexy body
Walkin' 'cross the stage
In those tight, hip-huggin' jeans
De sure don't look his age!

Bones, Bones, Bones McCoy
He's a sexy guy
When you see his big blue eyes
It makes you want to sigh.

Hug, hug, hug De's bod
Just don't video
What goes on at a con
Our guys should never know!

(And I thought KAT was the only sex maniac in the bunch!)

To the tune of GILLIGAN'S ISLAND

Just sit right back and we'll tell a tale
A tale of a world-famed Doc
Who started as a bad guy
In B-movie schlock.

He played out a famous gunfight
At the OK Corral
He did a lot of guest spots
It was good for his morale.

The Great Bird of the Galaxy
To De one day did come
"Please come and join our family
As we head out for the sun."

The adventure still continues
After 25 short years
With De's star always rising
In the eyes of all his peers.

To the tune of HAPPY DAYS ARE HERE AGAIN

De Kelley is here again
The fans are gonna cheer again
And we're glad that he is near again
De Kelley is here again.

Carolyn is by his side
Looking on with so much wifely pride
It's been such a meteoric ride
Carolyn is by his side.

We sure hate to see them go
They put on a real terrific show
They are people we are glad to know
We sure hate to see them go.

To the tune of YELLOW ROSE OF TEXAS (lyrics by Kris)

De is the rowdy cowboy
We girls just love to love
His eyes are even bluer
Than Texas skies above
You can talk about Roy Rogers
Or the dudes from Lonesome Dove
But De's the only cowboy
That we will ever love.

He was such a bad-ass cowboy
Most girls would run in fear
But we knew behind those blue eyes
Was someone very dear
You can take us in the hayloft
We won't even raise a fuss
You can take us out behind the barn
And have your way with us!

My mama told me not to trust
A man with big blue eyes
He'd only steal my heart away
And tell me lots of lies,
But let him tell me all those lies
And play me for a fool
And leave me layin' in the dust

I'd think it's really cool!

De is the rowdy cowboy
We girls just love to love
His eyes are even brighter
Than Texas skies above
You can talk about Roy Rogers
And the dudes from Lonesome Dove
But De's the only cowboy
That we will ever love!

HOPPY HALLOWEEN

Kat and I hand-made a pair of truly grotesque (by design) bunny costumes that we had planned to wear to AC Lyles' place in Bel Air on Halloween. (We had never perpetrated a got'cha on AC and figured it was time.) We each had a pair of panty hose over our heads, with cardboard pushed into the legs to make them resemble crude bunny ears; we had white jogging pants on with men's BVDs outside them (to hold the cotton tails we had made). Two women have never, in all of earth history, looked so ludicrous as we did in those get-ups. We were hysterical thinking what AC's reaction would be when he opened the door and spotted us standing there with a gaudy, plastic basketful of Reese's peanut butter cups (his favorites).

We were planning to tell AC, when he answered the door, that we were there to audition for the sequel to Night of the Lepus, the last film AC had made with De. As bad luck would have it, President G.H. Bush called AC out of town on Halloween weekend to campaign for him, so…

We needed another victim.

Kat suggested De and Carolyn, and I said no. "Jeez, if the neighbors catch us looking like idiots…it'll embarrass the Kelleys. We can't do this to them!" (Up in Bel Air, where the Lyles lived, we knew that no one would know us, whereas the neighbors near De would recognize us.)

Kat moped and groused, and I finally conceded. We'd gone to some expense to make ridiculous costumes, so…it was decided. We'd go to the Kelleys. Still, I was nervous about it.

Kat called Carolyn before we left, to be sure our victims would be at home when we arrived. When Carolyn answered the phone, Kat said, "Boo! Happy Halloween!" Carolyn returned the greeting and Kat asked permission to stop by and drop something off. Carolyn said the threshold had just been painted and was still wet. Kat said, "Oh, we don't want to come in. We just want to drop something off and we want you to look out the window when we do it, if you can."

Carolyn said, "Oh, you can come in; I just don't want you to step on the threshold when you do it." Then she laughed, "Maybe Kris can carry you over the threshold, since Daryl isn't around!"

Kat mentioned what a beautiful, clear day it was and Carolyn said, "This is exactly how it was when we moved here: clear, quiet, no crime…"

Kat said, "Darn! We missed it!"

Carolyn joked back, "You weren't even BORN yet!" and Kat responded, "Details, Carolyn! Details!"

Carolyn then asked Kat, "Does Kris want to talk to me?"

Kat asked me, "Do you want to talk to Carolyn?"

I was so nervous about our impending got'cha that I said, "No!" (because I knew we were about to make complete asses of ourselves). Kat said to me, "Oh, come on!" and whispered, "She asked for you. She'll be hurt if you don't say something."

So I leaped over to the phone and said enthusiastically, "Hi, Carolyn!"

Carolyn asked, sounding a little hurt, "Don't you want to talk to me?"

I said, "Yes, yes, yes, I do!" -- and she laughed.

I said, "But --- we're gonna see you in a few minutes."

Carolyn said, "So we can talk then, right?"

I said, "Right!"

"Well, I'll talk to you then, then! Bye!"

We drove over. I was really traumatized by this little thing we were about to do, worrying that it was very much over the edge.

Kat had a rather large amount of Science Diet dry cat food pebbles clasped tightly in one fist as we got out of the car. I had the Halloween basket in one of my hands. We started up the sidewalk to the front door and then were surprised from behind. De had exited the garage door and come around behind us. When he saw us, he looked...perplexed. Perhaps a better word is troubled. By us. I immediately felt we had sinned, big time.

Kat went over to him and started with, "Oh, I'm so happy to see you....I'm so excited to see you...I can't control myself!" – and, back behind her cotton tail, she dropped the Science Diet pellets on the sidewalk, to make it look as though the bunny had pooped.

De looked down at the kibble mess and said, "Oh, my." He started to lean down to collect the joke, and Kat said, "Don't worry about that! I'll pick it up!"

De said, "Oh, no! You two get in the house. Get in the house right now! I'll take care of this."

Yep, it was definitely the neighbors he was concerned about. Me, too.

Kat and I went inside. Carolyn saw us and laughed. I handed her the basket of Reese's peanut butter cups and said, "Happy Easter. I mean, "Hoppy Halloween!"

She sat the basket down and invited us into the little room, their office. We began to chat. Not long after, De stepped into the room.

Kat said, "Sorry, De." De said, "It's all taken care of. Don't worry about it."

I said, "I'm really surprised you invited us in, the way we look, and after all that."

De studied our costumes a little more and said, "You know, you look a little bit like nuns with that head gear you have on."

Kat shot back, "This is the first time I've ever been thought of as a nun!"

De laughed. "Yes, Kat, I can imagine that. You might want to aspire to something like that."

Kat said, "Not on your life, Mr. Kelley."

De again studied the costumes. "You have your underwear on the outside of your jogging pants."

"Yes," I said. "We didn't want to put a hole in our pants, so we bought men's underwear to cut a hole in. It was funnier than women's, since we're – women."

De said, "If you had put them on backwards, you wouldn't have had to cut a hole in them!"

I said, "Good thinking, De. We weren't thinking. What could possibly lead you to believe we were thinking --- at all?" He laughed.

Kat joked to De, "If we'd done that, and hadn't cut holes, we could have given you the underwear afterward!"

De laughed and joked, "That's right. That's why I said that!" We all laughed.

I acknowledged, "Kat and I both have bigger butts than you do. These shorts would fall down around your knees!"

True to form, Kat commented, "That would be good!"

Carolyn said, "That's quite enough, girls!"

We visited for about an hour, chatting about much less controversial topics, and then Kat and I "hopped" home…

A PERMANENT JOB AT LAST!

In November 6, 1992 I was given word that I would be hired on permanently at Warner Bros. I called Carolyn right away to give her the good news. She wept! I joked "For heaven's sake! I'm going to have to stop telling you good news! You can't handle it!" She said she knew how hard I had worked for this and how long I had waited.

"I'm just thrilled for you!" Then she asked, "Have you called your parents and told them?"

"No, I just found out, thirty seconds ago. My boss doesn't even know, yet!"

"I'm the first person you called?"

I said, "Yes." She continued crying. "Carolyn, get a grip!"

She repeated, "I'm just so happy for you!"

Murphy's Law. A week later, the producer of Bay Watch called. He said his wife had started a new production company "up there in the San Fernando Valley" and that he had recommended me to be her assistant. I was flattered, and I was torn. I had just accepted full-time work at WB, the studio I had felt intuitively drawn to for a number of years.

I called Carolyn and De, and explained the situation. De was the voice of reason. "You have the option of WB which is settled, stable, and permanent; you have this other option, which is a start-up concern with no real history."

"Yeah, but the new one is working in production, where the action is!"

"Production is the least stable area in the industry, unless the show is already a hit—and then it's staffed."

I sighed and said, "I know." I paused again, thinking, and then said, "It's nice to have a steady, permanent position."

Carolyn appended, "In a company that's going to be here for another thousand years."

De said, "I realize the other offer is flattering as hell, and you take it, if that's what your heart says to do. We're not directing you. You will be a success in any direction you choose. These are just our thoughts."

I said, "That's why I called and why I asked. You're more level-headed than I am when it comes to stuff like this. I'm just glad you confirmed what I've been thinking."

Carolyn said, "I think you're smart to stay at Warner Bros. You can be there forever as long as you don't 'screw it up,' as they say!"

I assured her, "Oh, I don't intend to 'screw it up', as they say!" She then said quietly, "That's not what they say, you know! They don't say 'screw it up'!" I whispered back, "Yes, I know. But we won't say what the men folk say, will we?

We are ladies, we are!"

She laughed and said, "Yes, we are, Kristine Marie!"

THANKSGIVING 1992

Mom and Dad drove down from Washington State to spend Thanksgiving with me. I was very excited about that, because Thanksgiving without family members can be a truly pathetic time. Mom and Dad had never met De and Carolyn and, because they hadn't, they were under the mistaken impression that I was over the edge about this mythical couple. Dad in particular thought I was nuts. That was kind of okay with me, because I thought he was pretty nuts, too. I dropped a note to the Kelleys inviting them to share Thanksgiving dinner with us that year. I knew they probably wouldn't, or couldn't, but it didn't hurt to ask. I'd be giving special thanks for them at the table whether they were there or not.

So it was a big surprise—and a relief, and a scare—when the Kelleys called. Carolyn said that although they couldn't partake of the dinner since they had other plans with another couple, they would like to drive over for an hour or so early in the day to meet Mom and Dad. I hung up the phone and made the announcement; Mom and Dad looked a little like deer caught in headlights. I got goose bumps. This was going to be Really Something: the moment of truth. Mom and Dad were going to be able to proclaim, at the conclusion of this visit, whether or not I was bonkers.

On Thanksgiving Day, Mom and Dad dressed up a little more than usual and Dad jabbed me with the caustic comment, "We'd better dress up for these gods who are visiting with us today!" I could tell he was ready to pronounce me insane well in advance of the event. Needless to say, I was a basket of nerves when the doorbell rang. I went to the door and opened it. De had a lovely little plant in his arms for me. I said, "Thanks!" and hugged him and Carolyn. I made the introductions and we all sat down. I sat as far away from everyone as I could get, hoping they'd settle into couches and chairs close to each other. Much to my relief, they did.

I poured everyone coffee, and they began to chat. Before long, Dad and De were chatting up a storm, and Mom and Carolyn were conversing. Then it became a kind of free-for-all. This occurred rather quickly, the moment the Kelleys decided my folks were comfortable with them and not at all intimidated by the circumstance. They got into a sort of gabfest about me because initially that was their common frame of reference. Instead of Dad's usual caustic remarks, I heard him saying some of the sweetest things about me! Then I thought that he was probably just following the Kelleys' lead, since they were being so complimentary. Then I decided, no...I guess Dad really did think I was worth claiming as a kid; he just had an uncommonly weird way of showing it.

Acutely embarrassed by their comments, I finally directed, "Okay, you guys. Knock it off."

Carolyn grinned, "Just stick your toe in the rug and take it, like a good little celebrity."

I laughed. So did De!

Dad told De a bald-faced lie: "I never did like Star Trek much (hah!) but I enjoyed the hell out of your westerns." That was music to De's ears. He enjoyed nothing better than having people recall and recognize his non-Trek roles. Dad said, "I tell you, now that I've met you and see for myself the kind of guy you really are, I think you deserve an Oscar for those sons-of-bitches you played in westerns! Sitting here, you don't look like you could act at all!" De threw his head back and laughed. That was Dad. He had a way of complimenting people that just never came out quite right. When De laughed, Dad realized he had said something a little amiss and made a course correction. He amended, "What I mean is, you are such a gentleman, such a nice, quiet, reserved man. Your roles in westerns—I just don't see how you managed to do that so convincingly. You don't look like the kind of guy who could find something that alien to his own nature. I mean, even your good guy, McCoy, is crabbier than you are!"

De got the point and was touched by it. "Well, thank you very much. That's a very great compliment."

Dad zeroed in finally and sincerely with, "You deserve an Oscar!"

I agreed, "Yes, he does!"

Carolyn nodded, "Yes, he does!"

Mom said, "It's unanimous!"

When the door shut and the Kelleys were gone, I was pretty well convinced that the visit had been a whopping success. Dad turned to me, sighed then said, "Kris, I apologize. I thought you were out of your mind. I really did. I was afraid for you. But now I see you were absolutely right about those two."

Mom said, "They're precious. You're very lucky to have them in your life."

It was then that I said, "And I'm lucky to have you in my life..." and then I joked, "and on my side after all these years!"

Dad shot back, "We've always been on your side!"

I hugged him and said, "I know." After that, I couldn't even joke about the Kelleys without Mom or Dad coming straight to their defense! Now who was over the edge, I mused, smiling.

One morning De called. He started out saying that an L.A. Times columnist had retired, and that he thought I should apply for the opening and write a daily or weekly column. We discussed that for several minutes. I told him what a tough job it would be to come up with stuff anyone would want to read on a daily or weekly basis. He said, "Well, you manage to do it for us on a daily basis, so I know you can do it for others, too." He said the

139

reports of my trips to Builder's Emporium and everywhere else I went were always very funny, and that the newspaper would probably jump at the chance to sign me up and write for them. He said he didn't know how to go about getting something like that started. I said I did.

He said, "Then do it!"

I said, "Yes, Boss!" But I never did follow up on his suggestion.

FUN CONFRONTATION WITH CAROLYN

Carolyn called one afternoon and mentioned that she had been going through her black book on De, trying to find when he had done a certain show.

"While doing that, I ran across the date we met you for the first time!"

Delighted, I said, "You did?"

She said, "Yes. It was January 6th, 1969!"

I said, "No, it wasn't."

She said, "Yes, it was. I have it right here in my book."

I said, "Sorry to have to disagree, Carolyn, but the date was May 4, 1968. The date you have is probably the publication date of the magazine in which my article appeared about meeting you."

She wasn't convinced. So then I supported my claim with facts: "The festival is called the Apple Blossom Festival. How many blossoms are on trees in Washington State in January? There's still snow on the ground in Wenatchee in January!" She admitted that her date suddenly didn't make much sense. I added, "As it mentions in the article, Mom and dad were seeding the fields in Cle Elum that weekend. That indicates it was planting time, not snow shoveling time." Then I said, "And Star Trek was canceled after '68…and your letters to me say that De had just begun the third season, and mentioned Spock's Brain. I have the letters." Then I joked, "You didn't write to tell me you had submitted the article about meeting you before you had met me, did you?"

She laughed heartily at that and said, "I guess not!"

It was a fun argument, but she was upset over how she could have written down the date incorrectly. I reiterated, "I know for a fact that January '69 was the newsstand date for the magazine. Maybe it was a reminder to you to pick up a copy?"

She said, "That might have been it…"

I was at work and another call came in. I asked if I could put her on hold. She said that wasn't necessary, as we were through "arguing."

About two hours later, she called again on another matter wanting me to make her more of the stationery I had computer-generated for her. I let her know I was happy to do that.

About two minutes later, De called. He again mentioned the L.A. Times columnist that had retired. Then he said, "You know you have the ability. I got you started with that Wenatchee visit in…January, 1969." A-ha! Had he been enlisted to continue the argument?

I joked, "Mr. Kelley, excuse me? Did you say January, 1969?"

"Yes," he confirmed.

I asked him, "Who you gonna believe? Me or your wife?"

De laughed, caught between a rock and a hard place.

I said, "It was May 4th, 1968, De. It is etched in my memory for all time. Trust me on this!" De said he remembered that it was a very cold day and that they drove through snow on the way from Seattle to Wenatchee.

I said, "Yes, you did. On the way from Seattle to Wenatchee, you drove over two mountain passes. But there wasn't any snow in Wenatchee. It was hot there, as I recall."

He said, "I remember a trip through Georgia when my father was still alive. I remember smelling apples up there then, and I thought that was in October sometime, but maybe it was in January," and laughed.

I laughed, too, and reminded him "Georgia in January and Washington State in January are two very different animals, De!"

He was working hard to get my goat and make me laugh. I knew he was only kidding with me, or placating Carolyn, or something significant like that.

CREATION CONVENTION
PASADENA CALIFORNIA 4/4/93

Reported by Krazy Kris Smith

DeForest Kelley was an honored guest on the final day's roster of events, so of course Kat Lane and I had to be there to droo—I mean, to watch—De cast his spell over the entire audience.

Paramount producers AC Lyles was asked by Creation to introduce De (as a surprise), and AC cast his own spell briefly over the proceedings with his glowing words regarding De. He said of his long-time friendship: "I've known and worked with just about producer, director, actors and executive on the Paramount lot over the past 55 years, and nobody is more well loved at Paramount than DeForest Kelley. He is so well loved that Kat Lane and Kris Smith go down to Hollywood Boulevard every Sunday morning to polish his star on the Hollywood Walk of Fame. I have a star, too, in front of the El Capitan, and because I'm a friend of De's, Kat and Kris polish my star, too!" (Reporter's note: This is malarkey. If we polished all the stars of people who are friends or fans of De's, we'd never get off the Hollywood Walk of Fame!) There was warm humility in AC's voice. He continued: "De is everything a Boy Scout is. He is respectful, reverent, kind, all of that. And there's something else he is, too." (Someone yelled, "Sexy!") and AC chuckled at that. "I'd add lazy. It takes him five minutes to smile! I've seen some laid-back people on that lot– Perry Como, Bing Crosby, Hank Fonda, Dean Martin—but De is so laid back he makes these people look like Robin Williams!

"My three favorite people in this industry are James Cagney, Ronald Reagan and DeForest Kelley. I don't know which one I love best, but today I love De best. My arms will always be around him and his wonderful wife, Carolyn, who is just as sweet and wonderful as he is. (Applause.) He is the sweetest, nicest guy in the whole wide world. I want to give him a big hug and welcome him: DeForest Kelley!"

De was greeted by a two-minute long standing ovation and thunderous applause, screams and whistles. He thanked the audience when it finally quieted down and sat down and then said of AC, "AC says what a sweet guy I am. I'm gonna tell you what a sweet guy he is. I very seldom made it through one of his westerns alive! (Laughter.) One time he tied me to a wagon wheel and shot an arrow into my chest and turned on the rain birds, and then had the Assistant Director call, 'Lunch!', and left me there tied to the wagon wheel! So that's what kind of guy AC Lyles is!

"But really…I feel as if I've passed away already. I know I'm lazy, but I'm not that lazy! Any time AC has called me out of my rose garden to go to

143

Arizona or somewhere to do a movie, I've always packed my bags and run to him. I hope I can live up to the nice things AC said about me."

He mentioned the recent torrential rains and said he was glad they finally called off the drought before everyone drowned. He asked how many people in the crowd were from far away, and the responses included England, Germany, Texas, Georgia – and Vulcan. He said this was the biggest crowd he had seen since the 25th anniversary at the Shrine Auditorium. Then told the story of what happened at the Shrine when he got even with Shatner for stealing his English muffin during the filming of Star Trek VI. Then he explained how Shatner got even for getting even, right there on the spot at the Shrine…and then how he almost got Shatner with a stage hook…and how Shatner got even when De left the stage hurriedly, thinking he'd be murdered otherwise by the Cap'n. It was hysterical.

De then told the stories revolving around the filming of WARLOCK with Henry Fonda and Edward Dmytryk, much to everyone's delight.

He asked Kat and me to stand up so he could spot us, and thanked us for polishing his star. Then he got me into trouble by asking if my boss, Michelle Sucillon, had come along. When I said, "Yes," he asked her to stand up and immediately proclaimed her beautiful. I went over to where she was sitting and she immediately told me I was fired. I assured her I had nothing to do with it. She laughed and assured me she was just joking. (She had never seen De before and had never been a Star Trek fan nor visited a convention of Trek fans, so she was astonished to see how beloved he is. "He's an icon!")

After De was finished raking us over the coals, he said he was told by a fan (who had attended one of Shatner's and Nimoy's conventions) that Bill and Leonard couldn't figure out why De was given the most space to sign his name at Mann's Chinese Theater. With a big smile, joking, De said he had told the fan to tell them, next time he saw them, that "they finally figured out who the real star of Star Trek is!" The crowd went nuts applauding and whistling and agreeing with him.

He added: "But I tell ya, when I saw that huge space for my name, I thought, 'Boy, that's sum'pin'…and the emcee had said that some stars got so nervous that they misspelled their names. Well, I was down there spelling mine, and photographers kept tellin' me to look up and smile and wave, which I did, and then I crossed the T but forgot the S! Boy, Shatner and Nimoy got a big kick out of that!"

At that point, De opened up the floor to questions and one of the fans mentioned that Walter Koenig had said that De saw a flying saucer. De repeated the question: "Walter Koenig says that I saw a flying saucer." Several people laughed at that, and De, in mock exasperation, said, "Well, you're a hell of a crowd to be laughing at that!" The whole place came unglued with uproarious laughter. De then described what he saw on that night in the early 1950's and said that other people reported seeing similar sightings that night to the newspapers, so he and Carolyn and their friend weren't the only eye witnesses to the strange craft. He finished with, "That's all I know. I know what I saw."

A woman told him that he had a great influence on her life and that she had recently become a doctor. He thanked her for telling him that and said that it is always heartwarming for an actor to find that they will be leaving something significant like that as a legacy. He said he had heard from many, many medical people who had been influenced by McCoy, and hopes to hear from many more. "I wish I had kept more of those letters."

Someone asked if he really drinks mint juleps. He said that he has had them, but that his favorite drink is vodka and water with a twist of lemon in it. "I call it the Kelley julep."

Another fan asked how he liked being an Admiral, and he said, "I loved it, but the minute I got home I was immediately stripped of my rank!" Everyone laughed. "But I have my little insignia in the bedroom."

Another question involved whether De knew that Star Trek would be the big hit and legend it has become, and he said, "No idea in the world, until about 1972 after it went into syndication. I was at a convention in New York where 500 fans were expected and 10,000 showed up. I went home and told Carolyn, 'I don't know what's going to happen with Star Trek, or when it's going to happen, but something big is going to happen.' I knew then, but not any earlier. You are the people responsible for the success of Star Trek, and I want to thank you right now." There was much applause.

One of the final questions involved whether we will be seeing De in any more movies. De said, "I really don't know. That depends on AC Lyles. Star Trek really took charge of my life after 1966. Before then, I was doing something that was very unusual in this business: I was crossing over between movies and television, which was rare at that time, but then Star Trek grabbed hold of us and I became so identified with this role..."

At that point, he queried the audience: "Just out of curiosity, how many of you would like to see a Star Trek VII with the original cast?" The house came down with roaring, stomping, cheering, whistling and other ear-splitting jubilation. De said, "The reason I ask that is, I don't think Paramount even knows the amount of mail we receive regarding this, and I know there are some Paramount people here today. We, who do see you so often, know what the feeling is..."

He turned back to the original question and continued: "I will have to sit down with my agent and decide, okay, this is where I want to go, or where I don't want to go. I have to re-align my life."

Someone asked about the episode For the World is Hollow and I Have Touched the Sky (the love story between McCoy and Natira) and De said, "Oh, yes! That was the episode where they gave Shatner a break from the broads…but it almost killed him!" (Laughter.)

At that point, De read his most recent poem, The Dream Goes On and On and On, and the audience loved it. Then he thanked everyone for coming and received another standing ovation as he left the stage.

He was DE-lightful, as always.

Wenatchee Washington May 4, 1968…
Place and date of Kris' first up close and personal encounter with
Carolyn and DeForest Kelley

De and Kris at the Spokane Convention, 1988

PARAMOUNT
TELEVISION

Miss Kristine Smith
Star Route #4 - Box 60
Cle Elum, Washington 98922

August 12, 1968

Dear Kristine:

I was so impressed with your letter and story that I turned it
over to Teresa Victor, Leonard Nimoy's Girl Friday with a
suggestion that it might make a good magazine piece.
She in turn contacted Pat Langdon of T.V. Star Parade who is
interested in using it for a Holiday Story.

Enclosed is the note Teresa sent to me.

Seems you are in for more fame.

Live long and prosper,

DeForest Kelley

DK/tv
Encl.: 1

DEFOREST KELLEY --- ACTOR

A DIVISION OF PARAMOUNT PICTURES/5451 MARATHON STREET, HOLLYWOOD, CALIFORNIA 90038/TELEPHONE (213) 463-0100
... and friend !!!

148

STAR TREK

A PARAMOUNT TELEVISION
PRODUCTION IN ASSOCIATION
WITH NORWAY PRODUCTIONS

FROM THE LOG OF THE STARSHIP ENTERPRISE

8455 Beverly Boulevard
Los Angeles, California 90048
September 17, 1968

Hello Kristine,

Thank you for both your letters, received just recently. We
had a 10-day vacation a couple of weeks ago, so I was delayed
in getting some of my mail. Now we are back shooting episodes
for the third season which will begin for our show on September 20th with one called "Spock's Brain" which I think you will
enjoy.

Carolyn and I both are so glad that you finally got in touch
with Pat Langdon - and that your cute story will be published.
Maybe that will be the beginning of something interesting for
your future....we hope.....and we shall be looking forward to
its publication. That should really make you a celebrity in
your own right in Cle Elum!

Stay happy as you are now - and "live long and prosper"....

Sincerely,

DeForest Kelley

D
K
:
c

PARAMOUNT TELEVISION PRODUCTIONS
780 NORTH GOWER STREET, HOLLYWOOD, CALIFORNIA 90028 • PHONE (213) 463-0100

Remember this crazy letter I sent to De after
his "penpal" message at the Dearborn Convention?

Dear Penpal:

Why haven't you written? I've been sitting here
looking forlorn for almost a year now. (OK, so
it's only been seven months. Time STANDS STILL
when one is forlorn...)

I'm NOT one to notice these things, and I KNOW
how busy you are--but where's MY autographed
photo? I am INCENSED! I've got an empty spot
on my wall (there's only ONE small empty spot
left) that's JUST the right size for a picture
of --- who? But, of course, I SUPPOSE I could
put a picture of SPOCK there--but it wouldn't go
with the rest of my De-cor, if you get my drift.

So, if you want to stay in my good graces (and,
good gracious, of COURSE you DO!) SEND ME A
PICTURE!!! And sign it something short and
sweet like "To my dear penpal (who belongs in
a pen!) with warmest regards and hugs and kisses
and Saurian brandy, "Bones." (And don't worry
if you can't see the picture afterwards: I've got
lots of pictures but no SIGNED ones!!!)

Grin!!!! It looks great on ya!

XOXOXOXOXOXOX,
Krazy Kris

P.S. I lock HER up when I see you. Aren't you
GLAD?!!!

A NOTE FROM...DE

Dear Kris,

Maybe this a little shut
you up until I'll
send you a big one
for your wall de-cor.

DeForest

P.S. Stick it in your
wall — I —

The "breakthrough" letter, August 1987

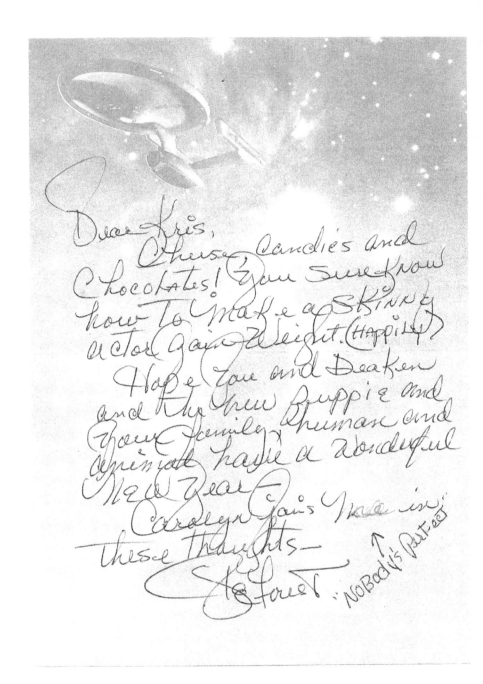

Dear Kris,

These candies and chocolates! You sure know how to make a skinny actor gain weight. (Happily)

Hope you and Deaken and the crew puppie and your family human and animal have a wonderful New Year.

Carolyn joins you me in these thoughts —

Lve S De Forest : Nobody's Perfect

Note De sent Kris after receiving a bunch of fattening "get well" goodies following one of his surgeries

TRUST ME
I'M A DOCTOR

316741

Maybe you can use
this in Denver —

USA

~ March 5, 1988 ~

wish you a whole year
of feeling good and being happy,
a whole year of good times
and good places
for them to happen,
a whole year of bright beginnings
and dreams come true.

Happy Birthday

All good wishes,

DeForest & Carolyn

Card, balloon and gift certificates De & Carolyn sent after
reading skits Kris and Kat Lane wrote about having
(an imaginary) dinner with them at upcoming
Denver convention.
(Subsequently, she had an actual dinner with them in Denver.)

We hope Deaken will enjoy having his very own traveling bag to accommodate all his gear on his trip here. We saw this bag the other day and decided it was just made to be Deaken's "luggage".

Sue sent us the tape of your Pacific Outdoors show — we thought you came over just great, very un-self-conscious camera-wise. Are you sure you don't want to be an actress? I can't remember if I ever told you that we enjoyed the tapes you sent us long ago, with your stand-up routine. Very good! And the shots of Deaken are terrific. Thanks even tho it's late.

My days lately are taken up with physical therapy visits, all this month, relative to my hip problems — but all will be well one of these days.

Between you & me, want to tell you that Di called Ann Harner and gave you a boost — but told her, truthfully, that you had no knowledge of the call. Maybe it will help.

Hope you're enjoying the bachelor days and no more kitchen tragedies. Di says hello & don't forget the chin-tickle for dear Deaken. Myrtle says hello too — she's loving all the extra attention these days. Bye — love,

Carolyn

Letter from Carolyn about Deaken's travel "luggage"
for his relocation trip to southern California

154

Deaken loving his travel bag from the Kelleys

De's rendering of what Deaken *actually* heard when
Kris told him that Deaken heard an ant
walking behind her wood stove
sixteen feet away in Eatonville.
Yeah…right!

Happy New Year, Deaken!
Please give this to Tippi, with
all good wishes for a happy
New Year to Shambala & all
the friends there who have been
good to you.
With our love — ♥ & 365
Chin-tickles (one for each
day in 1990.)
    De & Carolyn

Deaken Smith
c/o Kris Smith — Apt. 39
8717 So. La Cienega Blvd.
Inglewood, CA   90301

Carolyn Meets Deaken at Shambala, 1991

De, Deaken, Kris and Carolyn in Elephant Straw Pile, Shambala, 1991

Photo Carolyn included in Kelley Christmas Card   Photo by Bill Dow

Carolyn, Deaken and De in Kris's back yard   Photo by Bill Dow

Carolyn, Kris and Deaken

Carolyn, Tippi Hedren, De **at Shambala** Photo by Kristine M. Smith

De's favorite photo ever!

Hangin' with Deaken in Kris's Encino Backyard   Photos by Bill Dow

De, Deaken, Carolyn

Deaken, Kris and De in Kris's backyard

De with photographer Bill Dow after the photo session in Kris's back yard. Photo by Kristine M. Smith

"Doggie" De and "Kitty" Carolyn   Photos by Bill Dow

When Kris saw this photo, she wrote to De, "You'd better sign this one, 'Forget it, Kris!'" — so he DID! (One of the sexiest McCoy photos, ever, in her opinion!)

Photo De sent to Kris's Dad to take to the hospital
with him. It worked! He was treated like royalty!

Upper: Portrait   JoanneGraham.com   Lower: Seattle convention

OktoberTrek Shenanigans '92

This Pachyderm Poop Plaque was DE-livered to the
Kelleys at OktoberTrek '92

De picking lemons for Sue Keenan and Kris after trip to Shambala

De Farmer….

De Artist…

Delightful!

Success (more or less…) at last!

De's blue-and-white-striped *got'cha* shirt, Oakland CA   K.M. Smith

Kris's Standup Debut, Oakland, "Husband-Hunting on the Enterprise"

Sacramento
Photo by Greg Heimbigner

Starland, Denver
Photo by Kristine M. Smith

173

Photo by Kristine M. Smith

Happy (75th) Birthday to De

Wearing the **Star Trek VI** Crew Cap De got for Kris since she so
narrowly missed appearing in/working on the movie

De at home… date unknown

Harve Bennett speaking at De's star ceremony 12-18-1991
Photo by Kristine M. Smith

Please join a group of special friends
who will be on hand to celebrate
as

DeForest Kelley

receives his star on the
Hollywood Walk of Fame

11:30 am
Wednesday, December 18, 1991

7021 Hollywood Boulevard
across the street from the New Hollywood Galaxy

Reception to follow at the
Paramount Dining Room Patio
5555 Melrose Avenue
Hollywood

R.S.V.P. to Allison Jackson's Office
(213) 956-4880

SPECIAL GUEST
OF THE
DeFOREST KELLEY
PARTY

Leonard Nimoy hugs De prior to speaking at De's star ceremony
12/18/1991

Trek Cast handprints and signatures in cement in Hollywood

Photos on this page by Kristine M. Smith

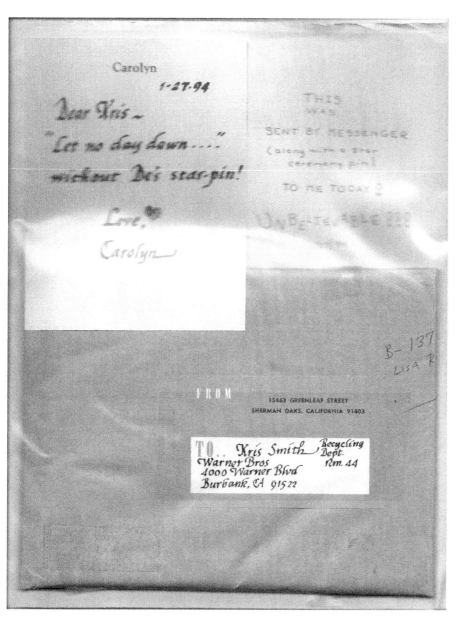

Carolyn

1-27-94

Dear Kris —
"Let no day dawn...."
without De's star-pin!

Love,
Carolyn

THIS
WAS
SENT BY MESSENGER
(along with a star ceremony pin)
TO ME TODAY!

UNBEATABLE!!!

FROM
15463 GREENLEAF STREET
SHERMAN OAKS, CALIFORNIA 91403

TO... Kris Smith — Recycling Dept.
Warner Bros   Rm. 44
4000 Warner Blvd
Burbank, CA 91522

B-137
LISA R.

Special DE-livery after Kris lost her
DeForest Kelley star pin in the bushes!

O Happy Day! 6/25/95

Carolyn and De posing with Kris's new car, which they paid for in a
surprise switcheroo… July, 1995

Carolyn and De enjoying Deaken at Kris's Encino home, July, 1995

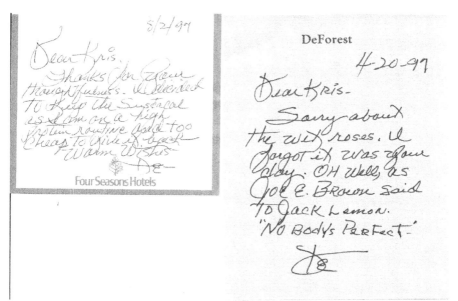

"Dear Kris, Thanks for your thoughtfulness. I decided to keep the Sustacal as I am on a high protein routine and too cheap to give it back. Warm wishes, De."

WE ARE THINKING
ABOUT YOU AND
HOPING THAT YOU
ARE FEELING
BETTER..
L♥VE
DeForest
AND
CAROLYN
7-24-98

Drawing and note De sent Kris's mother

OCTOBER 27, 1998

Dear Kris,
Consider this a note of
Congratulations for You and Your
family for the magnificent care
and devotion that all of You
have given to a terrific Lady.
We know and understand
Your Love for her for we
could feel the goodness
that she reflected in those
moments that we knew her—
With deep Sympathy
Love
De and Carolyn

Note De wrote after learning that Kris's mother had passed away…

182

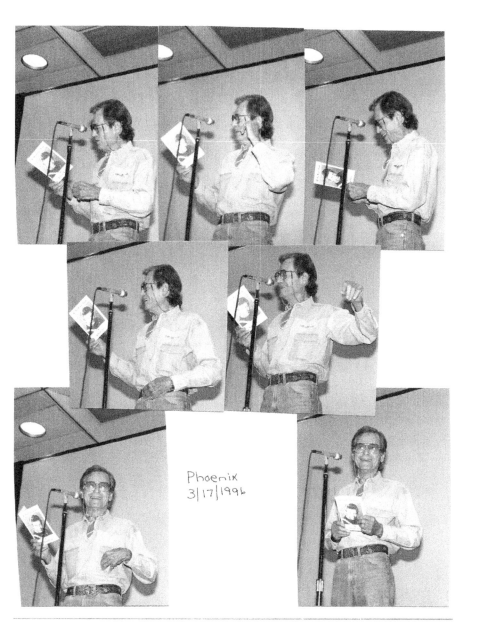

Phoenix
3/17/1996

Photos by Kristine M. Smith

183

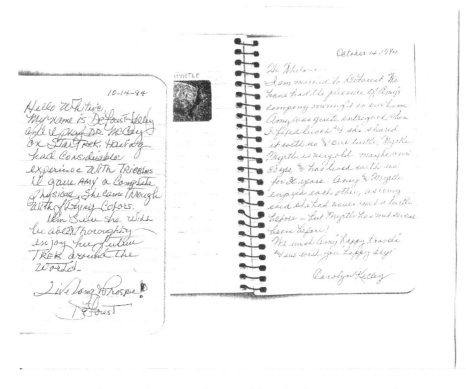

Notes to Whitnee, who sent a bear-with-a-backpack on an adventure

Carolyn and DeForest Kelley at home with Cheers, date unknown
Photo given to Kris on one of their many visits)

See you 'round the galaxy

Dear Kris,
I hope the quote
below meets with
your approval—

"a fast paced book,
full of laughter.
Written with Comedic
skill. It's a delightful
read."

DeForest 7/26/95

Raccoon Birthday Delivery

Carolyn and Poppy—Bill Dow

187

Kris, Dorothea Smith (Kris's mother) and A.C. Lyles at A.C's star on the Hollywood Walk of Fame, 1995

Hot air balloon anniversary gift for De and Carolyn:
"For two love birds who really know how to stay high on life!"

Sadly, the Kelleys' modest home at 15463 Greenleaf Street in Encino, California was leveled by the new owners in 2006 and replaced by a much larger dwelling. Photo by Kristine M. Smith

Dear, dear Deaken
...my heart smiles.
With our very best
wishes for your happiest
of birthdays!
De Forest & Carolyn

* Sheri from
  MOBILE VET
  called to
  wish Deaken
  a happy birthday!
* KAROLA gave him
  a blanket
* The Kelleys sent
  this card...

29 USA

Deaken Smith
17820 Collins Street
Encino, CA 91316

Carolyn's beautiful calligraphy is on full display here…

191

Upper: De with Fancy and Myrtle at home in his back yard
Lower: Carolyn with her birthday balloons

"Dammit, Kris, I'm an actor—<u>NOT</u> a writer!"
Foreword De wrote for Kris's book, **Let No Day Dawn that the Animals Cannot Share** (She thinks he did a fine job…)

He must have known that "Mom-cat" (KRIS) approved of us for he greeted us warmly with head rubs and licks - I refer to KRIS as the best "Mom-Cat" I know - She has a touch of Magic with both Wild and Domestic animals - She is deeply concerned for their welfare and care. She is concerned about their environment as well as our environment on this planet we inhabit. She possesses a real talent for expressing these feelings as you will see when you read this lovely book of poems. And make no mistake about it - She also has a wild sense of humor. She is known among some of us as "KRAZY KRIS" - - - She's CRAZY alright - CRAZY LIKE A FOX - - NOT A CAT

DeForest Kelley

P.S. Dammit Kris, I'm an ACTOR - NOT a writer! -

194

12/23/98

Dear Kris,

We think your condo looks great. Hope all is well with you and your dad and that your holidays will be peaceful — With good wishes — De, Forest & Carolyn

The last note De wrote Kris before she became
his personal assistant and caregiver in March 1999

In Memoriam
When Kris finally got to the star again… she left these roses from the
Kelley's garden to grace De's star on the Hollywood Walk of Fame

VISITS AND CALLS AND SUCH, OH MY!

On May 16, 1993, Deaken's 14th birthday, he received a card from Carolyn and De. The inside was hand-printed in exquisite calligraphy by Carolyn. She called that afternoon to ask how Deaken was enjoying his birthday. I said, "Great, except that he just about ate your card." I thanked her for sending me a newspaper article about dress codes in different industries and joked, "It's reassuring to learn that I haven't violated the entertainment industry dress code yet, which is 'no bare chests'." She laughed.

In June 93 my nephew Phil graduated from Franklin Pierce High School in Tacoma. The Kelleys had kept close tabs on him ever since we reconnected in 1986, and as the big day approached, I decided to fly up and be in attendance for the event. I asked De if he would sign a Star Trek tie to Phil, and he happily consented. He and Carolyn added a few more items to Phil's graduation stash and sent me merrily on my way to Washington.

When I got back from the graduation, I sent the Kelleys a program, since Phil was near the top of his class and had won significant honors, including recognition for his athletic endeavors, particularly in football. De called to say he enjoyed the commencement program, but then, joking, wondered why Phil hadn't won the "McCoy Award"!

I told him, "I was pretty upset by that, myself!" Then I joked, "I'll tell him you noticed!"

De said ruefully, "You probably will tell him that, won't you?"

I said, "I sure will! He'll love knowing you were joking about that. You really studied that program, didn't you?"

He said, "I sure did. Tell Phil congratulations for us. We're proud of him."

Not long after I returned home, the Kelleys received a letter of thanks from Phil. It was so touching, they called to tell me about it and then said they were putting it out in the mailbox for me to pick up and keep. "We think you will really treasure it."

I retrieved the letter and read:

"Dear De and Carolyn,

Thank you very much for the tie and the comic books and the autographed football. All are going to be cherished, I assure you. Kris wasn't lying when she said, "You'll love what De and Carolyn got you." That was an understatement. I thank you for the autographed football. I feel honored and proud. Soon I will have it in a glass case to show everyone I know that De and Carolyn care for me. It's hard to believe that a movie super-star actually knows me and cares for me. I will always look at it and it will remind me of you two. This sounds like I'm thanking you a lot, but I can't thank you enough. Well, that is about it. Thank you again! Sincerely, Phil McNiven."

Carolyn called me later and said, "If you're not careful, you're going to have some real competition in the writing field with that nephew of yours! He can make me cry, too!"

While in Washington for Phil's graduation, I visited Cle Elum (my home town) and neighboring Roslyn, which was famous for having been a childhood home (for a time) of Bing Crosby and, more recently, the setting for the television series Northern Exposure. I wandered around in Roslyn shops and found a coffee mug that was just perfect for De, so I snared it. It reminded me so much of the story De often told at conventions about the time he was dismounting from his horse in a western and accidentally kicked the horse next to him. The offended horse bucked and kicked him, causing him to flip in mid-air and land, hard, on the ground very near the tie rail. The director, Edward Dmytryk, smoking a cigar, immediately came over to see how De was. When De reassured him, "I'm fine," Dmytryk drawled, "Gee, I'm sure glad I hired real cowboys!"

The mug I sent De depicted a cowboy in a corral, nearly flat on his face, with a horse's front foot propped on the cowboy's upraised butt. The legend on the mug asked, "What Did You Think of My Performance?"

De thanked me for the mug. I could hear the grin in his voice. He said he hadn't seen one like it before, which was lucky on my part. I told him, "Belatedly, I wrote a limerick that I should have delivered with the mug." De said, "Let's hear it."

Now, De was a cowboy with flair
He rode side by side without care
Till one day, while dismountin'
He spurred the next mount and
Spent half of his scene in midair!"

De laughed. "I like that. Send it to me."
I said, "You got it." Then I said, "I have another limerick for you and Carolyn. Ready?"
"Okay."

It isn't all a bad dream
I'm as stuck on you as I seem
If you had your druthers

198

You might prefer others –
Or even the transporter beam!"

De guffawed. "Send us that one, too!"

He said Carolyn cried reading my letter about my trip to Washington and my visits with family members there. "I thought she was crying because it was so long, but finally figured out it was because it was sentimental."

I told him I was going to have to stop telling her sentimental stuff.

He said, "That's the worst part about family gatherings. The leave-taking is almost not worth the reunion."

He handed the phone to Carolyn, who again reiterated how the letter had made her weep uncontrollably. I then told her about Mom and me kissing, multiple times, all along the way to the airport. "Dad told us to knock it off, finally. I told him, 'If we do this for thirty miles, maybe by the time we get to Sea-Tac, you'll kick me out and say, 'Get the hell out of here!' instead of getting misty, which is my choice!" Carolyn agreed that leaving is always terrible.

On July 10, 1993 I had a wonderful visit with the Kelleys at my home in Encino. As De and Carolyn got out of the car, they headed for the trunk, so I went to the screen door and peeked out to see what the deal was. Carolyn spotted me and motioned for me to come out. De was pulling boxes of stuff out; I could see they were treasures still in their original packages. Also inside the trunk was a small sack of miscellaneous goodies. De loaded me to the gills with all the trunk stash I could possibly pack. He picked up the remaining sack of oranges and held them out to me, grinning, "Here are some oranges, too!"

I joked, "Put 'em in my back pocket. I think they'll just fit."

We headed indoors and sat the goodies on the dining room table. Then everyone met my newest addition, Rowdy Catboy, Deaken's newest playmate, an eight week old black and white kitten. De and Carolyn petted him while he remained snuggled in my arms. Carolyn showed me pictures of Fancy, Cheers and Maggie, her dearly departed pets (two dogs and a cat). Then she showed me the card and x-ray she has to show to Security at airports to prove she has an artificial hip so they would let her through the metal detectors at the check points. She said that De always wore cowboy boots with metal in the heels "and is always detained and practically asked to undress to get through security."

After a while, I opened one of the boxes they had brought. Inside was a Tholian Web globe. Carolyn said, "If you look right here, you will see what happens." I looked and looked and nothing happened.

She shook it a little bit and exclaimed, "There it goes!" I looked again and noticed little stars floating in the water and said, "That's neat."

199

De said, "Turn it on." I tried.

Carolyn said, "There it goes!" and I watched and watched but could see absolutely nothing different at all.

De asked me, "What's happening?"

I confessed, "I don't know; nothing that I can see."

He said, "Maybe you should check to see if it has batteries in it!"

So I checked: no batteries. I looked at Carolyn, "You've been seeing things, and I was trying to see them, too!"

Carolyn asked if I was ready and eager to go back to work, and I said, "Oh, yes!" I told her I got some new duds, and they asked to see them. I went into the closet and pulled them out on hangers.

De said he liked the Indian one best. "It must be my Cherokee blood."

I queried, "Cherokee blood, did you say?"

He said, "Yes."

I said, "I have a little Cherokee blood in me, too. Oh, God! Maybe we're related! Palefaces weren't exactly on friendly terms with Cherokees, we're they?"

De said, "Apparently somebody was on friendly terms with them!" We all laughed.

I brought Deaken into the house and they watched him groom RC for a while. As he did that, De mentioned that watching Deke do that was as relaxing as watching an aquarium. I agreed.

De told me he was doing an infomercial the following week regarding the 25th Anniversary Star Trek Game. Then he said, "It looks like a tough game." I asked if they had seen the MCI commercial he had just finished, and neither had yet. Deke suddenly became intensely interested in some noise in the next room somewhere, and seemed to be staring right through the wall, so I asked Deke, "What is it, Baby?"

De mused sarcastically, "I'll bet he hears another ant." I looked at him and scowled.

Carolyn said, "He's not going to let you forget that, Kris—ever!"

I said, "I guess not! But damn it, it's a true story!" De grinned.

Carolyn was amazed at how large Poppy had grown, and mentioned the photo she had taken of her a year earlier when she was a kitten. She said it was the best photo she had ever taken, and I agreed, saying it was good enough for a magazine and that I had it on my refrigerator door, and always would. We sat outside and watched Deaken for a while. De noticed Deke's weight loss and said he was looking good. De asked how long it took me to get to work, and I said, "About 35 minutes. It's twelve miles."

Carolyn said, "De goes to Beverly Hills for a haircut, and that's too far anymore, with this terrible traffic."

Very soon thereafter, Carolyn looked at her watch and exclaimed, "It's 4 o'clock. We've got to go!" and De agreed.

Carolyn added, "We have to get to the market," and joked, "They're waiting for us!"

I escorted them back to their car and noticed the sunroof on their '91 Lexus for the first time. De joked that he'd only had it open once. "It almost sucked me out, so I haven't had it open since!"

TV GUIDE ANTICS

The July 24, 1993 issue of TV Guide carried a large section in it about STAR TREK. In a sidebar, "What's Kirk's Crew Up To?" the cast was profiled and interviewed briefly. The paragraph regarding De read as follows:

"DeForest Kelley – the star's who's been most reluctant to milk TREK for all it's worth – is still waffling about his autobiography prospects. "I'd want it to be richer, more encompassing, and maybe more novelistic than just the 'I...I...I' thing," says Kelley, whose pre-TV career included such movie hits as Gunfight at the OK Corral. So what's the holdup? "It would involve a tremendous amount of digging and research," sighs 73- year old Kelley. "And I'd have to go out in the garage..."

(Reprinted with permission from TV Guide, 1993 TV Guide Magazine Group, Inc., volume 41, No.30)

On July 23, Carolyn called. I asked if she had seen the new TV Guide yet, and she exclaimed, "Oh, yes! We just got it yesterday!"

I directed her, "You tell De to go out into the garage and pull something out and go 'I-I-I' or 'we-we-we' but to do it!"

Carolyn turned to De right then and there and told him, "De, Kris says you're supposed to go out into the garage, pull something out, and go wee wee!" She cackled loudly and I nearly deafened her, protesting loudly, "That is not what I said!" hoping De would hear me.

I said, "Carolyn! You straighten him out right now! Tell him I didn't say that! Carolyn! Please tell him I didn't say that!"' I was mortified; Carolyn thought it was hysterical.

After we had settled down, she mentioned that a noted Star Trek chronicler had called De sometime recently to try to get an okay to write a biography on him, or to help him write his autobiography, and De had thanked him but said no, he wasn't going to do one.

I protested, "I wish he would. Can't you just get him to turn on a tape recorder when he feels like reminiscing?"

She said, "Oh, he'd clam up right away if I did that."

I said, "It's important!"

She didn't respond to that. She said she wanted to give Sue and me some Star Trek cachets.

I queried, "Those smell-pretty things?"

She said, "No, those are sachets. These are postal service envelopes celebrating Star Trek."

She described them to me. She said they had four of them left and wanted to give two of them to Sue and me.

I said, "That's wonderful. Thank you."

She asked if I wanted De to inscribe them to us individually, or just to sign his name. "They'll be worth more as collector's items if he just signs his name—in case you want to sell them somewhere down the line."

I said, "Oh, Carolyn! Of course have him inscribe it to me!"

I said, "I can't speak for Sue. I'm afraid you'll have to ask her individually."

I told her about a young collector I had met in an autograph line once.

I told her I had come awfully close to offering to break his neck for him, because of some of the things he had said about how valuable his collection would be after the original cast croaked.

She laughed and said, "Yes, we're aware of why an awful lot of these requests come in here."

On August 25, 1993 Carolyn called to ask how I felt. I had been under the weather, so I quickly reassured her I was fine again.

I asked how she was and she said, "Oh, I'm fine, but De has a cold. He was dyin' yesterday, but he's better today!"

I heard De, in the background, joking, "Don't tell her I'm dyin'!" (Perhaps he thought I might report it in a newsletter!)

She said, "De caught the cold in Detroit last weekend after he got out of the shower in his shorts and stood watching television under air conditioning for a few minutes."Commenting on her sentence structure, I joked, "He got out of the shower in his shorts?"

She laughed and said, "No, that wasn't how it happened."

I said, "Oh, that's good. I was a little bit concerned for a minute there."

On a fall afternoon I visited with Carolyn at her home. After about an hour, De wandered in. I didn't see or hear him until he was in the room next to me, offering his hand. I stood up and said, "Howdy! Er, How! De!" Indian-like, referring to our Cherokee heritage. He pulled up a chair and sat on it. The chair gave out a large cracking sound, and he jumped up quickly, then sat down on it again.

Carolyn told me, "It's just settling."

I said, "I'm glad. I was going to offer to trade chairs with you, De, but you weigh less than I do, so you just stay right there."

He laughed and nodded, "I will."

I managed to diagnose the problem of a "chirp-less" mechanical bird for Carolyn—dead batteries—and left briefly to facilitate its rehabilitation. De and Carolyn were very pleased with my veterinary services. We visited for an hour or more and discussed a lot of topics, some serious and poignant, others humorous. At one point, we were discussing Underground Atlanta and Underground Seattle. Carolyn exclaimed, "I didn't even know there was an Underground Seattle until after I left there. It's down there near where the Space Needle is now, isn't it? Near Yesler?"

I said, "I think so."

She said, "Well, when I lived there, Yesler was the red light district, and good girls like me didn't go down there."

De joked, "Yesler, That's My Baby!" I scowled at him and then laughed.

Then I said, "I suppose those ladies were familiar with Underground Seattle!"

De chimed in, "It isn't too likely they'd be 'entertaining' right there on the street, I don't suppose!"

A day later I called Carolyn to be sure they would be home to accept a delivery the morning before their anniversary (September 6th). Carolyn told me they would be home that morning but then had to fly to a QVC station in Pennsylvania in the afternoon.

Then she said, "De was just trying to call you, but your line was busy."

I said, "I was arranging for tomorrow's delivery to you." She said, "Oh!"

I said, "So! What did De want?" She said, "Here. He can tell you."

De got on the line and sounded very sincere—momentarily. He said, "Kris?" I replied, "Yes, sir?"

He said, mock-sincerely, "I can't think of a nicer anniversary present than the one you've already given us…Nothing will ever top it…so don't even try. *You have given us the bird!"* I laughed real hard!

Then he said, "Here's Carolyn again."

Carolyn got back on the line and said, of the bird, "You know, it's really a silly little thing, this little bird, but we got used to sitting here and having it chirp at us, and it means a lot to have it chirping again."

I said, "I know. I know how much that little bird means to you!"

She said, "They say, if you need something done, ask a busy person to do it! Thank you very much, Kris."

I said, "My pleasure. Any time."

SURPRISE TRIP TO VALLEY FORGE

The next day when Carolyn and De called to thank me for the anniversary basket, I was expecting just that: a brief call of gratitude. But the conversation took an unexpected turn almost immediately.

"Kris, the hot air balloon just arrived. It's sitting right here on the floor of my office. De just carried it in."

At that point, De got on the line and joked, "We've cancelled our flight for Tuesday and are going to ride to Pennsylvania on this!" Then he handed the phone back to Carolyn.

She said, "It is just magnificent! You're spending all your money on us again."

I protested, "No, I'm not!" I added, "Did you read the card?"

She said, "No. It just got here. De just now carried it in to me. De, get the card." De handed her the card. She read it aloud, choking up as the meaning sank in, "For two people who know how to stay high on love. Kris and Furballs."

At that point, she dropped the bomb: "Listen. We've made arrangements this morning for you to go to the [upcoming] Valley Forge convention, unless you don't want to go." My mouth fell open. I was just speechless.

I managed to say, "Oh, Carolyn!" then just went silent.

She said, "I've got flight schedules here and I want to know when you want to fly." She gave me a couple of options. I was so hesitant, knowing I couldn't afford any of the trip, not just the flight, but didn't want to admit that was what was troubling me.

Finally, though, the truth had to come out. "It isn't just a matter of the flight. I can't afford the hotel or the shuttle or anything. That's why I decided a month ago that it was impossible."

Carolyn asked, "Well, how much are the rooms?"

I said, "$80 something a night, I think. But maybe I could stay with Sue and Sandy one night— they told me I could—and get down to only having to pay for one night. I could handle that."

About an hour later, she called again. "Kris, I got you a Weekender's Special at the convention hotel for $82.00 night for Saturday and Sunday nights in a special suite with two TVs, a coffee pot, a whirlpool bath, and including a free breakfast…"

Oh, man. I thanked her and then reported, "Then in that case, I can afford the con tickets."

She said, "No, I'm going to arrange for those, too." She started to repeat the amazing room amenities.

After listening through the lengthy list again I laughed, "Gee, I hope I can drag myself away from the room long enough to see De's appearance!" Carolyn howled.

During the QVC show the next day, I was astonished and tickled pink to hear De relate the story about the day I got batteries for their "phony little" bird! The next time Carolyn called, she asked me, "Did you catch the show?"

I said, "I sure did. It was great!"

"Did you collapse when De mentioned your name?"

I said, "God, Carolyn! I just about did! I couldn't believe it!"

She said, "I was sitting back stage in the green room, and when I heard him start to tell that story, and then when he said your name, I thought, 'Kris must be losin' her mind!'"

A few days later I went to the Kelley home to pick up the tickets. I got to the house and walked to the porch. The front door was wide open, but the screen door was shut, so I rang the doorbell. After about 20 seconds, De peeked around the corner from the hallway. He smiled and opened the door, saying, "Come on in."

I hugged him. He motioned me toward the living room. De sat down on one of the love seats, and I sat in the other one, across the room from him. Presently Carolyn joined us. I asked if they had seen Myrtle yet that day and De said, "Yes. She was circling the wagons out there about an hour ago. She'll be back at around five looking for dinner. She goes over by the garbage cans and rattles things there when she wants our attention, and then I go out and feed her."

Carolyn said, "Well! I guess we'd better dig out the tickets for you now." She got them, handed them to me, and said, "Now, don't lose these."

I said, "Lose them? Never!"

She said, "Go ahead and look at them. Make sure everything's there." I looked inside and reported to them that Mom had joked, "Make sure they're round trip tickets!"

Carolyn assured me, "They are!"

De, playing on Mom's comment, exclaimed, "They are?" feigning surprise and dismay.

I looked at him and scowled. I asked if I could take them to dinner one night at Valley Forge as a thank you, and she said, "No! Merry KrisSmith early!"

We talked for a while. I asked if they dream in color. Both said yes. Carolyn said to De, "But you didn't always. I remember when you started dreaming in color. You were astounded and told me about it when it first started happening."

I said, "I remember having my first Technicolor dream. I was about ten. It was just after I'd seen The Music Man for about the tenth time. Robert Preston came to my ranch home in his band uniform and danced around on the green grass!" They laughed. I theorized, "We still had a black and white TV at that time, but that's about the time that motion pictures started coming out routinely in color."

De said, "Perhaps that's about the time I started dreaming in color, too, for the same reason."

I joked, "Because you loved Robert Preston?"

He shot me a look and said, "No."

I said, "Maybe our brains switched over as soon as movies showed us that color was an option."

He said that was very likely.

Carolyn asked what year I was born and I told her, "1951." She said, "We were living in New York when Kristine Marie came into the world."

I said, "Yes. You were working at Warner Bros. just a short walk from your home."

She said, "Yes! You know all about us by now."

We returned to the kitchen where she handed me a sack of six home-grown tomatoes. Knowing that I didn't relish tomatoes, De joked, "We only give my tomatoes to people who don't like them, so they don't ask for any more!"

On September 29, I got another call from Carolyn telling me they had received more studio samples and she asked if I'd like to drive over and pick out what I wanted of it. While visiting with them Carolyn mentioned having lost four pounds recently during her cold and the many weeks she spent coughing.

I said, "Coughing is hard work! It's no wonder you lost four pounds."

"Especially the way I cough! I don't cough like a lady; I cough like a lumberjack!"

I told her, "I do, too. I also blow my nose like a fog horn. It's real embarrassing, because without thinking, I'll do it at work and people will just stop everything to marvel at it!"

De threw his head back and laughed. He told a hilarious story about a loud belly flop Carolyn essayed at the Riverside Hotel many years ago. "We laughed about that for days afterward!"

Carolyn said, "We're still laughing about it, as you can see, fifty years later!"

I straightened up and asked, "So! You swim?"

She shot back, "Not as well as I dive!" and we all cracked up again. We talked about exercise. I said I'd walk, but don't feel secure doing it alone.

De said, "It's getting to be a scary world, isn't it? Twenty years ago I wouldn't have thought twice about going for a walk, but I do now." I told them that my Arrest, Search and Seizure class—to become a Humane Officer—trained us how to avoid looking like victims or easy targets.

De pulled the Trek box over to me and I went through it, piece by piece, to see what I wanted to keep. De had a set of Starfleet insignias in a case and asked if I would deliver it to Sue some time.

I said, "Sure! You bet."

He added: "No hurry. Just the next time you see her." We watched their backyard critters and I was able to spot a mutant ground squirrel they had been telling me about. I said it looked as though it was put together by a committee.

De told me about a tall tree that used to be in their back yard. It had a jay living in it that grew fond of De and Carolyn and would even land on their shoulders. The jay raised a family. One of the little jays fell out of the nest and De rescued it and put it in a cage and then sat it near the air conditioning unit next to the house. "The mama jay would fly over and feed it through the bars. We thought it was such a phenomenal thing that we called the L.A. Times and a photographer came out to do a pictorial on the situation. Because the photographer was a stranger, the bird wouldn't come back in and feed the baby. So I had the photographer hide, and I went down by the cage. The mama jay came back in right away. The photographer got some fantastic shots. Sometime I'll dig 'em out and show them to you."

On October 5th, her birthday, Carolyn underwent surgery to alleviate severe pain she had long endured in her lower back. She called two days earlier than the surgery date to let me know what was happening, but made it clear that she didn't want visitors in the hospital or flowers. She said De would call me following the surgery to let me know how everything went.

De called at about 4:30 the afternoon of surgery and said, "Hello, Kris. This is DeForest."

I said, "Hi!"

"How are you?"

"How am I? I'm on the ninth fudgesicle of the day, waiting to hear how Carolyn is!"

He apologized, "Well, she came through the surgery just beautifully. She has a young doctor from the east coast who really knows his stuff and loves his work, and he told me she lost only 22 cc's of blood during the whole thing."

"How long did the surgery take?"

"Four hours."

"Good Lord!"

He said the incision site was heavily bandaged and that her legs were in a leather-like get-up to help with circulation. "She has a little pain medication bulb that she can squeeze whenever she feels any pain, but she hasn't needed to at all, and seems to feel fine during her periods of wakefulness."

He said the flowers from Sue's club were delivered to her at the hospital, and when I said I wanted to send some too, but Carolyn had told me no earlier, De said, "Oh, please don't. There's no room for them there, and your cards are all she wants or needs. Don't strap yourself. Just call her tomorrow evening and keep those cards and letters coming."

I said, "Not to worry. I'm on top of that!" He gave me Carolyn's phone number at the hospital. I asked how long she'd be there, and he said, "Four days."

I said, "Good. Back home on the weekend!"

He said, "Yes," sounding relieved. I asked if he was tired, and he responded, "Oh, yes! We didn't sleep at all the night before, and then—as Carolyn told you—we had to be there at 5 a.m. for the preparations…"

I called Carolyn every day. She reported that the doctor was very pleased with her progress. She said she had no pain in her legs at all when she walked. "It's my best birthday present ever!"

But her stay lasted a couple days longer than anticipated. On the 8th, she called and, after visiting on the phone for a while, reported, "I wanted to tell you that I won't be going to the Valley Forge convention."

Heartbroken, I said, "Oh, Carolyn!"

She said, "Well, you probably had it figured out anyway, didn't you?" I said, "Well, I was hoping you'd be able to make it."

She said, "No. It would be too much, this soon after surgery, with that long flight and the long drive at both ends." I sighed, very disappointed, but of course understanding. Then I offered, "Can I stay here and help you, then, while De's gone?"

She said, "No! You have tickets! I arranged the trip for you! You have to go!"

I called De a few minutes later and offered, "I'll be happy to go shopping or do other errands for you to free you up to be with her, or just to rest."

He said, "That's very thoughtful, but I shopped just before she went in, and I'm in like a bear."

I said, "Well, I'm serious…so, if there's anything I can do to help out, you let me know, okay?"

He said, "Okay. Thank you very much, honey. Thanks a lot."

VALLEY FORGE

On October 20, 1993 Carolyn called to wish me a happy trip. Then she asked me, "You *will* write me every day while you're gone, right?" I said, "Oh, sure!" She laughed and said she was just kidding. I told her that Mom had called to wish me a happy trip, too, and that I had told her, "Oh, Carolyn has seen to that!" She giggled.

At the Valley Forge convention, De introduced me as his star polisher on both days. On the second day, he said to the crowd something along the lines of, "You really know who loves you, when a fan will do something like that." He said it very sincerely, and the audience accepted it as such. Afterwards, several fans came over to me to talk about their love and respect for De, and one of them said, "If I lived close enough to his star, I would be honored to polish it, too." Then she thanked me for keeping De's star the shiniest star on the Walk of Fame.

At one point, De was talking about Pennsylvania's gorgeous autumn leaves, and then he said, "We Angelinos are happy just to be able to see a tree, let alone one that changes colors for us!" That got a laugh. "Carolyn and I do have one magnificent tree—an oak or a maple, I guess—out over our back fence that changes color in the fall." At that point, he turned back toward me, sitting in the audience, and asked, "You know the tree I'm talking about, Kris? You've seen it." I nodded, confirming to him that I had seen it. "Well, it's a beauty, and we love it."

As a result of that statement, a fan came up to me following De's appearance and said, "You know him! You've been to his house and everything!" I nodded and let her know that De was every bit as sweet as she felt he was—which made her day.

De relied on me a couple of times to relay questions from fans in the rear of the auditorium, since the acoustics in the place weren't entirely adequate.

De got downright philosophical and spiritual for a short period of time each day. At one point, an Iowa man told him, "Our children think it's wonderful that you are the son of a minister, too."

De responded, "Oh? Are you a minister?" When the man nodded, De cautioned him, "Go easy on your children. They have a rough row to hoe. It isn't easy growing up perfect, you know. It's one of the reasons I moved to Hollywood from Georgia and became an actor!"

Then the minister's wife chimed in: "Our daughter wants to be an actress, too!"

De said, "See? There you go!"

The next day, De said, "I guess it's not possible to kick all the religion out of a preacher's kid. I wrote a couple little poems. Hope I can remember 'em. There's a Catholic Church not far from us, over our side fence, and most of the time I can go out into the back yard and see the cross that's on the roof there. But not long ago, a tree that stands between us and the church sent branches out that obscured my view of the cross, and I couldn't see it anymore, so I wrote a little thing...let's see if I can remember it...just a minute, now....

A branch has blocked my view of the cross
I always thought God was boss
Then again He must be
For only God can make a tree!"

The audience applauded and roared its approval. Then he said, "A little while later, I saw that someone had pruned that tree back, so that I was again able to see the cross, so I wrote...I won't get this one exactly right...I wrote something like...

I'm happy again, I'm able to see
The cross that stands above the tree
I know it's silly but I like to think
Someone did that just for me!

Then De said, "One more." He pulled this one out of a pocket.

Time is really
The blink of an eye.
Where do they go
Those who die?
What is below?
What is above?
What is in store
For those we love?
All that's been written
And all that's been said
Still does not answer
What happens to the dead?

The audience was awed and silenced by that briefly, then they applauded warmly, at which time he promptly changed to a happier subject.

"Hallelujah and amen! What else is on your minds today?"

In early August 1994, seven months after the Northridge earthquake that had devastated Sherman Oaks where the Kelleys lived, I arrived at the

Kelley's close to 6 p.m. and parked across the street, then walked up to the front door and rang the doorbell. Carolyn opened the door. De was standing in the hallway near the living room and I went over and hugged him and said hello. I walked into the living room. We had refreshments. I sat a coaster on a table which was supporting a huge box next to where they had motioned me to sit. De saw where I had placed the coaster and where I planned to sit my cola while opening the box, and said, "Sodder theah." (Meaning "Set her there.") Then he chuckled and said, "That's what Grandma Casey used to always tell me: 'Sodder theah, F'ost.' She called me F'ost."

Then he said, "I really hated that. So one time my mother helped me buy her a scarf—I was eleven years old—and I said, 'Grandma Casey, I have a present for you, but to get it, you have to promise me you'll never say, 'Sodder theah' to me ever again.' She promised me. So I gave her the scarf, and she loved it, and then put it on the table and said, 'Sodder theah, F'ost!'" De threw his head back and guffawed at the memory.

I laughed too and then said, "Your first real lesson in giving: Don't give with any thought of reward in your mind, or you may be disappointed!"

He laughed and nodded, and then I fantasized, aloud, portraying him in conversation: "Now, Grandma, let's go ovuh this again! What did we just discuss?"

He laughed and said, "Sodder theah, Kristine Marie..." (Move the coaster to the other table). I looked at Carolyn and she indicated where to put it down, so I did.

I said, "Yes, suh."

De said, "Christ! Can you believe it's August already?"

"I cannot. It feels like it should be about April to me."

"That's exactly how I feel. I've never had a year travel the way this one has."

"I really think that quake had something to do with it."

He pointed at a remaining chink in the ceiling, and said, "I'm sure of it." Then he said, "You know, when you're ten you can't wait to be twenty. You get from twenty to thirty without thinking a thing about it at all, and then—I just don't what happens to the years after that. They just disappear! Suddenly I'm near the end of the road— real near the end!"

He said it with a laugh and with a degree of startled realization that had poignancy in it, but without disappointment, fear or frustration. I paused and didn't say much, and Carolyn said, "Open that box and look what's in there."

I went into the box and began to pull out a bunch of Star Trek paraphernalia. She said, "There isn't very much that's De, but we thought you might like it anyway." I pulled each out piece by piece, commenting on all of it, some with genuine joy and other stuff with humor. I pulled out a Kirk doll. Carolyn said, "I don't know why they send us everybody else's stuff and none of the McCoy stuff." As I pulled out some bookmarks, Carolyn said, "I must confess something here. There were two De bookmarks, but I kept 'em. I want to send one to Ann and I want to keep one." I pulled out helium Enterprises, a puzzle, a medallion, several ties, magazines, a T-shirt, two mugs—of Kirk and Spock.

At that point, De said, "I want to call Bill and Leonard and ask 'em, 'Who got my cup?'"

I said, "Do that. Hold theirs hostage until you get yours!"

When the Star Trek collector's edition scripts came out, De said he would sign them if I wanted, and I said, "Yeah! That would be great!" He got up to get a pen, and then I remembered, and said, "Oh! Since you're doing this, would you also sign a photo to Joe? He's a consultant to my boss and a big Trekkie."

De said "Sure," and headed into the workroom for pens.

Carolyn hollered in to him, "Get the big black marker for these scripts!" She opened the cellophane that had been protecting the scripts with a razor blade knife that De brought back, and De said, "Just sign them, right? Or do you even want me to?"

I said, "De! Yes, I want you to!"

He said, "I'm just going to sign my name. They'll be worth something someday—probably already are!"

Carolyn said, "Oh! We've waited until you got here to feed Myrtle her dinner! Would you like to go out and watch her eat?"

I said, "Yes!" We all got up. De headed out the back door to locate her. I called to him, "If she has waited this long, it will probably be real easy to find her. She's probably about ready to knock on your door!"

I followed Carolyn into the kitchen. She took the tortoise salad out of the refrigerator and we went out the side door. Myrtle was at the edge of the lawn. Carolyn gave Myrtle a chin-tickle before setting the salad down. Myrtle liked the chin tickle. I got down on the grass. The creature cocked her head, looked at me, and didn't eat for the longest time.

I said, "Maybe she's nervous because she doesn't know me."

De said, "Oh, no. She's just slow. It always takes her this long to take her first bite. She's gettin' slower, too."

Carolyn said, "Yeah, she's slower than her old man, now." I looked up and shook my head and laughed. So did they.

I said, "Deke's getting slower, too..."

De said, "Well, he's old. But he's happy."

I said, "Oh, yes. He is that, for sure, still."

He said, "That's what matters."

213

Myrtle finally started eating. De asked me if I thought they should scrub the top of her head because it looked dry. Carolyn said, "Oh, no. It's a lot better than it was."

I looked up at De and said, "She's a wild animal. In the wilds, there'd be no one scrubbing her head. She looks fine to me. Her eyes are clear; her nose is dry. She's got a great appetite! She's fine."

Carolyn said that if the tortoise didn't eat everything, the mockingbirds would descend and scarf the rest down.

On August 16 Carolyn called to tell me the essay I had written for a L.A. Times essay contest, "Why I Live in the Valley" was a "sure-fire winner."

I said, "Oh, I wish you were the judge!"

She said, "I'm just sure it's going to be a winner." I asked her to let me know if it appeared, so I could be sure and get a few copies. I told her the expected publication date—"Sept. 6th, the day before your anniversary"—and she said, "Oh, yes, I won't forget that!"

Several days later, I was informed by the newspaper that my essay had won first place. I called to let the Kelleys know. They were ecstatic, and Carolyn hastened to remind me, "See, I told you it was a winner!"

I said, "Yes, you did. Sure am glad I listen to you!" Then I added, "But I have to do something goofy to publicize it." The photographer wanted me to wear a fairy godmother costume, hold a wand and make a spectacle of myself on Ventura Boulevard in the middle of the street. I reneged on the costume but agreed to the wand and to the mid-street photo shoot during rush hour, against my better judgment. Somehow the photographer and I survived the ordeal—but not without soiling our reputations as sane human beings, I'm sure.

On September 5th, the day before the article was scheduled to appear the Kelleys visited me in Encino. Sue was with me. Carolyn mentioned that she hadn't seen Sue in two years, since the last time Sue was in my back yard. We all went outside to see Sue's new car. She was still smarting over having sold "Tony," her classic car. De said, "I know how you feel. I still feel terrible for having sold the Thunderbird. We never should have done it."

After about an hour and a half, the Kelleys said they had to be on their way. I asked if they wanted to say goodbye to Deaken, who had been sleeping on my bed all afternoon, and they said, "Oh, yes, of course."

As the visit came to an end, we hugged all around and I said to Carolyn as we hugged "I love you."

She said, very sincerely, "Well, we love you, too—all you girls. You know that, don't you?"

214

I smiled at her and said, "Oh, yes. If I'm sure of anything in this world, I'm sure of that!"

The next day "Why I Live in the Valley" appeared in the newspaper.

Carolyn called and left a funny message on my answering machine, which I treasure. "This is your press agent calling, and I'm calling to see if you have a suggestion on what we can do for the next—pardon the expression—layout on you."

I called her back and she was so excited! "You won first place and look at that big, beautiful, color picture, too!" I was less-than-ecstatic that nearly all the humorous references had been edited out but she said, "Oh, don't let that bother you at all. It's just wonderful and you should be proud and happy. I've already received a call this morning about it!"

Surprised, I said, "You have?"

She said, "Yes! The lady I bought my pantsuit from yesterday called me up this morning to tell me my husband was mentioned in the newspaper. So I got to tell her about you. And De got some publicity. It's just a wonderful thing and we're real proud of you, and happy!"

I said, "Good Lord. Then I'm happy, too! Okay, I'm happy, too!"

The next afternoon, on their 49th wedding anniversary, Carolyn called to thank me for their anniversary gifts. At first, she seemed nearly overcome with emotion and the love-filled things I had gathered for them and by the sentimental cards I had found to give them. She said, "I just love it all." Then she added, "We don't open our presents until around 4:00 every year, because we were married at 4:20, so I hope you don't think we opened them early and have been ignoring you all day." I assured her that I did not think that.

Then I joked, "So! You're getting hitched in about ten minutes, huh?"

She said, "Yeah…" with a big, nostalgic smile in her voice. "We're gonna drink some wine at the exact moment."

I joked, "Aren't you in the least bit nervous? Sure you don't want to back out? Are you absolutely certain you're making the right decision on the love of a lifetime?"

She said, I'm sure while looking at De, "Absolutely." I said, "You were married in the Los Angeles County Courthouse, downtown, right?"

"Yes. We did it right in the courthouse—" then joked, "real fancy!"

"Well, that just goes to show it doesn't have to be fancy to last!"

"That's for sure!"

She said, "AC called a little while ago, and since De was outside, I got to talk to him. I told him all about your wonderful article and picture in the newspaper. He said he was going to go in search of a copy this afternoon and see if he could still find one. The Lyles don't get the valley edition, you know."

"I've sent him a copy already."

"Oh! I didn't know that. I hope I didn't steal your surprise!"

"Not at all. It wasn't planned as a surprise; I just wanted to be sure he got a copy. I'll call him after I hang up with you and let him know one is on the way, so he won't go nuts looking for a copy."

Then she said, "The moment is arriving, so I'll hang up now."

"Happy anniversary, you two lovebirds!" I said.

"And again, thank you for making this anniversary so memorable! We love you! Good-bye!"

In mid-August, it was discovered that Dad's chronic and increasingly debilitating back problems would require surgery. Carolyn hastened to reassure him that the surgery would be no problem at all and that he would feel immediate relief, knowing how nervous he must be to have to undergo surgery.

The first week of September, while being put through standard tests prior to his back surgery, it was discovered that he had heart complications, and that before his back could be fixed, his heart had to be repaired. He was at serious risk for a heart attack.

Carolyn called me four days after her anniversary to commiserate over Dad's diagnosis and prognosis. Then she said, "I want to thank you for sending me Dennis Morgan's obituaries from the trades."

I said sadly, "You're welcome. I sure thought of you when I heard the sad news on Gregg Hunter's radio show." Dennis Morgan had been Carolyn's favorite actor for over fifty years.

"That's when we heard it, too. De and I were in bed, listening to Gregg's program, and when he announced dear Dennis's death, I just froze. I couldn't speak. De reached over and patted my hand. And then I cried."

She started crying again. Then she said, "I suppose it's silly, but it was almost as if I'd lost De. I loved Dennis for a very long time…"

She cried a little more. I consoled her with, "I know…and it's not silly. Not at all." She quickly changed the subject. "Cutie is outside eating her sunflower seeds."

I told her how much Deaken loves cantaloupe, rinds and all, and honeydew melons, and Carolyn said, 'Oh, we love honeydews, too. They're getting toward the end of their season now, so you' better get them now!"

Then it was back to Dennis Morgan. "I received lots of calls about Dennis. Everybody knows how much I love him." She told about the time Bert Marks, an agent, called them at 11:00 at night. De answered the phone and Bert told De that he had Dennis Morgan at a party and wanted to know if Carolyn wanted to talk to him. De asked Carolyn, and Carolyn said, "Forget it!" "I wouldn't talk to him. That was about 1952 or

216

1954…no…later than that…about 1959. You are going to know everything about me pretty soon!"

I said, "Good! Then I can write the Carolyn Kelley story!"

Carolyn said, "You might as well. De isn't going to [write an autobiography]."

I told her, "I guess you know that if I write it, it will be the inadvertent start of a new world religion!" She laughed like hell at that, and repeated it to De, who also guffawed.

Later on De told us, "I did a Trek retrospective interview recently. It will be on videotape once it has aired, and the video will have more on it than what airs." Then he said, "You get a long interview and imagine it's going to be really sum'pin' when it airs and then you see the final version, and you wonder what happened! You're on there for only a few seconds, and you were interviewed for hours! I hesitate telling anyone about upcoming things I've done, because sometimes they'll sit through it for an hour—as friends did during the recent Bonanza retrospective—and I'm in it for two seconds at the very end. It's embarrassing!"

In September I accepted a full-time position as an executive secretary in Technical Support (MIS) at Warner Bros, after having worked there for five months as a temporary. My bosses, Dan Kronstadt and Paul McDonald, were such terrific people to work for and with that I fell in love with the department. It hadn't been what I was looking for—in fact, I had been terrified of accepting work there even on a temporary basis, as I knew so little about computers and "tech talk"—but the chemistry among the people was so marvelous that I decided to stay.

I called Carolyn on her birthday to sing Happy Birthday and to update her on Dad's upcoming heart surgery on the 11th. She said she and De were in stitches over that morning's letter from me, in which I had regaled them with Dad's recollection of my conception. I said, "Oh, you think it's real funny that I was conceived on a rock in the middle of Lake Cushman, huh?"

Carolyn laughed, "Yes, we do. We think it's wonderful!"

I said, "It's now readily apparent why I'm a little rocky, isn't it?!"

She laughed, "Oh, yes!"

I added, "My father is Fred Flintstone!"

I flew to Washington for Dad's heart surgery. It went well. De sent a signed photo to him in the hospital. The photo was of De in hospital scrubs and he had inscribed, "Dear Jack, If they give you any trouble, you know who to call! DeForest." Dad pinned it on his wall and the nurses and doctors treated him like a celebrity! One of the doctors told Dad, "We'd better take good care of you, if your Primary Care Physician is Bones!"

Several of the physicians and medical technicians asked Dad if he could get signed photos for them, so he asked me. When I called the Kelleys

217

with an update on Dad, I asked De if he would mind signing three more photos to Dad's medical team.

He said, "Not at all."

I joked to De, "I begged him to hide that photo, so you don't get any more requests, but he refused!"

De chuckled and said, "It's okay. Don't worry about it." Dad was so cheered and encouraged by De's kindness and by the response of his medical team to it that he perked right up, worked hard to recover quickly, and earned the "Best Patient Award"!

Mom wrote the Kelleys a note some time later:

Dear Carolyn and De,

I apologize for being so late in thanking you for the pictures and good wishes. As you know by now from Kris, De's picture made such a hit with the doctors and nurses. Several nurses even followed him from floor to floor on his many moves to visit and bask in reflected glory!! Believe me—it sure raised Jack's spirits! I wish I had the same sort of magic to make Carolyn feel better! Our thoughts are with you.

With love,
Jack and Dorothea

Anne Richardson, president of a DeForest Kelley fan club in Australia, visited California in October shortly after Carolyn had contracted a severe case of shingles. The Kelleys had planned to meet with her while she was in town, but Carolyn was in such sad shape that their plans had to be scuttled. I asked her if De would be able to meet with her, and she said, "Oh, no. He won't do anything like that without me along." She asked if I would call Anne when she got in and say hello.

I told her, "I'll be happy to do that. I can go meet her and take her star polishing, if she wants."

Carolyn said that would be wonderful. "I'll call her when she arrives to express my regrets and to let her know you'll be calling and getting in touch with her."

I said, "Give her my phone number, so in case I miss her, she can contact me."

She said, "Okay. Thanks."

I said, "I'm happy to do it. I've wanted to meet her!"

She said, "I really wanted to meet her, too, but you can't understand how miserable these [shingles] are."

Anne arrived on October 23rd. I took her star polishing. It was such a terrific day I didn't want to drop her back at her hotel when the day was over. I didn't get her back there until nearly eleven at night.

The next day, De called me at work, asking "Are you terribly busy right now?"

"No."

"I wonder if you'd do me a favor."

"Certainly!"

"I want to get Anne on the Paramount lot sometime this week, if I can find out when she wants to go. Will you call and see what her wishes are? When you find out, call me back and I'll call Rick Berman and see if his schedule can accommodate her."

I called Anne and got the information, then got back to De. "Get a walk-on for Anne, because she says she'll take a cab from her hotel."

"I'll do that. Thank you for the help and for taking Anne around the sights last night."

"I am, and was, happy to do it."

"Well, we sure do appreciate it."

About 20 minutes later he called back to let me know he had arranged a private tour of the Deep Space 9 and Voyager sets with Rick Berman's assistant, and that Anne would be met at the gate by the assistant, who would escort her on the tour. I told him, "I'll let her know. She'll be tickled pink." Then I said, "You'd better get back to your duties now, Nurse."

He half- chuckled, half-guffawed at that and responded, "I'll have to think about that one!"

Carolyn called a little later to thank me and to get a report on all I had done with Anne the day before. I told her, "We went to Hollywood to see and polish De's star; then we went to my place so she could meet Deaken. You'll be happy to know he treated her real special. We went through my De collection. I guess you know that took quite a while!"

She said, "I'll bet! I was so looking forward to meeting her. I shuffled around the house today gathering what I could find to give to Anne: an audio tape De made a long time ago; some photographs. She might like them."

I assured her, "She'll love them, Carolyn!"

She said, "It's wonderful that Deaken was so sweet to Anne."

I said, "I think he must have known she was special to you. He treated her just great, and I was really glad. She loved it." I let her know how high off the ground Anne sounded when I told her that De had procured her a special tour of the Trek sets. Carolyn said she was sorry the next movie wasn't in production yet, as she was sure Anne would have preferred to visit that set.

219

I said, "She's happy with what she has."

Then she said, "It's too bad you can't get away to go too, but you work at a studio and all of this stuff is probably old-hat to you."

I told her it was, and that I had to stay put and work, as I borrowed vacation days from next year's calendar already to fly up and be with Dad for his surgery and to go up for Thanksgiving.

Even though she was still battling shingles and a painful hip, Carolyn continued to stay in touch. At work I had been handed a little teddy bear named Amy. Amy wore a knapsack and was attempting to make an around-the-world voyage in one school year. A little girl, Whitnie Sill, had started the bear on its journey from a school in Battle Mountain, Nevada. I was the little bear's second or third stop. I asked De and Carolyn if they would like a little visit from Amy, the jet-setting bear, and they said, "Oh, yes, we would!" So I dropped it off.

De and Carolyn pulled out the journal in the little bear's knapsack and wrote Whitnie hand-written notes, letting her know that the bear had visited them.

De wrote:

10-14-94

Hello Whitnie,

My name is DeForest Kelley and I play Dr. McCoy on Star Trek. Having had considerable experience with tribbles, I gave Amy a complete physical. She came through with flying colors. I'm sure she will be able to thoroughly enjoy her future TREK around the world. Live long and prosper, DeForest

Carolyn wrote: October 14, 1994

Hi, Whitnie,

I am married to DeForest. We have had the pleasure of Amy's company overnight in our home. Amy was quite intrigued when I fixed lunch and she shared it with us and our turtle, Myrtle. Myrtle is very old, maybe over 80 years, and has lived with us for 30 years. Amy and Myrtle enjoyed each other, as Amy said she had never met a turtle before – but Myrtle has met several bears before! We wish Amy "happy travels" and we wish you "happy days."

Carolyn Kelley

The little bear continued its world tour, spending time in several foreign nations before returning to Whitnie. Whitnie wrote to me later, "Amy came back to Battle Mountain, Nevada. These are some of the places Amy has been: Oregon, California, Hawaii, Virginia, and seen DeForest Kelley of Star Trek fame. From there she went to France, Germany, Russia, and Japan. The most interesting place she visited was with DeForest Kelley."

On December 18 Carolyn called to ask if I had gone star-polishing. I of course said, "Yes! The Anniversary Boy's star is shining like gold this morning!"

She said, "I can't believe it has been three years already." She then said, "You sound a little tired this afternoon. Are you okay?"

I said, "I just got up from a nap. I had another bout with Deaken last night."

She said, "Oh, I'm sorry to hear that. What happened?"

I said, "He just has what I will describe as power failures. He'll start across the floor, go just a few steps, and then will pant, lie down and almost faint. Pretty soon he comes out of it and acts as though nothing has happened."

She said, "Is it old age?"

I said, "It's something. I'll take him to the vet as soon as I can get an appointment and have some tests run. He did that once as a kitten and scared the stuffing out of me, but this is the first time he did it as an old guy."

She said, "Try not to worry, if it has happened before and he was okay."

I said, "I'm trying not to, but it isn't normal, and I'm going to find out what's up."

Soon after I returned with Deaken from the vet the phone rang. "De asked me to call and ask you how Deaken's check-up went," Carolyn began.

"His blood work checked out ten months ago and they expect it to check out again. The lump is probably fat or an infection in a salivary gland; it's not a tumor."

She said, "De wonders why he collapsed then."

I said, "If everything checks out, it's probably just age and his weight. He wore out and laid down until he got his wind back."

Carolyn said, "I don't know how you'll ever get the extra weight off him. He's just like his Aunt Carolyn—can't exercise at all, can he?"

After a while I said, "Well, we'll just do all we can for him and he'll live with it for as long as he can happily. Like the rest of us mortals."

Still, I knew that time was running out on my wild one. I spent some time talking with De and Carolyn about his eventual demise, and we often choked up reminiscing over the many wonderful times we had shared with him through the years. Carolyn and I occasionally even sniffled and cried over the situation. De counseled, "Keep a stiff upper lip."

I told him, "I am. Deaken keeps me smiling even through my tears."

De and I had tummy problems with diverticulitis that month, too. I suggested to De soaking as often as needed in a tub of hot water, saying, "It always gives me such relief that it's impossible to think I hurt so much only moments earlier."

Shortly after the New Year (1995) Carolyn called to check up on me, and to respond to an inquiry, telling me that De did not want a gift from me for his birthday "in any form whatsoever. A card is enough." I said, "Okay. I just wanted to be sure. That's why I asked. 'If De says no, ask Carolyn, and if Carolyn says no, forget it!'" She laughed and said, "Carolyn says no and I'll put De on the phone, too, if you want to hear it from him!"

She told me that Cutie squirrel was on the screen that morning. "De took her some walnuts. She's the only squirrel we've seen today, so she's the only one that's been fed. But it's raining, so the others are smarter."

I said, "Not necessarily! Next she'll be on the screen asking you for a teensy, weensy little raincoat!"

Carolyn laughed and said, "And we'd get one for her, and I'd put it on her!" and we both laughed.

We talked about Bruce in the meat department at Pavilion's, and about what a great guy he was. "He saw my De shirt and told me, 'DeForest shops here all the time.' I told him, 'You're not supposed to tell fans that!' and he ducked as if he was about to be busted for some heinous crime. Then I told him it was all right to tell me because Mrs. Kelley is the person who turned me on to this place because of your great deals on Ensure."

De was on the other line and chuckled, "One time I went to another store where we frequently shop, and there was a new checker there. I hadn't seen her before, and she hadn't seen me before, but I ended up going though her line. I could tell she knew who I was—that was pretty obvious—but she wouldn't say anything; kept lookin' down at the groceries and working. I guess she didn't want to risk how I might react. A lot of stars don't like to be acknowledged when they're shopping, you know, and can be pretty obnoxious if you approach them. Anyway, her subconscious must have been bothering her, because pretty soon she starts humming the Star Trek theme!" He laughed. "She never said another word; didn't even seem to realize she was doing it!"

On January 20, De's 75th birthday, he called me, sounding tickled as heck. I soon found out he was embarrassed, not tickled. "I have to tell you,

I just got back from the DMV, and—this is so embarrassing—I flunked the written test the first time."

I laughed and said, "You didn't!"

"I did! Then I talked to another man there and he said he did, too! And the man told me, 'I consider myself a reasonably intelligent human being, but these questions are—'"

He paused, and I filled in the blanks: "— worded in such a way that you're not sure what the hell is being asked?"

"Exactly! Plus, on one of them, I just accidentally marked the wrong answer even when I knew the right one. That's the one that put me over the limit. It was about parking on a hill; whether to turn the front wheels toward the curb or away from the curb. I marked 'make 'em parallel to the curb!'"

He laughed heartily at that and then said, "That way the car can shoot down the hill at full speed unobstructed!"

On January 29th De called me. I had written a heart piece earlier in the week for De's and Carolyn's eyes only called "Dammit, Jim, He's My Hero, Not A Doctor!" I had shown it to Mom, who said she thought it would be a wonderful magazine article. I said, "I don't think so. It's too personal. I don't think De and Carolyn want very many people knowing this kind of stuff about them." Mom said, "Well, that's a shame. I wish more people did know this about them, so people know why you're nuts—about them!"

I said, "Gee, thanks, Mom!"

I dropped off the article to the Kelleys in a sealed envelope. De and Carolyn read it, and then De called. "Hello. Kris. It's DeForest." He had on his business voice.

I said, "Well, hello, DeForest" in my best, albeit much less-believable, business voice.

He was very serious and said, "I've just finished reading your article for TV Guide—and I think it's fine."

I inquired, "For TV Guide?"

He said, "Yes."

I said, "Serious?" I'd long since lost my business voice, but he still had his.

He said, "Yes. TV Guide is doing a special on Star Trek in March and they are interested in me again. I'd get it in right away, and I also suggest that you request to see a copy of the edited version, so that you'll be satisfied with what goes in. Oftentimes, you'll see an interview and think, 'Gee, that isn't what I said or intended at all,' and it can be very frustrating."

I was in shock. I asked, "Are you sure you want this published?"

He said, "Well, it's very flattering, of course, but it's also well-written and it's all true."

I said, "So, then, you think I should submit it?"

He said, "I don't see why not. I have no objection to it."

I said, "Wow! I'm surprised. I thought you'd think it too personal."

He said, "No. I think it's fine." A day later De called again to say he had re-read the article and thought it was "just wonderful. I think it might even be used as a special article, possibly not even in the Star Trek issue, but all by itself at some point..."

I joked, "From your mouth to God's ears!"

I slapped that puppy into an envelope with a cover letter and mailed it to TV Guide within the hour! They didn't publish it, considering it "too fannish." I subsequently placed it on the Internet on every DeForest Kelley website that would carry it. Thank God there's more than one way to shout good news from the rooftop!

In mid-April Carolyn called to ask me, "How's dear Deaken these days?"

I said, sadly, "He's winding down, I'm afraid. He's very old. He's healthy and happy, but old age doesn't last very long in kitties once they begin to show it, especially in wild ones. They try to stay as hale and hearty looking as they can for as long as they can, because the minute they start to show their age in the wild, some other predator capitalizes on it and enjoys a serval snack." I told her, "He hugs my neck at night with his forepaws, several times each night. He'll even wake me to do it, and then he'll purr and head rub me. I know it's anthropomorphic, but I sometimes wonder if he knows our time together is coming to an end and that's why he's more huggy and kissy than he has been in the past. He has always been sweet and loving, but now he's kind of smothery about it." I started to get a little bit misty, and so did she.

"It's making me cry, too."

I said, "I'm sorry. I had no idea this was going to happen when I started this subject. Sometimes I can discuss it totally dry-eyed, and other times I get surprised like this." I told her, "Deaken has been a special pride of mine. Raising a wild cat who is healthy and happy and unstressed in captivity, and well-socialized is something that's rare and beautiful. Domestic animals have been genetically designed over thousands of years to cope with people, but wild ones are genetically engineered for self-sufficiency and autonomy."

She said, "I understand completely the attachment and pride you feel in what you've accomplished with Deaken."

FATHER'S DAY 1995

On June 13, 1995 I was at work when the phone rang. It was De. Deadpan, he said, "Hello, Kris, this is DeForest. I'm calling to let you know that a package for Father's Day arrived here at the wrong address this afternoon."

Thinking he was serious, I hastened to assure him, "No, it didn't, De. It went where it was supposed to if it's made of chocolate."

He said, "Hush up, loudmouth, and listen!"

I smiled. "Yes, sir?"

De continued: "This must have come to the wrong address because I'm not your father—although I'm certainly old enough to be—but I have a proposition."

I queried, "Yes?"

He replied, "Since it came to this address—and happens to be Chocolate Decadence Cake—I thought I would keep it and we'd eat it anyway!"

I agreed, "That's a very good plan! Just don't tell my father: he'll be very jealous. He's getting a healthy food basket for his Father's day!"

De chuckled and said, "I won't say a word."

TRANSPORTATION TRAVAILS AND TRANSITIONS

Later in June it became obvious that my car was in its last days. I called Carolyn and told her the story. She said, "I wish you could get a new car so you'd be sure of its reliability. We didn't want to sell the 'Bird and get a new car, either, but it got to a point where we couldn't rely on it. It's a terrible feeling when you don't know whether or not your car will start when you need it." Carolyn asked me, "Guess how many miles we have on our '91 Lexus."

I thought about it and guessed, "12,000?"

She said, "Cut it in half. We've gone 6,000. The farthest we've gone in it is Long Beach."

Three days later I reported to Carolyn that my bucket of bolts had left me stranded again and that I wouldn't be by with their letter or to go star polishing. Carolyn interrupted me with, "You and that car!"

I said, "Have no fear! I was approved for a $5,000 car loan at the credit union and just today my mechanic told me he has knowledge of a tremendous buy for $3,000, so we drove out and looked at it. And I love it, and he's going to go through it—put it up on the rack—and be sure it hasn't been abused and that it will be reliable transportation for me."

She got real excited and said, "Tell me about it!"

I told her, "It's red! Boy oh boy, is it red! But that's okay—I never speed anyway! I've never had this new a car before! I'm excited!"

Then she said, "Listen: why don't you let us loan you the $3,000 to get the car and you can pay us back when you can—in ten years or so!"

I just about cried. I misted up and sputtered, "Carolyn! It isn't necessary! First Entertainment gave me a loan."

She said, "It's no interest with us!"

That stopped me cold. "Really?"

She said, "No interest. That would save you a pretty penny, and you won't have the worry of having to come up with a payment every month, if you get strapped for some other important reason."

I sighed. "Let me think about it."

She giggled. "The little business analyst wants a conference."

I laughed and said, "No, the little business analyst wants to cry!"

She said, "Cry, then call me back. But first, talk to De."

She handed the phone to De, who said, "Congratulations! It sounds as though you've found a new set of wheels, if everything checks out on it okay."

I said, "Yeah! I'm excited! It's just the cutest little car!"

He said, "Well, I hope it checks out for you and is everything you want."

226

Referring to a book of humor I'd just written about being a floating secretary in the entertainment industry, De said, "I enjoyed it very much."

I said, "Carolyn told me you have some suggestions to make it even better."

He said, "Now, I've been known to be wrong a time or two, so these are just my ideas. Put one or two of your best anecdotes up front. You have plenty of them. That first one brings a smile, but not a guffaw like the later ones do. You have to catch the reader right away, as soon as they open the book, or they won't take it from the shelf and buy it."

I agreed with that.

He said, "That's it. That's my only suggestion. I thought it was thoroughly enjoyable. I wish it was longer; that's my only gripe. It was so much fun, I wanted there to be more of it...Well, I hope you get that car, if it's the one you want."

He handed the receiver to Carolyn, who said, "We're holding all good thoughts that it checks out all right!"

I said, "Thank you again for your sweet offer!"

She said, "We'd love to do it for you, Kris. You just let us know. I'll put your book out in the mailbox and you can pick it up whenever you get by again."

A few minutes later, she called me again to say, "De asked me what kind of car it is you're looking at, and I couldn't remember. Tell me again so I can write it down and tell him. He wants to call a friend and see what he has to say about that model."

I said, "Okay."

I gave her the specifics again and she said, "Okay. I have it all now. Thanks!" Then she said, "Kris, when you get the car, our check is a gift to you. You don't have a thing to worry about, so stop worrying."

I cried, "Oh, Carolyn!" then sighed, silent and overcome.

I called the Kelleys on the 27th to let them know the Mazda had checked out. I told Carolyn everything was ready.

Carolyn said, "Let me call the bank and see if I can transfer the funds and write you the check. I'll call you right back." She called back a bit later and reported, "The check is writ."

I sighed and said, "I can't tell you how much I appreciate this, Carolyn."

She said, "I know you do. We're happy to do it. Just don't copy the check before you cash it."

I said, "I won't. I'll be by at about six, so you can put it in the mailbox then."

She said, "Oh, no. You come on in when you get here and get it."

I said, "Great! I need a hug!"

227

She said, "I bet you do! See you soon."

When I got to their house, Carolyn invited me in and I hugged her. She got me a cola and a party napkin with the words "Indulge Thyself" on it. At that moment, De sneaked up behind me and poked me in the ribs. I jumped, startled, and then gave him a hug and a hello.

They invited me into their living room and sat me down on a love seat. There was an envelope on the table near me. Carolyn sat in a rocking chair next to my love seat. De sat across the room in another love seat. De and I talked about growing up on ranches or in the South. We had similar experiences regarding animals, using them for food (subsistence hunting, etc.). He mentioned eating squirrels and opossums and rabbits; I mentioned ducks, pheasants, deer and rabbits. We spoke about veal, the cruelly-raised kind. They wanted to know how to tell which veal had been raised in tight little stalls, so they would avoid buying it in the future. De mentioned how they trapped rabbits and treed 'possums and squirrels and told how they quickly and humanely dispatched the animals with a quick blow to the head. Carolyn interjected, "This was done by a minister, remember!" De said, "We were not a well-to-do family. Often what we caught was all we had to eat. A minister's life is not lucrative."

Not long after, they asked me to open the envelope. I did. Inside was a check for $3,000, made out in Carolyn's exquisite calligraphy. I marveled at it and then said, "You can't know how much I appreciate this…"

De said, "You just get that car and I hope it gives you years of fun and good transportation."

I assured him, "Oh, it will!"

Carolyn again repeated, "Please don't copy the check before you cash it."

I reassured her, "I won't. I'll just memorize it right now!" and sat and stared at it as they laughed. Pretty soon thereafter I looked at my watch, eager with anticipation, and Carolyn said, "Go get your car."

I asked, "When do you want to see it?"

They discussed that and said, "Tonight, if you can manage it before 7:30 or 8 o'clock."

I said, "I can manage it if I leave here right now. I'll be back before 7:30 or let you know otherwise."

They said, "Okay."

I hugged them both, sighed, and said, "Thanks again. This is just tremendous. I'm never gonna get over this!"

In two shakes I was back at the Kelleys with my new car. I didn't even have to knock. De was out the front door and heading down the sidewalk the moment I pulled up. I asked, "Where's Carolyn?"

He said, "She'll be out in a minute. She's getting something. Let's take a look at this little jewel." We walked out to the car, and by the time we reached the hood, Carolyn was walking out, holding her camera at the ready. I walked back to greet her and hug her. I pointed at the car and said, "Isn't it just the coolest?" She admitted that it sure was. I went over and opened the hood so De could peer underneath. He spotted a rubberized cap that was up and not doing its job over the battery cable, so he pushed it back down.

By this time Carolyn had positioned herself in the middle of the street with the camera and said, "Look up, you two. I want to get a picture." I wrapped my arm around De—he reciprocated— and we stood still for the photo. The grins were genuine!

I asked Carolyn to come over for a picture and she said, "Oh, no. Not now!" and then joked, "I don't have my eyelashes on!"

She positioned me around behind the car and took a few more photos. When we finished with that, they studied the car minutely, inside and out, and agreed that it was quite the deal and that it was in terrific shape. Then De said, "Just don't screw it up with those [DeForest Kelley] window stickers you have on the other one."

I feigned anger and blustered, "Excuse me?"

He laughed.

I asked him, "Whose car is this?"

He said, "Yours."

I agreed, "Mine. It's gonna look like my car, too!" I hugged them no fewer than six times each during the course of all of this, and they grinned mightily and kept saying that my joy was all the thanks they needed.

The next morning Carolyn called me at work and asked, "Did your new little car get you to work okay this morning?" I assured her it did.

I told her, "I just love it—and it has a new wax shine on it and new floor pads and a new Club and a sun visor and—what else?"

She asked, "Did you doll it up with stickers again?"

I asked, "Are you kidding? Do you even have to ask me that?"

She laughed and asked, "What did you put on?"

I said, "I have my NO BONES ABOUT IT, I'M A DeFOREST KELLEY FAN license plate holder and a MAY DeFOREST BEWITCH YOU window sticker—and on the rear view mirror I have wooden key chains that say DeForest and Carolyn on them."

The Kelleys asked me to keep mum regarding the car, so at work I had to pretend nothing unusual at all had happened. I managed to do that only by divorcing myself almost entirely from the happy event. But after a month passed, and on the day I would have had to make the first car payment, I was in the parking garage at Warner Bros. Placing the key into the lock to unlock it, it hit me that the car was mine, then and there, paid in full, and I started to bawl. I quickly jumped into the car and sat there sobbing, hoping no one would come by and ask me what was wrong. What could I have said?

No phone calls came in from the Kelleys between June 29 and July 5. I was used to hearing from Carolyn or De no fewer than three days a week, so this was odd; worry material for my brain. It put me into Mother Hen mode with a vengeance. I wrote and asked them, "Is everybody okay over there?"

Carolyn called on July 5 to tell me, "I felt I should call to let you know not to worry about me."

I said, "I do worry when you make yourself scarce for so many days running like this. It isn't like you. I can't help it."

She said, "Well, don't worry about it."

I explained, "I love you, lady and gentleman!"

She didn't say a word, so I added, "So big deal, right?"

She laughed at that, sounding a bit surprised that she could laugh. The call did nothing to alleviate my concern regarding their uncustomary absence since Thursday. It heightened it.

She called again on July 12 and sounded wonderful. She said, "We have been real busy and I realize we haven't been in touch for a while, but I can't call all the time."

I said, "I know that. I'm just happy to hear from you when you can. You sound real happy, too!"

She said, "I am. De has been having some tummy troubles again—"

I said, "Oh, no!"

She said, "He had a test this morning. It came out fine, so we're relieved."

I cautioned her, "It's those nuts, Carolyn! Hide those nuts! They're murder on a person susceptible to diverticulosis!"

De called on July 21. I had asked if he would be willing to write either an introduction for Floating Around Hollywood or a blurb for the back cover. He thought about that and then called with his response.

"Hi, honey. Do you have a minute?"

I said, "Sure."

He said, "I'm going to back out on writing a foreword for your book."

I said, "Okay."

He said, "I have a couple of reasons. The first is, you've already written about me in the book. It wouldn't be politically correct for me to say much more on it."

I said, "Okay. And you don't have to give me any reasons, De!"

He said, "The second reason is, I'm just no good at this type of thing. I'm a poet, not a writer."

I joked, "A long time ago, in a state far, far away…" mimicking his earlier Star Trek poems.

He said, "I will try to write a little something for the back of the book, though."

I said, "Cool! Super! Thanks!"

He asked if Deaken would be in the book, and I said, "No."

He said, "He should be in the book."

I asked, "What would he be doing in a book about floating around Hollywood? He'll get his own book someday, probably."

De said, "I'd imagine so. It'll be a good one." Then he said, "Deke could be on the acknowledgments or dedication page."

I said, "Okay, okay! I'll think about it, De." Then I got serious and said, "Uncle De loves his nephew—my little serval son—doesn't he?"

He said, "We sure do."

Within a week of this conversation, my landlord, pushed over the brink emotionally and financially by the effects of the Northridge quake and the expense of repairing his two rental properties plus his own place, mentioned to me that he and his wife were considering selling out and moving to Florida. The news panicked me. He wanted out. I recalled how long it had taken to find a landlord willing to let me have Deaken. Still, with the landlord's pressing concerns and incessant fear, I could well understand his need, so it seemed to me a dead certainty that, before too long, I'd be searching for new digs, the difficulty of such a search be damned.

I considered moving back to Washington. Mom and I both vetoed that idea, with Mom saying, "Much as I'd love to have you move back here, you'd be insane to move back solely for a cat that's about to expire anyway. That just doesn't make good sense at all." So it came as a big relief when the landlord reconsidered and told me I could stay for at least another six months. It would buy enough time for a sane, rational approach to the next housing option—and who knew, perhaps Deaken wouldn't even be a factor in six months, since he was obviously sliding downhill health-wise. Searching for a housing situation sans Deaken would be a picnic in comparison to looking for a place for him and me.

Out of the blue Carolyn phoned one day, "Do you have any plans for tomorrow?" "No."

"You sure?"

"I'm sure, Carolyn."

"Would you enjoy a little visit?"

"I'd love it!"

"You don't have any other plans?"

"No."

"Okay, we'll come by."

"Here? Awright, when? Morning?"

She said, "Not morning. I'm not out of bed in the morning! How about 2:00?"

I said, "Okay. You can see Deaken again!"

She said, "I'll bring my camera."

They arrived at about 3:30 after phoning earlier to let me know they would be delayed in getting over. Carolyn accidentally hit the car horn when backing into the street parking spot, so I ran out there and joked, "So now you're honking at me!"

De got out first, so I went over and gave him a hug, and then went to the driver's side and waited for Carolyn to emerge. I gave her a big hug and we started up the sidewalk to the house. De spotted the Mazda and said, "There's that little red gem."

I sighed, "Yeah…Ain't it purty? I called and told Mom I put another coat of wax on it today and she said, 'If you keep doing that, pretty soon it won't fit in one lane of traffic! You'll have to get an Over-sized Load sign and blinking caution lights!'" They laughed.

We went indoors to escape the heat. Deaken was lying on a bunch of strategically-placed pillows in the living room. They immediately started exclaiming, "There's our boy! Hi, Deaken! Hi, sweetie!" Deaken lapped it up and gave De a kiss on his hand.

Carolyn said, "Oh, look! He kissed you! Oh!" Carolyn put her hand out to Deaken and he kissed her and started rubbing his chin all over her hand, drooling a little bit, ecstatic. Carolyn exclaimed, "Oh, thank you! Thank you, Deaken!" Deke was pretty laid-back and sleepy, and almost fell asleep with his chin in the palm of Carolyn's hand. She exclaimed, "Oh, his head is heavy! He's weighing me down!" She said, "I have to get my camera out. I want pictures." She handed the camera to me with her free hand and said, "Get some pictures of us with him, will you?"

I said, "Sure." Deke remained lying in her hand, so I got a photo of that, then additional photos of De and Carolyn with him.

De stepped behind me to get an ashtray and inquired, "Does Deke mind if I smoke?"

I said, "Not at all."

Carolyn said, "Oh, that's right. I forgot about not wearing perfume. Some smells upset wild animals."

I told her, "Whatever you have on, keep it. He obviously loves it. I don't know of any scent Deke doesn't like."

De joked, "Bleach, elephant dung, armpits…"

I said, "Those are just his favorites, De. He likes Dioressence and White Linen, too."

De reached out and Deke enjoyed chin-tickling again, then they straightened up and sat properly on the couch. I got a Gatorade for Carolyn, and De and I shared a diet cola. I gave the Kelleys cups that had their pictures on them. When Carolyn noticed hers, she exclaimed, "Oh, look! This cup has me all over it! And Fancy! Oh, look, De! Fancy! Oh, it makes me cry!"

De looked at his cup and he said, "This one has me on it, too." They exchanged cups and studied them minutely.

I said, "I only use them for special occasions. In fact, I think this is the only time I've ever used them."

Carolyn said, "Let's go out and take pictures with the car."

I asked, "Already? We were just out there. Want to go again so soon?"

She said, "Sure, if you want to."

I said, "It's fine with me." They stood up, Carolyn grabbed her camera, and we went back out into the hot sunshine.

I backed the car out. De took a couple pictures of Carolyn and me with the Mazda, and then Carolyn took a couple of De and me with it. Then I took a couple of them with the car. After that, we went back indoors. Of course, they greeted Deaken again, petted him, and let him know he was a handsome boy. Carolyn went into my bedroom to study the "Kelley Shrine" on the walls, so De followed her. I did, too. Then De noticed the Native American dream catcher and we commented on the legend behind it. I told them "It works!" Carolyn noticed again the many photos of her with Fancy and she mentioned how much they loved her and how much they missed her.

We went back to the living room, where Carolyn looked lovingly at Deaken again and asked, "How are we going to survive losing Deaken?"

I said, "We'll survive it, but it's gonna be a trial. I can't think of it for more than about three seconds these days without falling apart."

She said, "It's so hard."

De offered, as consolation, "He'll probably out-live all of us."

I said, "No way. Who would be here to take care of him and love him the way we do?"

De said, "That's right." Then he said of Deaken, "A part of you is in him, isn't it?"

I said, "Forever. I'll never be without him, any more than I'll ever be without you two. It just ain't possible."

On August 31, I was a woman with a mission. When Carolyn called to chat, I wanted to somehow steer the conversation around to find out the call letters of her favorite radio stations. Then I planned to call those stations and let them know that the Kelleys' 50th anniversary was coming up, so they'd wish De and Carolyn a happy 50th and play their favorite courting songs in honor of their long union. But first I had to get the information out of Carolyn without her becoming any the wiser.

I told her, "You know—I feel real dumb—but you have mentioned several times that I ought to tune in to the radio stations you listen to most often, because the music on them is so good, but I can never remember which ones. If I promise to write them down this time, would you tell me one more time?"

"Sure!" she said, delighted. "They play all our music: music of the 40's, 50's and 60's, sometimes even earlier." She listed four stations; I wrote them down.

Eventually I even found out their theme song from Carolyn. "Our favorite is Twilight Time. Do you know it?" That information made its way to the radio stations, too.

A few days later I called Carolyn at around noon, shaking like a leaf, after Entertainment Tonight called me in response to the anniversary date notice I had sent to them. The photo coordinator reported that she didn't have a photo of De and Carolyn together to air during the announcement of their 50th wedding anniversary. I had told the woman, "I have a photo of the Kelleys together that was taken in my back yard," and she wanted me to bring it to the studio post haste if we owned the copyright. I told her Carolyn owned the copyright, and that I would have to ask her. So I called her, not knowing how she would receive the information. She also wanted a photo of the Kelleys on their wedding day, if one was available.

As soon as Carolyn answered the phone, I cried, "Don't be mad at me!"

She asked, "Is this Kris?"

I said, "Yeah. I told ET about your anniversary, and they called me today and say they need a photo of you and De together that they can show during the announcement of your 50th anniversary. I told them I have one that was taken in my back yard, and they want me to bring it to them, but I want to know if that's all right with you."

She said, "De isn't here right now to ask—but—oh, I think it would be all right. Go ahead and do it!"

I said, "ET also wants to know if you have a wedding day photo you can provide."

She said, "No, we don't."

I said, "OK. I'll go with what I have, then. Thanks!"

She said, "Thank you!" I told her I loved her and we hung up.

Sadly, the photo never aired and the announcement was never made. The lady explained that they had wanted to do something more extensive, and when the photos weren't available to do a larger piece, it fell by the wayside. She did say that the photo might be used as a later date, possibly on

Valentine's Day, as part of a larger piece on the few celebrity marriages that have stood the test of time and all the temptations. I told Carolyn that and she said, sarcastically, "They'll probably use it after we're dead."

Mom and Dad arrived on Halloween Day while I was at work and called in to let me know they were at my home. Then they took a nap. Carolyn called at about 2:00 to wish me "Happy Spooks!" I excitedly and enthusiastically reported Mom's and Dad's arrival. Just before we signed off I told her that a co-worker, Greg Heimbigner, had heard a commercial for the upcoming Pasadena convention with De, Leonard, and Bill. "Funny thing is, the announcer said that McCoy and Bones will be at the convention! Greg told me, 'I guess De is going to be beside himself at that convention!'"

Carolyn laughed at that and added, "Two for the price of one!"

On November 30th, the axe fell. The landlord sent a move-out notice, giving us 90 days to find other digs, as he had made the decision to move out of California and re-locate to Florida. I was beside myself with worry. I was enormously glad that Mom and Dad were in Southern California for the winter and could scout out options while I worked. Carolyn and De called often to tell us of places they'd heard of, and to try to keep my panic at a manageable level. Deaken was the obstacle. And I wasn't about to have Deaken euthanized out of expediency. No way. I'd give up my career and everything I had going for me in Southern California if it came to that. The commitment I'd made to Deaken the first time I held him in my arms, at five hours old, was inviolate.

In December, Emese Fisher, my guardian angel Realtor, kicked around the idea that rather than locating a rental, we should go for the purchase of a house or condo. Dad was for it. "You'd own the place; you wouldn't be pouring money down a rat hole."

The decision made, I let the Kelleys know of the new direction. Carolyn wanted to know how I would come up with the down payment. I said, "Dad and Mom said they can help with most of it. I just have to be sure and get it back to them by summer."

"Why?"

"Well…they're both retired and on a limited income."

She said, "We could loan you the money. No interest. Up to ten years to pay."

I countered, "Carolyn, I have heard this story before, with the Mazda, and you wouldn't let me pay you back."

She giggled and said, "Oh, have you?" Then she got serious and said, "No, you'll have to pay this one back."

"Promise!"

"I promise."

"Will you please let me pay you interest on the loan?"

"No. It's no interest, or no deal...Now you can relax a little bit and find the perfect home for you and Deaken with much less strain and trouble for everyone."

That same week, a producer called and left a voice mail message at home asking if he could interview me at De's star for a segment he was producing for the Popcorn Channel. Mom encouraged me to take a few hours and do it. "It will be good for you. You need to do something fun during this, too." I called him back and asked if his crew could meet me at De's star on Sunday at my usual star polishing time. He said, "Certainly."

On Sunday morning, we did the shoot. It turned out so well that the producer called the next day to proclaim me a star. He said, "You were just fantastic. We interviewed other polishers, but you have the preponderance of time in the edited version that will air. I think DeForest will be very pleased."

I asked if he would provide three copies of the segment. "I want to have two, in case one breaks, and I'd like to give the third to the Kelleys."

He said, "Certainly. I'll have a messenger take them to you this afternoon at your studio. Give me your particulars."

I called the Kelleys to let them know the producer was satisfied and that we'd be getting copies to see and keep. Carolyn said, "Oh, we don't need a copy to keep. We'll just look at it and give it back to you. We can't keep everything that's sent to us, you know. We'd have to move out!"

I said, "I understand. That's cool. I'm more than happy to have three copies of my two and a half minutes of fame!"

I dropped off a copy on the way home. They didn't look at it until the next morning, but when they did, it was all I could have imagined. They called to tell me they truly loved the segment. Then Carolyn said, "May I retract my earlier comment that we'd return the tape? We want to keep it."

I said, "You certainly may!"

She said, "Kris, you looked so comfortable and natural."

I joked, "I did? Where's my Emmy, in that case!"

At that point, De jumped on with a hearty "Congratulations! That is a magnificent piece." I thanked him and told him I was very glad, and very relieved, that they liked it.

Carolyn got back on and said, "We'll take it to Long Beach to show our friends—if we ever go there again."

On March 13, 1995 we moved my belongings to the new condo unpacked with our remaining, albeit lagging, energy. I'd just recently had Deaken's necessary permits transferred to the new location, but kept quiet about him to the condo association and to my new neighbors. I'd had enough crises for the time being; I certainly intended to avoid any others that were attributable to sharing my life with a geriatric, three-legged, rapidly-failing wild animal.

That afternoon a lovely plant basket arrived at my doorstep. It contained three plants and three flower blossoms. Atop the arrangement was a vinyl balloon which proclaimed, "Best wishes." The attached note read "Happy new home and happy days ahead, De and Carolyn." I called to thank them during one of the rare breaks Dad allowed us to have. Dad knew if we quit for long, we'd collapse. Carolyn said she had also procured a complimentary seat for me at the upcoming Arizona convention.

I protested, "I can afford this now, Carolyn."

She said, "I know you can, but we wanted to do it anyway. We got you one for Sacramento, too."

I said, "Thank you. You two are just too much!"

Carolyn called on the 21st to ask if it would be all right if she and De drove over for a little while on the 24th to finally meet my visiting sister Jackie, visit with Mom and Dad, and see my new condo. I was totally thrilled that they wanted to do that, and told her Mom would make lemon meringue pies for the occasion.

Carolyn said, "Oh, we won't stay long—maybe just an hour—but we'll eat pie or take it home with us!"

I said, "Mom will make you a pie. You can have a piece of ours and then abscond with your own." She said, "Your mom makes the best pies. I accused her to De of getting them down at this famous little bakery in our neighborhood."

I said, "No way! Your famous little bakery can't even compare with my mom's pies!" She said, "I think you're right. We're not big pie eaters, but we sure do manage to choke down every last morsel of your mother's pies!" We both laughed.

On March 24th, De and Carolyn visited. They met Jackie and then took a short tour of the new condo. De confessed, "We're surprised you found a nice place for such a great price! We were a little concerned. I must say, we are very impressed. It's small, but it's certainly everything you need and it looks just terrific."

They gave chin tickles to Deaken, who was luxuriating in my bedroom during the get-together. They studied the Guest/Kelley Room briefly, and then returned to the front room to sit and visit with Mom and Dad, Jackie, Poppy and me.

At their departure, Carolyn said, "Your mother sat way off in a corner by herself most of the time. Is she all right?"

I said, "She says she feels fine, but she has mentioned a stuffy sinus, and she keeps wiggling the upper part of her nose with her fingers, as though trying to dislodge stuffiness. But she's all right, I'm sure. My Mom's the healthiest soul on the planet. She never gets sick." Famous last words.

The Kelleys got into their car, waved good- bye, and were gone.

Some days later, Carolyn said she really enjoyed talking with everyone on Sunday and then made the observation, "Your mother is the saint in the family."

I confirmed, "You have that right! We thank God for our mommy day and night, night and day. Dad can be a real human hemorrhoid sometimes—but we love him, anyway!"

She guffawed at that: "Human hemorrhoid! That's very funny, Kris."

I joked back, "Not when you're living with one, it isn't!"

MEDICAL MALADIES MULTIPLY

On May 16, Deaken's 17th birthday, Carolyn called. She sounded tired and very subdued. After a brief few sentences, she said, "I want to tell you something, but I want you to keep it entirely confidential. I don't want you to tell anybody. Can you do that—keep a secret?"

I said, "I can."

She said, "I'm only telling you, because I'm friendly with you, and because De said I could."

I said, "Okay…"

She said, "De's in the hospital."

I took a deep breath and said, "Okay…" and waited for more information.

She could tell I wasn't entirely surprised, and said, "You knew something was up, didn't you?"

I said, "Well, it got awfully quiet over in your neck of the woods recently, so I was concerned that something might be up."

She said, "He had surgery a couple of days ago." I waited for more information. She said, "They removed a tumor from his colon."

I said, "Oh, God."

She said, "It's okay. The doctors say he'll live to be 95, as slowly as these things grow, but they wanted that one out of there."

I said, "I imagine that's what's been causing him the tummy problems."

She said, "Oh, absolutely. He should have had this done years ago."

I said, "As long as he'll be okay…"

She said, "Oh, yes! He'll be okay. He said I can tell you and one other person—no one else—and that he doesn't want flowers or balloons—and please don't send anything to him at the hospital."

I said, "Can I send cards to the house?"

She said, "Absolutely. I'll take them to him whenever I go."

Then she said, "I'm exhausted. I've been there from eight to eight both days. They have a tube down his throat that's giving him fits, and tonight he just told me to get out of there and come back later in the morning tomorrow. He worries about me being there all the time."

I said, "Well, he's probably just sleeping most of the time right now, anyway."

"He is, but every time he wakes up, I want him to see I'm there. But he doesn't think it's good for me, so he sent me home. I'm very tired…"

"Well, sweetie, my arms are around you."

She started to cry a little bit, but caught herself. She said, "I know you want to do something—help me out in some way—but the little gal across

239

the street is doing everything I need to have done. If I need anything else, I will let you know."

"Okay." I added, "My thoughts and prayers are with you."

She said, "I know they are. I'm going to try and get some sleep now. And remember: this is totally confidential."

"Oh, Carolyn, I swear, I won't even tell my Mom!"

"Good. That's the way we want it."

"Thank you for telling me."

"Well, I knew you had to be wondering what was going on."

"Yeah, I was."

"Well, now you know, and you can stop worrying. All's well that ends well." I told her I loved her and we hung up.

Carolyn called the next day to thank me for the stuffed bunny I sent her and the stuffed wild kitty and the box of goodies I sent De.

"Everything's fine here. De hasn't done anything more than smile at his serval and goodies and then go back to sleep, but he'll look at them more closely later on."

"Squeeze the kitty's toe for De. It will roar if you do that." I told her I had a friend staying with me over the weekend, so I wouldn't be stopping by to drop anything more, so she'd feel comfortable coming and going without risking running into us. She thanked me for my thoughtfulness.

Then she said, "We very much appreciate all you've done."

I told her, "I love you both, Carolyn!"

On May 21 Carolyn called to report that things were going fine. I asked when De would be home, if he wasn't already, and she said, "Maybe tomorrow."

"Cool..."

"I don't want you to worry. All is well." She added, "It upsets me when you're upset."

"Don't worry about me. As long as you two are okay, I'm fine."

I asked if I could take any of the workload off her, and she said, "No, I have to take care of it all myself."

"Okay, but if you need me, I'm here."

She thanked me and we hung up.

A few days later we celebrated. Carolyn reported, "De has no more lower extremity pain at all anymore, and he's been eating like a horse and walking around the back patio to satisfy the doctor's orders for exercise. He's asleep right now."

"He's probably hungry now that he can eat without it hurting afterwards."

"That's it exactly!" She sounded relieved and happy. "You can go ahead and tell your folks now."

Finally when De was up to talking, I asked him, "And how are you?"

"Well, it's a slow process, but I'm doing fine. I'm hugging my leopard right now that you gave me and I enjoyed all of your cards."

"I thought you should have at least two a day from me."

"I certainly did—and I appreciate them. Thank you."

"Did you squeeze your little leopard's toe?"

"I squeezed him all over."

"Did he roar for you?"

"Roar? No."

"Then you haven't squeezed his right toe yet. When you do, he'll roar for you."

"I'll have to try that."

I was weathering some news about Mom's health on top of worrying about De.

On June 9, De called. When I answered the phone, he said, "Well, hello, Santa Claus!" He was in great spirits and thanked me for the large sack of decadent food I dropped on his doorstep that morning, and then quickly added, "Now, stop that!"

I giggled and said, "Yes, sir!"

He said he had so much food there, sent from well-wishers, that he was thinking about opening his own grocery store.

Carolyn motioned for him to give her the phone, so he did and she said, "Hello. I'm still really busy but I want to tell you I hope all goes well for your dear mother."

I said, "I'm sure it will."

She said, "I'm sure it will, too." I said, "The doctor will probably just tell my Dad to lay off her and let her retire!"

"What does he have her do for him?"

"Everything! Tote and fetch and shop and carry and wash and clean and build bunk houses and RV trailers—you name it, she does it."

"Heavens! I can understand why she might be having problems!" She then asked, "Did I tell you that De quit smoking?"

"No! That's great!"

"I'm so proud of him. He hasn't had a ciggy since May 11th."

"Oh, that's just terrific. I'm gonna cry!"

"Don't cry!"

"It'll be a happy cry! Give him a big hug for me and tell him I'm proud of him. That makes my day!" I told her he would probably automatically gain some weight as a result of having stopped—everyone does.

She said, "Oh, really?"

241

I said, "Yes. Eight to twelve pounds on average from what I've read."

"That would be wonderful."

"It'll happen. Just hang in there." I asked her to be sure and hug De for me for quitting smoking—she said she would—then told her "I love you" and we hung up.

Carolyn called first thing in the morning after reading an updating letter about Mom. "We read your letter and we're so sorry that your dear mother has to have surgery." I started sniffling right away, but managed to keep talking, giving further details and answering whatever questions she asked. She asked how Dad was doing over this thing.

I said, "Oh, he's hanging in there. He almost lost it once on the phone, but got it back. I'm sure he's a basket case inside."

"I wish we could wave a magic wand and make your mother's problem just go away!"

"I know that, and I can hear you waving one wildly, and that means the world to us. Thank you."

"It's awful to want to do something to help, and to know there isn't a darn thing we can do about it." Then she said, "You take good care of yourself. Try not to worry too much."

"Don't worry about me. I'll handle it."

"I know you will. We just wish you didn't have to."

"Oh, well. I guess it's my turn."

I told her, "I hope it's a sinus infection, because tumors in the head tend to come back often, the doctor said," and she said, "Oh, don't even think about that. It may never happen again. Everyone is so different."

I said, "Okay. I just do not want my mom in the surgery room every three months. She'd hate that."

Carolyn said, "Just think positive."

I said, "I am. I'm just real scared once in a while." I sniffled when I said that, upset again.

She said, "I know. We'll be thinking of you up there constantly, sending all of our good thoughts your way."

I sniffled again and said, "Thank you."

She said, "You take care. Give your family our best."

On June 19, 1996 I called the Kelleys from a hospital waiting room in Seattle at about 10 a.m. to give them the bad news about Mom's prognosis. I told them I didn't want to lay the bad news on them right at bedtime the night before, so I had waited. I told them, "The doctor thinks it's a grade 3 or 4 cancerous tumor, and if it is, it will be back in 2-4 months without radiation and chemotherapy, and within a year with radiation and chemotherapy." I became upset talking about it again, but managed to control my emotions enough to answer their questions.

242

They gave me their love and good wishes and Carolyn ended by saying, "Take good care of yourself."

In that blur of days the Kelleys made known their loyalty and their love. I told them their flowers gave Mom a big boost and that she went from "probably not leaving the hospital this weekend" to "out of there the next afternoon" following Phil's delivery of them to her.

She said, "Oh, it would be nice to think they made that big a difference."

I said, "She was very happy to get them and you can call it a coincidence if you want, but I think they had a very positive effect on her."

A couple days later, I let the Kelleys know that Mom's liver tests came back normal so the decision to go ahead with radiation and chemotherapy had been made.

"Had that liver test come back showing liver cancer that would've been the end. The doctors wouldn't have suggested chemo and radiation. Once cancer gets into the liver, I guess that's it—no time left to try anything else. So, Mom and Dad are dancing on the table tonight; on the ceiling, too, if they can get to it!"

She said, "That's wonderful. Give our love to your mother and father when you see them over the 4th, won't you?"

I said, "I sure will."

When I got back from the 4th of July visit, Carolyn wanted to know how it had gone. I told her Mom was doing just great and her spirits were terrific.

"She's a case study in centered living. Nothing seems to rattle her. She just keeps on smiling and joking and living!"

Carolyn offered, "She's a very special lady." Then she said, "I'm still so proud of De. I was on him for years to quit smoking—and he finally did it." I asked if he had gained any weight as a result, and she exclaimed, "Oh, yes! He's up to 128! I'd like to see him put on another twenty, but I'll be happy with ten."

DEAKEN'S DEMISE

On September 11, 1996 after a full month of dedicated attempts to see if I could find a way (medical, surgical or natural) to keep my dear Deaken from suffering from acute pain and disability after he had either suffered a stroke or twisted his spine horribly during the night, my veterinarian and I decided that, at age 17 and one quarter, the kindest thing to offer him was release, since surgery would be risky at his age and recovery (if he survived the surgery) would be prolonged and painful.

De and Carolyn insisted on paying for his final vet bill and cremation. They called me often and commiserated with me. We all cried. Deaken blessed many lives—especially mine. I have written another book about him (Serval Son: Spots and Stripes Forever, You Are Responsible for All You Tame) so I won't recount his leave-taking here or the many ways in which his life touched so many others. You can read his story there.

On September 29, 1996 I was late getting to the Kelleys on Sunday to deliver my letter and to pick up stuff from them, and by the time I got there and was picking roses, Carolyn was up and opened the front door and exclaimed, "There's our girl—stealing roses—and her little red car!"

I went to over to her and gave her a hug and said, "Hello! Good morning! Am I late, or what?"

She didn't respond to that. I showed her my guardian angel cat necklace, which she thought was adorable and asked me where I got it. I told her, "Some catalog, but I can't remember, now, which one."

She mentioned the program from Huntsville (in the plastic bag she left for me) and I pulled it out, and she said, "De's article starts on page sixteen." I opened it up to that page and oohed and ahhed over the pictures and said I was interested in reading it, and thanked her for giving me one.

She said, "Can you come in for a few minutes and visit?"

I said, "Well...sure!" very delighted, and tried to wipe the mud from their garden off my shoes.

She said, "That's fine, that's plenty...don't worry about it...Come on in!" I spotted De at that point standing in the entrance to the kitchen.

He was grinning and I said sarcastically, "Well, if someone wouldn't water the roses ten minutes before I arrive, I wouldn't be having this problem!"

He chuckled and said, "I'll remember that!" I stepped in and gave him a big hug and a hello, and Carolyn motioned me into the kitchen to see the magnets that Sheila Werner created and sent her. They were adorable. She asked if I'd like to have a Coke or something else to drink, and I said, "No, thanks."

As she was showing me the magnets, she saw the "cowlick" in the back of my head and said, "Oh, you have one, too! I'm getting so bald in back, here. Take a look." I looked but didn't see much of a problem.

De said, "I have that same problem in the same place. I think it's where the swirl starts when you start to get hair. It doesn't seem to grow any right there."

Carolyn said, "We just comb something over it."

I said, "When I have a permanent, it hides it better, but what the hell!"

We went into the living room and Carolyn and I started to yak nonstop. Pretty soon De stuck his head out of the kitchen and asked, "Do you want a Cola or anything else to drink?"

I reconsidered and said, "Yes, please!"

Carolyn said, "I just asked you that, and you said no!"

I said, "Well, I been talkin' and now I'm thirsty!"

As De was bringing the cola in, I noticed that my shoes still had mud on the sides and told them I ought to go out and get rid of it. Carolyn said, "Oh, no, don't do that. Don't bother. If it hasn't fallen off by now, it won't."

I said, "Okay…" and a few seconds later a big clump fell off. I said, "Oh, great," and took my shoes off and started to pick the mud clumps up and put them into my shoe.

Carolyn said, "Oh, don't do that! Don't worry about it. Really! I have a little man who cleans up all those things for me whenever they happen." I glanced over at De, and he raised his hand and waved it, indicating that he was her "little man".

I said, "Some little man!" and indicated his 6'0" height. We all laughed. I got up and took the shoes, and the detritus from them that I could pick up by hand, outside, then came back in.

We talked about their charming Berber rug, and De laughed, remembering how much they hated it at first. He said, "We walked in here and thought they hadn't laid the carpet yet! We thought it was the mat underneath!"

Carolyn said, "We cried about that for days – but we really love it, now. It cleans up like a snap, and when you vacuum you don't see any ridges. We just love it."

I told her I thought I'd get it next time.

She asked, "Don't you have a brand new rug?"

I said, "Yes, but it's only going to last about eight years."

They asked if I still like condo-living and my condo, and I told them I do. They asked how far I am from the pool, and I told them it was only a few steps on the other side of my bedroom patio. De wondered why they

245

hadn't seen it when they were there, and I said they parked right in front of the condo and never walked around the outside.

I told them that Dad was happy because I don't have to drive the freeways anymore; he was always worried about that, although I seldom actually drove them. Carolyn said it was great that I can go home at lunch and swim and take care of kitties and the like, and De said the time savings and the wear and tear on the car would be reduced tremendously, too.

I was gulping cola like mad and De said, "If you keep gulping soda like that, you're gonna belch."

I said, "I drink everything like this!"

He said, "That's what John Carradine used to do in order to let out a big belch when we were doing Tobacco Road on the east coast. Just before the second act, he'd drink an entire cola down, so he could come on and do his line, which included this tremendous belch and the words, 'Damn' turnips!' Carolyn played the impoverished old lady and was always beggin' John for a turnip for her aching tummy. John did that play later with a real elderly woman playing the part of the old lady, and he told her 'I had a twenty year old who made a better old lady that you do!'"

Carolyn grinned at that.

De said, "The night that play closed, we were playing to a house with about 35 people in it – I'll never forget it – and John came out onto the stage for the curtain call and announced, 'You'll be happy to know I'll be back next season in King Richard III!'" He guffawed at that, remembering. "Last time I saw John was at Universal a few years ago. He was crippled with arthritis. It was very sad."

Carolyn said, "Everyone is all gone now. But we're still here!"

They both laughed and I said, "You just stick around, too!"

We talked about Mom's case and about Dad's problems and anguish. I showed them the photos from the trip north and they enjoyed the pix of the lot in Cle Elum. De mentioned that Dad had told him about blasting those lakes with fertilizer, and smiled at the memory of the story. He and Carolyn both said Mom looks very good, and I agreed. They saw the photos of Laurel's family and when I mentioned that Sirkka was only 14 and starting college this year, Carolyn said, "Uh-oh, she's such a knock-out she might get into trouble if she isn't careful!" De nodded, in complete agreement.

I said, "She knows karate. She may have to use it on a few boys, I think!"

We discussed the new kittens. I told them I think their names are going to be Archie (because the silver tabby arches to get petted) and Ashley (because the other one is the color of ashes), and Carolyn said, "You always have dumb names for your pets."

I said, "Thank you very much, Carolyn!" and we all laughed.

We talked about dear Deaken (what a wonderful life he had) and we spotted Myrtle out and about. De said, "She was just over getting a blessing from St. Francis, and now she's headed west along the back fence."

I spotted her and said, "There she is! I see her now."

De said, "Did I tell you how we got that St. Francis statue?"

I said, "No."

He said, "Bill Shatner bought a new house – the one just before this one he has now. His Realtor was a friend of ours, and she invited us to take a look at it after Bill bought it. We spotted the St. Francis statue in the yard –"

Carolyn added, "Bill's Jewish, you know."

I said, "Yeah…"

De continued, "…so I went to Bill and said, 'You don't want that St. Francis statue in your back yard, do you?' and he said 'No,' so I told him, 'We'd like to have it, if you'll let us,' and he gave it to us. I went into the back yard and lifted that heavy piece of concrete all across the yard and into a car and into the back yard. I look at it now and don't know how I managed it!"

I told him, "I have a St. Francis a third that size, and I can't imagine lifting one even twice that size. You're one strong puppy!"

He then told about lifting a massive piece of marble from another back yard, up steps, and showed me the piece. Carolyn told me to go over and try to tip it, let alone lift it. I went over and tried, and about croaked. I was amazed.

I said, "It's amazing what you can do when you want something badly enough. Forget the crane – I can handle it!" We all laughed.

Carolyn and I went and sat back down and I asked how they're doing. They said they're doing fine but that Carolyn will have to get hip surgery eventually – probably sooner than later. I commiserated with her over that. She asked me not to spread it around, as she doesn't want to be inundated with cards and gifts and flowers from well-wishers, as it just makes more work for her (she has to answer them all).

I said, "I won't tell anyone. You just lie in the hospital and be miserable; no one will be thinking of you at all." She giggled and I said, "I really won't tell."

She said, "No flowers, either. There are always too many flowers to bring home. It's just a waste."

I said, "Cards are okay – as long as I don't send seven a day, right?"

She smiled and said, "Yes."

I said, "Oh, good." I added, "It's a pain to have to go in, but in twelve weeks you'll be glad you did, once it's over."

247

She sighed and said, "Yes. I don't recall it taking twelve weeks last time, though."

De said, "It was a long time; I remember that."

She said, "I don't remember that at all."

I said, "That's good."

De asked if I had heard that Bones (Daryl's cat) died. I said I did; that Carolyn had told me.

I said, "He lived through that cat. This has been a bad month for people's cats, hasn't it?" Carolyn said another friend of theirs just lost a fifteen year old cat.

She took me into their bedroom to show me photos of her/their pets throughout the years: Flossy (her first cat) in her arms when she was about four; Stardust (her dog); and of course Fancy, Cheers and Myrtle. She showed me the first little goodie I ever sent her, and said that she just loves the plaque I sent them a few years ago: "It doesn't matter where you go in live, what you do, or how much you have. It's who you have beside you." She showed me a pillow that someone sent them for an anniversary that reads: "Real love stories don't have endings" and I told her that one pillow I saw and loved read, "If you ever leave me, I'm going with you!"

She showed me a few of De's achievement plaques in the office/study and we gazed at Deaken's photo in there. Carolyn said it's her favorite – and I agreed it's mine, too. She got tears in her eyes.

I thanked them for inviting me in and went to the porch to get my shoes on. They came to the porch and we started to talk about different car waxes. De asked what kind I use on my little jewel and I told him Macguires. He asked if I know about the car duster that works wonders. I asked if he knew the name of it, and he said, "I don't recall, but I'll show it to you on the way out." He went into the garage and opened the garage door and showed me the name brand: California Car Brush. He said he has only washed his car about six times in the four years they've had it; "the rest of the time, all I've used is this. The dirtier it gets, the better it works!" He then laughed, "Except for when it rains. You can't knock mud off with it!" and hit me on the arm.

I told him I'd remember that and then said, "My little car never gets mud on it!"

He looked out at it sitting in the street and he said, "It certainly looks brand new."

I said, "You bet. Always. It hasn't gone a day without looking that good."

I told him good-bye and then waved to Carolyn (who was standing at the front door). They waited until I was driving away, so I added, "Have a

248

happy birthday on Saturday, Carolyn!" and she said, "Oh, I will!" I threw them a kiss and drove away.

A COMMUNION OF SORTS

On March 27, 1997 Carolyn called to let us know that she and De would like to drive over to my place the following Saturday and visit with my folks and me "if that's all right."

I said, "It certainly is!" and she giggled. I gave her careful directions, as they had only been to my condo once before.

Then she said, "Be sure your new kittens are on their best behavior and that they're looking good."

I said, "I can guarantee they'll look good—they always do—but, best behavior? They're eight months old, Carolyn. They don't have a best behavior unless they're asleep!"

She laughed and said, "They'll be fine!"

The Kelleys visited with us for an hour and a half. Mom was wearing a turban on her head to hide the fact that her hair had grown back in mismatched colors and textures. The hair was still patchy in spots. Instead of the silvery mane she had once enjoyed and been complimented on endless times, she felt she looked "like someone who would make babies cry in the supermarket." Despite the fact that the turban was warm and itchy, she insisted on wearing it when company was around or when she went out in public. The wig she had bought had long since been cast aside as too hot, too scratchy and too artificial-looking.

I was happy to see how good both De and Carolyn looked. The regimen of walking six blocks daily had given them a look of such robust health that they both appeared radiant. De had gained weight, too.

The Kelleys and Mom and Dad discussed their various health challenges. Carolyn bragged on De for having quit smoking. She said, "We're both real Puritans now."

Mom mentioned having developed a sweet tooth following chemotherapy. "I never had it before."

Carolyn said, "I've developed a sweet tooth for that bittersweet chocolate De always gets."

De leaned over to me and chuckled "Now you know where it goes!"

De told Dad that he was finished with acting.

Dad told De "You're a hell of an actor; I never knew how good until I met you. I thought you'd be a real son of a bitch after seeing those Westerns you did." Then he added, "Nothing against Star Trek, but you could hardly get a word in, with Shatner hogging all the time!"

De threw his head back and laughed at that, then clarified for Dad, "In the fourth and fifth years, we were supposed to get our due. Each of our characters was supposed to have episodes spotlighting them, but the fourth and fifth years never came to pass."

They met the kitties. As luck would have it, both of the little rascals had worn themselves out prior to the Kelleys arrival, so Ashley, the shy one, actually slept on Carolyn's lap while she stroked his long, silky fur and cooed to him. "He's the loveliest cat I have ever seen." she exclaimed. "His photos are beautiful, but they don't do him justice."

De and Carolyn mentioned how wonderful Mom looked. She said, "Well, thank you." Then she said, "I miss my hair!"

Carolyn said, "Don't worry, it'll be back, better than ever. Maybe even curly!"

That's when Mom began her personal contribution to the visit. "I don't normally do this, except around family. It's pretty frightening to the uninitiated. But I feel comfortable with you. Let me show you how my hair is coming in—then you'll know why I wear this turban!"

Slowly—painfully slowly, I thought—she pulled the turban from the top of her head, revealing the multiple colors of her hair and the remaining bare patches. I knew how much courage that took. I held my breath, knowing it might be a difficult moment for the Kelleys, as sensitive as they were.

De stood up at that moment and adopted a McCoy-like stance and authority, but he was still genuinely and authentically De. It wasn't false at all. Then he walked over to where she was sitting and said, "Yes, let's get a good look at you. It's time for your physical."

Mom stood up. He embraced her and held her for a long moment. Then he gently pushed her out to arm's length, gave her the once-over, head to toe, and proclaimed, "You are a beautiful woman, Dorothea, and you're going to be just fine!"

I never loved DeForest Kelley more than I did at that moment. Mom melted, hugged him again, and responded gratefully, "I know I'm going to be fine. I wish all you people would stop worrying about me." Then she joked, "I'm going to out-live all of you."

Mom left the turban off a lot more often after that visit. DeForest Kelley had told her she was beautiful and that she was going to be fine, and that was the only prognosis she was prepared to believe. She and Dad drove home to Washington with happier hearts.

By May 6th, the horizon for Mom was becoming ominously dark and cloudy. Carolyn called to say, "De and I were very sorry to hear about your mom." The MRI specialists had noticed "something more" going on in Mom's brain. It was too small to be seen as a recurrence of the deadly tumor, but something was going on at that location.

I let them know that Mom was handling the new information just great. "She doesn't seem to be at all afraid and is directing her medical team to wait until they know something more definite. If they wait a month and find out it's coming back, they can go in and take it out and do whatever else needs doing, all in one procedure, instead of opening her head up twice."

Carolyn said, "She seems to be the kind of person who has her head on straight about things."

I assured her, "She's amazing in that way. I asked her if she was scared, and she said she doesn't feel any differently about dying now than she did before this whole thing started. 'It's going to happen someday. I'll live until I die'—very straightforward and with full acceptance. She told me the drugs to keep her comfortable are great and that she didn't suffer a bit with the tumor taking up so much of her forehead or after the surgery, so she really isn't all that concerned about what might happen next. She says she's lucky she has what she has, and not a more painful type. She feels sorry for the little kids who have cancer and the young newlyweds and the young parents with kids who have it. She's just remarkable, all the way around."

Carolyn listened to this soliloquy and agreed, "Yes, she is." Then she asked me, "How's your dad handling it?"

I said, "Okay, for the time being—as well as can be expected for a control freak." She chuckled at that. We discussed how I was emotionally torn between staying in Southern California to live and work and my duty to my mother in Washington State. After a lot of soul-searching, I decided to stay in Los Angeles and fly home whenever possible.

Carolyn said, "I'm glad you decided to stay. I think it's smart, but I know it's hard to be so far away from them at a time like this."

I said, "Yeah, it is. The rest of the family gets Mom for hopefully another two years. I get her for thirty days, if I'm lucky. That's a terrible feeling!"

She said, "I'll bet it is."

In June, Carolyn called again in response to a letter I had written them, saying she was sad to hear Mom talking about her own cremation already. I said, "Well, it was a funny conversation, so it was okay. They are going to implant radioactive electrodes in her brain next week sometime—I told you that in the letter—and they said if she dies before a year is up, she can't be cremated, because the process would release radioactive particles into the air. So I told her, 'Oh, good! That means you can't possibly die for at least a year, 'cause you said you want to be cremated!' and she thought about that and then said, 'That's right! I'm safe for a whole year!' That's when she told me, 'If there's such a thing as reincarnation, I want to come back as one of your pets!'"

Carolyn laughed at that and said, "I know why! I'd like that, too!"

I continued, "That's when she got a little serious and said she doesn't care what anyone does with her ashes but she wants at least part of them in my bedroom near Deaken's ashes, so she can keep an eye on me and be my guardian angel."

Carolyn said, "Could you do that?"

I said, "To tell you the truth, at first the idea kind of gave me pause. But now I think, by golly, if that's what she wants, she gets it. And now I even love the idea!"

She said, "Well, I hope all this talk of cremation is premature. I think she's going to beat her cancer."

I cautioned her, "It's a long shot. It's the longest shot in the field of cancer, I think. But of course we're hopeful, too."

A few days later I had to call the Kelleys and thank them for a signed photo De had sent to Mom prior to her entry into the hospital for the clinical trials procedure. Carolyn answered the phone, so I started to thank her, but she stopped me and said, "Just a minute. Let me get De! De! It's Kris! She has news about her mother!"

De got on and I continued, "I wish you could have heard Mom's voice. She was so tickled. Thank you, De. You made her day, and her tomorrow and her weekend, by the sound of her voice. She's taking it to the hospital with her, so she gets the royal treatment!"

He chuckled and said, "It works that way sometimes."

I said, "I know it does. It did with Dad."

He said, "Well, I'm glad she enjoyed it. Just a minute. Carolyn wants you again."

I told Carolyn Mom's surgery was scheduled for the next day, and she said, "We're holding all good thoughts here for her."

I said, "I'm sure it will be fine. She's so positive and gung ho."

She said, "She's a great lady."

I said, "Yes, she is—and a very happy lady, too, with that photo in her mitt!"

She said, "It's nice to know that something that little can make such a big difference."

I said, "It does. It's a type of magic, pure and simple."

Carolyn called the next day to see how the surgery went. I told her it went well and gave her the good news that the surgery could offer her a year or more of the good, status quo quality of life, with other protocols that might also extend her life after the radioactive protocol wore out. She was thrilled to hear about that. Then I told her, "De's photo made such a hit at the hospital and Mom is getting such good treatment as a result that she says she's thinking of becoming a hypochondriac!" Carolyn howled at that.

When De called to thank me for his Father's Day gift on June 15 his throat was coated with the gift: Trader Joe's bittersweet chocolate. I didn't recognize who was calling, as a result, but it was certainly a happy voice. I could tell that much.

"Hello," he began.

"Hi." I sounded more noncommittal than I customarily was with him, so he figured out the problem and identified himself.

"It's DeForest. I'm eating your birthday chocolate. Thank you! And—hey! That's wonderful news about your mother."

I said, "Yes! Isn't that fantastic? She's stuck with us for at least another year."

De said, "Just terrific. Oh! And congratulations on your upcoming debut on E. [They wanted to interview De's star polisher.] You can do your stand-up routines and become a star."

I laughed and said, "Oh, right! That's what they're after me for—not your star!"

Then De said, "But my main purpose in calling you today is to thank you for the candy bars and to ask you to give our love to your mother."

I said, "I will! Thanks! And thank you for calling!"

The E! interview was canceled "for at least a month" just a day before I was scheduled to do it. I was glad, because I had fallen ill with a bad cold that suddenly and unexpectedly turned into bronchitis. So, on the morning I had originally agreed to do the interview, I was instead in an emergency room in Burbank at Saint Joseph's Hospital being rehabilitated and sent home with a prescription and doctor's orders for lots of rest and no activity for several days.

When the E! reporter called to cancel the interview, she let slip some information she shouldn't have. She said the cancellation was due to the fact that "DeForest was planning to come down to the star and surprise you while you were being interviewed by us, but he isn't feeling well just now and we want to wait for his availability."

I hadn't known De was feeling ill again—neither De nor Carolyn had alluded to it in months—so the news startled me in two ways. I was tickled pink that he wanted to surprise me, but I wondered how ill he was feeling and whether or not I should let the Kelleys know that I knew about the upcoming surprise. I decided to play dumb, deciding that De or Carolyn would tell me whatever they wanted me to know when they wanted me to know it. After all, the interview was still on; it would just be delayed a month or so. That didn't sound terribly ominous. And I remained giddy because De thought enough of me to want to surprise me in such a public way— on television, in front of millions of viewers. Yikes and egads!

CAROLYN BREAKS HER LEG

During an evening hour on April 4, 1998 De called and started out by saying, "Thinking this was Friday, I called you at work earlier today and asked you to give me a call. Now I realize it's Saturday, so I'm calling you at home." He continued, "Carolyn fell today and fractured the leg bone just below one hip—the femur."

Shocked and saddened, I responded, "Oh, no!"

He said, "I was away at the time—I had gone to the nursery for some flowers—and she stumbled and fell, and couldn't get to the phone. I guess she laid there for thirty five or forty minutes before I walked back into the house. I called the paramedics and they came and took her to the hospital. As they wheeled her away, she told me, 'Tell anyone you call No flowers.'" Then he chuckled, despite himself. He continued, "It's such a shame, because we have been walking for the past several months, and she was really getting around – walking all over the place." Then he said, "She had surgery and they set the bone. She's out of it right now—I can't even talk to her—but I will get a chance tomorrow again, I'm sure."

I was stunned into near silence by his report. I asked him, "How are you?"

He said, "I'm fine." (He sounded fine at that moment, but when I got back to work and heard the message he had left me just after she had fallen, he didn't sound fine then. He sounded muffled and a bit choked up, like a man trying to keep his emotions from running away with him.)

On April 13 Carolyn was transferred from the local hospital to another long term care and rehabilitation facility, when it became evident that her recovery period would be lengthy—possibly endless. On April 14 I called to ask how the transfer went. She said it went beautifully. I told her,

"I called the new hospital last night to get your new phone and room numbers, but asked them not to connect me to you, because I knew it had been a busy day for you." She said, "I sure do appreciate you checking up on me. It's very sweet of you…"

Months of non-stop hospital visits became De's life. I asked if he needed help or respite; he thanked me but said no, he was taking care of everything. I asked if I could visit Carolyn in the hospital. He said, "No, she isn't in the right frame of mind to accept visitors. Just keep those cards and letters coming. They really help keep her spirits up."

MOM PASSES AWAY

In early October 1998 I flew to Washington to spend Mom's final days with her. She was completely bedridden so I spent days and many nights sitting and sleeping near her. I gave her bed baths, rubbed oils on her body, and kept her feet well-scratched and tickled, which she loved.

About ten days before her death on October 23rd, she refused food and drink altogether. The Hospice people told us the time would probably come when she would do that, so we were advised, but far from prepared. The deathwatch had begun. I began to sing "Kumbaya" softly—leaking tears like crazy—almost every time she would doze off. The song provided the desperately-needed comfort my aching soul needed.

The final evening just before slipping into a coma, Mom gave Dad and me her last instructions. The first was, "Don't fight." (In Mom's presence, Dad and I had been discussing his health issues and why I felt so strongly that he should curtail smoking and drinking and take better care of himself.) The other one was, "Don't be upset [by my death]." I held her hand in mine and started to leak tears. I told her, "Mom, I'm not upset. When I cry, it's just the love leaking out." She nodded and her eyes welled up just a little. I continued, after a long pause, as hard as it was to hear myself say it, "It's okay for you to go whenever you feel ready. I will miss you: I will never forget you. I love you, my mommy."

Within two days, surrounded by her loving family, Dorothea Hope Smith passed away into The Loving Arms with delight on her face and in her eyes. I smiled, "She has one foot in heaven already, and is she ever okay with it!"

A large part of my mother's enduring legacy is that she never complained—and the only anguish or angst she ever caused was when she left us.

A few days later I received a letter from De, which I will always treasure:

October 27th, 1998

Dear Kris,
Consider this a note of congratulations for you and your family for the magnificent care and devotion that all of you have given to a terrific lady. We know and understand your love for her for we could feel the goodness that she reflected in those moments that we knew her. With deep sympathy, love, De and Carolyn.

THE FINAL FRONTIER

On March 14, 1999 A.C. Lyles called and dropped a ton of bricks on me. He said, bluntly, "Kris, I need your help."

"Sure, A.C. What is it?"

"De is dying."

I almost died myself. I managed to utter a wooden, "Oh."

"It wasn't unexpected, was it?"

I lied, "No, but it still…"

"He has cancer, you know."

I again lied, "Yes, I know."

"I need you to fax me a copy of De's biography. I don't have one and I have to be ready with information for the media."

"I can drive to Warner Brothers, access the Internet and get it off the Paramount Star Trek web site. Do you want it today?"

"Yes, of course, right away." A.C. replied. "I won't be home when you send it; I have to go out right away to do something for De."

"Okay."

"And don't call Carolyn. She's upset right now, as you can well imagine."

I drove to Warner Brothers half in shock, feeling alternately dazed and sick to my stomach. From my work station I faxed the information to A.C's home. When I got back home there was a voice mail message on my machine.

"Kris, this is A.C. I'm over at the hospital with De; he's doing a lot better today. He's been in the hospital a few days, dear, and he's looking at me now and nodding his head. He's doing better today, and I was talking to Carolyn and to De and we want to ask you a big favor, if we can. I'm sure you'd like to do this because you've told me in the past that you would be happy to do it while Carolyn's in the hospital. While De is here, he'd love for you to have the key to the house…and stop by whenever you can, every day or every other day, whatever. The man next door has been picking up the mail, but they just want to make sure that everything is good at the house, honey, and since you know the house so well and everything, De and Carolyn would be most appreciative if you could do that for them. De has a key here to the house, and if you could come get the key, De would appreciate it very much; I know he'd like to say hello to you…Ask for his nurse and she will take care of you. The key will be waiting for you…So would you—when you get back—I know what you're doing; you're doing something for me, and I appreciate it—when you get back will you call us, please, and De wants to say hello to you. Just a minute."

Maddeningly, the answering machine cut off at that point! While I was listening to this upsetting voice mail, the phone rang, so I stopped the voice mail and picked it up. It was Carolyn.

"Hello, Kris."

"Hi, sweetie."

"Did A.C. call you?"

"Yes." She sighed.

"Then you know."

"Yes."

"De and A.C. wanted me to drive out to De's hospital and get De's keys and take care of the house."

"Then let's not talk now. Call me back later. And thank you."

"I will…just as soon as I get back here." I called the hospital and spoke with the nurse. I asked if I would be able to see De when I came in.

"Oh, yes, of course!"

When I got to the hospital, I didn't recognize De. If A.C. hadn't been with him, I'm pretty sure I would have denied that the skeleton occupying the bed was he. He couldn't have weighed ninety pounds. His complexion was yellow. I hugged A.C. as he greeted me, then went to De's bedside and took his bony, emaciated hand. He had just eaten a slice of watermelon and was slowly working on a cola.

De was trying to help us not take his predicament so seriously; he was joking as much as his weakened condition allowed.

"My answering machine shut off before you came on to tell me what you had to say."

De joked, "That's because AC is so long-winded."

"What did you say?"

He smiled. "I said, 'I suppose when I get out of here, my car will be gone and my home will be wiped out!'"

I feigned serious personal injury. "Well, thank you for the vote of confidence, Mr. Kelley!"

He chuckled weakly. "Dear girl, if I didn't trust you, you wouldn't be getting the keys!"

His feet and legs were dry, felt like ice and looked nearly lifeless. I asked him if I could put lotion on them; he nodded. I did that for about ninety minutes, being careful not to hurt him. Eventually, with the lotion and light massaging, his circulation improved, so his legs became pink and warm again. I eventually did his back and left side, too. The nurse came in to give him whole blood and an IV with lots of nutrition in it. A.C and De joked that in three days I'd be ready to join her staff. De decided he and A.C. had a quorum now with me there and so could make decisions that would stick.

A.C. left at about 3. I walked him to the parking lot. AC said De had rebounded tremendously just in the few hours since we'd arrived. I told him, "You scared the hell out of me with that phone call. I didn't know De was ill."

"You're joking. I thought he told you everything."

"I think he was about to, but he hadn't yet."

"So, my call was a shock."

"It damn' near killed me."

"Oh, I'm so sorry."

"It's OK. You didn't know."

I went back into the hospital to sit with De for another two hours. He told me his story in harrowing detail: about how he had almost checked out at one point. "The room went all white, and it was just like a scene out of ER. I could see two nurses, and then a roomful of people trying to bring me back, but I was completely helpless to respond. I thought it was all over with me, for sure, but I just kept thinking, 'I can't go now. I still have things to do—the taxes, Carolyn…What a weird feeling!"

Then he said he had considered asking for my help sooner "but I was getting along pretty well up until recently; then everything happened all at once, and here we are." He said he had negotiated a bungalow for Carolyn to remain at her facility in the event she was unable to return home. I told him I had three weeks of vacation time coming and that I could probably fudge at work and get family leave or, lacking that, a leave of absence to take care of him at home with a Hospice crew, if need be.

He said, "Let's hope the need won't be." I assured him I'd love to help him out, and he said, "There's more to do yet."

I said, "That's fine. I'm your girl!"

He said he needed to write some bills, move some things, and check the answering machine. He said I should start the car every few days so the battery wouldn't run down, and to run the sprinklers as needed to keep the lawn and roses looking good.

As he was explaining to me what to do at the house and where to find things, I was concentrating hard, trying to memorize his words. He misinterpreted my gaze as a worried look regarding his condition, leaned forward and squeezed my hand.

"Don't look so worried. Don't you worry about me, or anything else."

I drew back, surprised. "I'm not worrying. I'm just concentrating real hard so I don't screw up!"

He said, "You can't screw up. Don't even worry about that. Call me if you can't find something." He mentioned what a dear man A.C. is, and what a long- time friend he had been.

At one point, De grimaced mightily when a nurse pushed a pillow behind him, accusing her of hiding a baseball bat in it. Later, I tried moving his hips underneath him more squarely, and he grimaced again. "Oh, I'm sorry!"

He said, "It's all right. They do it, too."

"Well, I'll find a way not to!" Then I used the sheet underneath him to move his hips into place; it didn't hurt a bit.

He became weary at close to five and kept nodding off so I told him I'd let him get some rest and go check out his house. He thanked me for my help. When I got to his house, I found out that he had given me one too few keys—I didn't have the key to the dead bolt—so I drove back to let him know. When I told him my problem, he joked, "I don't like to make it convenient for you to help me!"

I went back to his house, got inside, opened the garage door and started the Lexus. I checked on Myrtle, still hibernating in a cardboard box in the garage, and studied the sprinkler system. I got the messages off the answering machine and checked out the rooms to be sure everything looked okay. I lowered the thermostat to 65 degrees then called De's hospital. He was asleep, but his nurse assured me he was improving hourly. I called Carolyn and let her know what had transpired and that De was doing much better. She thanked me several times for "coming to our aid." I told her how much I loved doing it. Next I called the Kelley's neighbor intending to introduce myself and see if he had mail for them, but his line was busy, so I hung around a little while longer, familiarizing myself with the house. On a credenza in the workroom, I spotted a list of "Things to Do" which De had written. On the list, noted twice—once on the front and once on the back—was the notation, "Ask David about a fee for Kris." It was an indication that De had been seriously thinking about bringing me in to help him before he was hospitalized. When I again received a busy signal at the neighbor's phone number, I drove home.

At home there was a voice mail message from Carolyn. "Kris, this is Carolyn. Will you please give me a call when you can?"

I dialed immediately. She wanted my take on how De was. I told her he was much better and that she should get some rest. She thanked me again for my help.

Almost as soon as I hung up, the phone rang. It was De. He asked if he was interrupting anything.

"Absolutely not."

"I want to tell you, you did a good day's work. Thank you."

"I loved doing it. I should be thanking you for trusting and relying on me. You get a good night's sleep and don't hesitate to call me, day or night, if you want to talk or feel you need me to come over."

"Okay."

"Goodnight. I love you."

"I love you, too, Kris. Goodnight."

I called the nurse back and gave her my home and work numbers, asking her to call me, any time day or night, if there was a frightening change, as I wanted to get in there and be with him if he went critical again. She promised she would call.

The next day, I called Dan Kronstadt, my boss at Warner Bros to let him know I'd be late to work; that I was going to a hospital to be with a friend for a while and that I'd fill him in on details later.

I was with De four or five hours. The nurse and I gave him a bath. I was going to leave during his bath, but the nurse asked if I'd stay and help, so I asked De if that would be all right, and he said, "Certainly."

Back at the Kelley's home, I met their neighbor, Don, a lovely man who gave me their stacks of mail. We chatted for about 10 minutes. Then I went into the Kelley's house and did some chores. After that I reported to work and confidentially told my boss the situation, asking him what my options were for helping De. Dan was a big Star Trek fan; the news that De was dying upset him. He told me I had carte blanche to do whatever I needed for De for as long as he needed me; that he'd do his best to hold my job for me until I got back. I told him, "If De gets out of the hospital, I will probably have to stay at his house with him, but he won't be getting out for a while, so I'll just work here and do for De at lunch time, evenings and weekends." Dan said that would work; then, with genuine sadness in his voice, he added, "I wish there was something I could do for De." Surprised and touched by the sentiment, I told him, "Dear man, you just did!"

De was an ideal patient and a great storyteller. He recounted times he and Carolyn had parakeets and what naughty things they had said. "A friend of ours had taught one of them to say, 'F— Hollywood!' while we were in New York. This little bit of information made its way into one of the Hollywood gossip columns."

I said, "I'll bet that made your return to Hollywood problematic."

He said, "It sure did!" and scowled.

The hospital had moved him from ICU to the 4th floor. We wrote out only four checks and I outlined the next day's plan of attack for the rest of the bills, which he approved. Knowing he was exhausted, I left him as soon as he seemed ready to let me go. I returned to his house to look for his missing wallet because we couldn't find it in his pocket when we tried to locate it to get his Medicare card and supplemental insurance card to photocopy. The nursing staff said they didn't have it and that it wasn't locked up, so I was getting a little frantic. Then De recalled that his friend John might have it. "John is the one who drove me in the night I came in,

261

and I seem to recall that he may have taken it home with him." That relieved me somewhat, but I wasn't totally appeased since De also said, "I was so out of it with the pain when I got here to emergency that I couldn't even remember my home address when they asked me." By the time I got to his house, there was a message from him saying he had recalled John's phone number and called him, and that John had the wallet.

When I got home there was a wistful voicemail from Carolyn. "Hello, Kris, this is Carolyn. I'm just calling to ask how you're doing and how De was doing. He sounded pretty good to me. Give me a call, please, when you have time. I know you're a busy girl. Bye-bye." I called and gave her a full report.

On March 17 I went straight to De's hospital and received instructions on what to take out to the accountant so that he could begin working on De and Carolyn's taxes. The next day, I went to De's house to check on things, then to the hospital to find De sitting in a chair while six or seven nurses scurried around trying to get things done for him. Then we set to work on his affairs.

We discussed my offer to become his full-time, around-the-clock assistant when he got out of the hospital. I told him I had cleared it with Dan, who said I could take a Leave of Absence, and that he had said he would try to hold my job for me. "So I can drive you to your doctor appointments; take you to visit with Carolyn; do your shopping; work with your energy level whenever you want to work, even in the middle of the night, since we both have a tendency to get up and rattle around from 2 to 4 a.m. Then when you get tired and want to rest, I'll be able to keep going and finishing whatever tasks you want done."

He said, "That sure would be a wonderful thing; very helpful." He nodded his agreement and then said, "Would you call and tell Carolyn about this idea? You explain it so much better than I ever could." I nodded.

De's friend John arrived with his wallet. After a few minutes of conversation, a nurse entered and ushered John and me out of De's room and pulled the privacy curtain, but then six nurses went in. Two said they wanted to help him change his hospital gown. De said he didn't need six nurses to change his gown, but not one of the nurses left. Having been directed out of the room, I was in no position to protest the nurses' refusal to step out. I felt acutely embarrassed for De's discomfort.

Eventually John and I got back into the room and I learned that on an earlier date, De had been separated from his car by policemen. He was on heavy pain medication and still trying to function without help—go places and do things by himself and he was moving too slowly in traffic, so the officers stopped him and took him to the hospital when they determined he was ill. John and the next door neighbor had gone to the police station to claim his car for him. That's when I realized he'd needed help for quite some time but was refusing to ask for it. Not long after, De became weary again, so I bid him goodbye.

I called Carolyn and told her about the plan to become De's live-in assistant. "Oh, that would be terrific! Just wonderful! It would be such a help, and I wouldn't have to worry about him being there at home all alone."

When I got back to work, I remembered my concern about De's nursing fans and called Carolyn to report De's gawkers and asked her permission to raise humane hell at the nurse's station to be sure a repeat performance of the morning's antics would not be forthcoming. She agreed emphatically that I should do whatever it took to protect De's privacy, time, and rest. I told her I'd go back that night and be sure I'd spoken to the head nurse.

About an hour later, De called. He sounded good, except at one point he got a twinge of pain. He told me, "Take the night off and find out what real life is all about." I told him I had planned to come out to speak to the nurses about his need for rest, privacy, efficiency, and solitude so he could recover and go home. He said he had already done that and that it was taken care of. I said, "Okay, but if it happens more, let me know and I'll be sure someone gets a report."

I told him I wouldn't call that night because I didn't want to risk waking him. He said, "You have to decide what we should pay you for your help."

"De, I don't want you to pay me. As long as I remain employed at Warner Bros., there's no need. I'm just fine, unless we decide I need to take that Leave of Absence. That's unpaid, and I'd need something then, just enough to meet my obligations."

He said, "No, we want to pay you something. You decide what it should be, and write the check, and I'll sign it next time you come out."

"I don't have a blue clue."

He said, "It's all new to me, too."

Mid-afternoon, De called again, with bad news. "There has been a dramatic turn of events. The CT scan came back, and I have four new spots on my liver."

I was devastated. "Oh, I'm so sorry…"

"That makes two of us. In light of this, I think the smart thing for me to do would be to move to Carolyn's facility. What's your opinion on that?"

I was numb with grief over the liver involvement, but managed to say, "Yes, that's best." I asked if he still wanted me to take a Leave of Absence so I could help him full-time.

He said, "Oh, yes, there's a lot to do and to think about but I just won't be there at the house with you."

"That's okay. You're a good director. I can take instruction over the phone."

"Let's plan on that, then, okay?"

"You got it."

After work I visited Carolyn for about two hours. I told her, "The best way I can describe how I feel about this is I just hope that thirty or forty years from now, when I'm in your shoes, there will be someone who loves me as much as I love the two of you, so I won't even hesitate asking them to lend a hand, because I'll know what a blessing it will be for them to help, as it is for me to help you in this situation."

She said, "I hope you get your wish and that someone is there for you when you need it."

At about 7:15 I called De to let him know I was leaving. I asked if he wanted me to stop by on my way home.

"No. I'm throwing up. You go on home tonight. Next time you stop by, though, bring me about three pairs of socks, will you?"

"Sure."

"Thank you," he said, and hung up fast; I could tell he was very uncomfortable and close to getting sick again.

As I neared his hospital on the way home I just felt, intuitively, that I should stop by, even though I fretted that it might make De angry for having disobeyed. I went to his house, got the socks, and drove to the hospital. As I took the elevator, I started to get cold feet about disobeying his request to leave him alone and instead decided just to drop the socks at the nurses' station. But when I got to the nurses' station, there wasn't a single nurse on the floor. Then I noticed that De's call light was on. I hesitated only an instant before going in; I knew he wouldn't be calling for help unless he needed it.

I went into his room and found him looking nauseated. The head of his bed was elevated, but not enough: he was leaning too far back to be able to grab the plastic pan someone had placed near his ankles, nor could he lean forward enough to safely vomit. I said, "Hi, De. Can I help? There isn't a nurse on the floor at the moment."

"I feel lousy. I'm going to be sick."

I went to his bedside and grabbed the plastic pan, placing it in his lap. I put my arm behind him and pulled him forward. He was violently ill several times. He still felt lousy, so I started to press reflexology points in his hands, hoping to relieve the nausea. I heard several nurses at the nurses' station, so I asked De if he was all right for a minute while I went out to speak with them. He nodded.

I told the nurses what had happened and said that if I hadn't been there, he may have aspirated the vomit and choked to death. I told them he still felt sick and asked if they had something they could give him for it. One said, "Yes, we were just talking about that."

"Will it be soon?"

"It will take a little while."

"In the meantime, do any of you know about the reflexology point for nausea, so I can help him in that way until the medicine is ready?" They hemmed and hawed for about fifteen seconds, and then I said, "Do you have a reflexology manual?"

"No."

"Do you have access to the Internet?"

"Downstairs on the first floor."

"Well, can someone go down there and look up reflexology points?" One said she could, and I said, "Thank you."

I went back into De's room and related to him that the nurses were working on getting him something for the nausea. He said feebly, "Good."

"In the meantime, I'm going to rub and press some reflex points on your feet and see if I can help limit the uncomfortable feeling you're having. Is that okay, or do you think it might make you feel worse?"

"No, I think it will be okay. It might make me feel better. I hope so."

I re-positioned myself near his feet and started to deeply massage and press on areas on the underside of his foot, hoping to find the right spot. Sure enough—thank you, God!—I found the spot quickly and within a couple of minutes I could see his rigid, uncomfortable body relax and his breathing become more normal.

"Go ahead and fall asleep if you can. I'm right here. So don't worry."

"OK. Thanks." A few seconds later, he said, "I hated to put you through that."

"You didn't put me though anything. I volunteered. You told me not to come by, remember?"

He nodded. "I'm glad you did."

Within a few minutes he had relaxed enough to fall into a light doze. About ten minutes later, two nurses came in and said they had IV medication that would help with the nausea. De roused at that time and said, "Good."

I asked one of the nurses how long it would be before it would take effect.

"Ten to fifteen minutes."

I reported "The reflex points are working well, so he'll be okay until that stuff kicks in, I think."

265

At last he was truly asleep, so at close to 11, I decided I could risk going home as long as I got a vow from a ward nurse that she would plant herself at the nurses' station just outside his room and watch him closely. I said, "Mr. Kelley is a very sweet man, and he won't call for help unless he needs it, because he hates to inconvenience anyone—so if he calls for help, please get right in there."

She said, "I will. I promise."

"If you're short-staffed tonight and can't be sure you'll be here to help, I'll stay here in his room all night. I don't want him to be alone while he feels so lousy and is so dependent if he becomes ill again."

She said, "I will watch him. There's no need for you to stay."

"Okay, thank you. I'll be back first thing in the morning."

Just before leaving the hospital I whispered into De's room while he slept: "Goodnight, sweet prince." It made me cry, but it seemed a good way to ask the angels to keep a close eye on him.

The next morning, I got to De's hospital at 8 a.m. As I approached his room, I heard him leaving a message on my answer machine sounding rather urgent: "It's not terribly important. I'll get in touch with you a little bit later. Thank you."

I immediately poked my head in and announced, "You rang?!" He laughed and said, "My God! Now, that's service! You beamed right in!"

We discussed errands and chores, "Plus, there's the bedding, if you want to go to that trouble."

"Sure, no problem."

"You'll have to make the bed again."

"I think I can manage that!"

He mentioned he'd like me to find and buy him a new pair of thongs for the shower, as the ones he had at home were ratty.

On Friday I stopped by to see the Kelley's neighbor and pick up mail. I asked him, "Did you hear the news about De's new tumors?"

He said, sadly, "Yes. I didn't sleep much last night."

We went in and sat down; he got me a tissue when I teared-up as I poured out all the now-defunct plans about De returning home and directing my steps so that he could have everything taken care of. Don comforted me, saying he was glad I was a friend of De's because he knew I'd handle anything De needed so he wouldn't feel so out of control.

With errands run and De on his way to Carolyn's hospital I went back to work at Warner Bros. until 5:30 and then called A.C. with an update.

Carolyn called to report that De had a good afternoon and was very happy.

"Well, of course he is. He's back near his lady for the first time in what probably felt like forever."

"For him and me both."

"I know. I'm real happy for you. I'm a hopeless romantic when it comes to the two of you; you might as well know it, if you don't already."

Some days later, De asked if I got the sheets done. "Yes!"

"Carolyn tells me you decided what we'd pay you."

"We had discussed $100 a week; he approved it wholeheartedly."

Then I said, "By the way, this first week is a freebie."

He protested, "It was the worst week!"

"And you couldn't have kept me away with a team of horses. Warner Bros. paid me all week and I don't need the money. I can start the Leave Of Absence any time you say, but in the meantime I'll just report back to work and continue to help you part time until you tell me to go full time. How's that?"

"That sounds terrific. And listen: please tell Dan thank you for me. You've always told me what a great guy he is, but now I know. I'm very touched by his generosity"—he began to choke up—"so you tell him for me, will you?"

I said, "Sure."

Tuesday March 23 I saw De and Carolyn again for the first time in four days. De looked a lot better; he was gaining weight. I drove over in the Kelley's car; their neighbor Don rode along. He bragged to De upon arrival, "Not only is she a great gal and a hard worker, she's a good driver, too!"

Don and De yakked a lot; Carolyn and I mostly just listened. Carolyn seemed depressed—with good reason.

De and I did the business stuff and he approved the robe I'd bought.

On March 24 I called De early. He sounded half-asleep, so I asked if I had awakened him.

He said, "Almost."

I said, "Sorry, but this is important." I told him that Allison at his insurance agency needed a retrofit inspection on the foundation of his house and said she knew someone who would do it for $75.

He said, "Tell her to go ahead and do it."

At noon I drove the retrofit check out for De to sign. When I walked in, he was asleep. I planned to let him sleep while I made out the check, but a nurse came in for blood, waking him almost immediately. He spotted me in the chair and said, "Kris! I didn't know you were here."

"I wasn't until 20 seconds ago—just got my butt into the chair."

He said, "Oh, that's good."

I got the signature. He asked the nurse for a pain pill. I could tell he was hurting even while he had been sleeping. He told me, "I had a shower, a walk and too much other stuff going on all morning. It wiped me out." I told him I'd leave him alone and let him go back to sleep. He said, "No, sit here for a little while."

He asked if I'd bring his bottles of Clear Eyes and hair spray next time I came out, telling me where to find them.

"Sure."

I asked if he'd seen the Oscar telecast; he said he'd caught parts of it. I mentioned Roberto Benigni's acceptance speech and how he could've fallen on Steven Spielberg when he balanced on the backs of chairs in his exuberance over winning.

That reminded De of the "biggest mistake I ever made in my career." Steven Spielberg had asked De to appear in a court scene early in his (Spielberg's) career. "Although it was a wonderful scene, I turned it down. I regret it to this day. I didn't know who he was at the time; he didn't have much of a career yet, and it was such a small scene that I just felt it wasn't going to help much. What a mistake!"

De asked me to call and introduce myself to his attorney and give him my phone numbers. He asked me to be sure his accountant had my phone numbers, too.

De's arms and legs looked rehydrated, and his weight was coming back. At about that time Dr. Kaaren Douglas, Carolyn's visiting doctor and a personal friend, came in. They visited for about five minutes. By then, De was visibly exhausted, so when the doctor left I told him I'd leave so he could sleep.

I went to Carolyn's room. She had me wheel her to the bathroom; after that we visited for quite a while. I did little things for her—adjusting a curtain and putting lotion on her exposed leg. She seemed hesitant to let me go, but she knew I had to get back to work. But I didn't hurry out, telling her I had as much time as we needed for a good visit. So we talked about fifteen minutes more and then lunch was served so I took my leave.

A large part of my responsibilities entailed scheduling and cross-referencing the enormous number of things De needed to deal with. It quickly became apparent why the list of tasks had been a burden and a source of stress for him.

At one point Don wanted to know if Carolyn was provided for in case De didn't survive, and I assured him she was.

De was planning and wanting to get out of the hospital and go home, and every nerve and fiber of my being wanted it to work out that way for him eventually. Intuitively, however, I felt it was wishful thinking, unless he went home under Hospice care, with me as his around the clock assistant. I ordered a few reflexology manuals, in case he was able to go home, so I could keep him feeling well without drugs…or with as few drugs as possible.

I knew if he went home, I'd have to get some nutrition training from an expert at the hospital to be sure he got enough supplementation—either by eating or via IV drip—to maintain his nice weight gain.

On March 25 during a phone call made from my cubicle at Warner Bros., we celebrated his six pound jump to 104. "You're on the mend, boy!" I cheered. He asked how the family was up north; had I heard from them?

"Not real recently."

"How the hell could you? You've been workin' non-stop for me!" Then he said, "I thought you'd take today off and rest."

"No. I don't need to. I'm feeling good." I told him I got his hair spray and the eye drops he'd asked for and asked if he wanted me to drop them by at noon the next day.

He said it wasn't necessary; that he didn't want to run me around unnecessarily. "Just come out when you have more to do."

"Okay." Then I said, "You look wonderful with or without hair spray."

He grinned, "You're prejudiced."

"You think so?"

"You've got good taste, though!"

"Damn' straight, I do!"

"You sure have a wonderful boss."

"The best! He's at his desk right now. Would you like to speak with him?"

"Yes! I would!"

So I told him to hold while I transferred his call to Dan's line.

I ran to Dan and announced, "Dan, pick up the phone! It's DeForest! He wants to talk to you!"

Dan was tickled by the call. I closed his door more than halfway, so he wouldn't be interrupted, but listened to their conversation from just outside. De apparently thanked Dan for the loan of his secretary and they discussed me briefly. I heard Dan say, "Yes, she is wonderful." De said something else, and then Dan said, "Well, I'm happy to do it. And if there's anything else we can do—anything at all—just let me know. You've got it."

De was overcome by Dan's comments, so Dan put him on hold and had me pick up the line. De told me, "I have to hang up now. You two have me crying."

I spoke with Dan right away. He was deeply touched and visibly moved. He said, "I felt like I was talking to a legend. I was—and it felt like it." He said he was saddened to hear how weak De's voice sounded.

I told him, "It's worlds better than it has been—and, incidentally, just so you know, his actual voice is very quiet and reserved normally, even when

269

he's well. His stage- screen voice is projected a lot more than his normal voice."

Dan said he wished the whole world could know De's precarious health so he'd get the outpouring of love and affection that so many millions of people have for him. I told him I understood and concurred, but explained, "De's the kind of guy who would feel he should respond to each and every card, and he just doesn't have the time or the energy left; he has too much other stuff that needs doing." I assured Dan, "De knows he's loved—he doesn't have a blue clue how much, but he isn't exactly suffering from a lack of love or acknowledgment, either." Dan still felt it was sad that he wouldn't be shown. I offered, "Feeling the way you do, and being in on the fact that he's sick, it's okay for you to write him a note and tell him what you think he needs to know about how well loved and respected he is."

Dan said, "I think I'll do that this weekend."

After work I called De again to tell him he had affected Dan as much as Dan affected him. De said, "I didn't want to do that [cry], but he said such lovely things that I couldn't help it."

I said, "Don't worry about it. The feeling was mutual."

He told me his IV bottle of blood leaked while he was reading the newspaper and he looked down and saw the bed awash in blood!

"My first thought was, 'Sweet Jesus! I'm bleeding to death!' I called for help, and the attendant came in and assured me it was bottled blood, not my own. Boy, was I relieved."

I said, "I guess!"

I called Carolyn after that. We chatted for about 20 minutes. She asked me to buy her a new bottle of Dioressence at Macy's the next time I had a chance.

On March 26 I went to visit De to take him the eye drops and hairspray he'd been waiting for. I put lotion on his arms in profusion; had to wipe some off afterward because his skin wasn't absorbing it the way it was earlier in his convalescence.

De mentioned my boss again—or tried to—and then said, "This is crazy! Every time I mention your boss, I start to cry!"

"It's okay. You affected him, too!"

"It's getting really awful!" Tears were brimming, but he was grinning. "I cry every day over something!"

"That's wonderful! Don't worry about it. You have a lot of love inside and it's okay when it leaks out."

He handed me the piece of cake from his lunch tray. "Eat this. I saved it for you."

"Share your fork?"

270

"Sure." I put two bites into my mouth and then he asked me, "Are you gaining weight, or losing it?"

I said, "I'm losing it. But this isn't helping!"

He grinned. He mentioned a new drug the doctors were thinking of using on him—to starve the tumors of blood so they couldn't grow anymore. He said he had a doctor appointment on Monday to discuss it.

A volunteer came in then and mentioned that De had requested a milk shake earlier.

De said, "Yes."

I amended, "He'd prefer a malt if you have that."

She said, "I don't have malts, I'm afraid."

De said, "A milk shake is fine, dear. My assistant should sit idly by and be still!"

I flinched—for comic effect—and said, "Yes, sir!"

De looked at me, wondering if he had hurt my feelings. "I was joking, Kris. You know that, don't you?"

"Yes, De, I do."

The volunteer said, "The milk shake will be my own concoction, but I think you'll like it."

De replied, "I'm sure I will."

He mentioned that he hoped he wasn't appearing cranky as a result of all that had been happening to him. "Not at all!"

"I hope not. Sometimes it's hard, you know?"

"If you want to be cranky, do it. I won't take it the wrong way. It's real normal to feel like throwing things when stuff like this happens."

"I don't want to do that."

I reassured him, "But if you do, it's okay. It helps you deal with it. You can't hold it all inside." He was never short or snappish in my presence, not once.

He was getting tired, so he asked me to tell Carolyn he was going to write a letter and then he'd be over.

"Okay. You have a great day and I hope you get some rest." I mentioned that I'd written him a little book and that I was leaving it on the tray for him, "for when you feel up to reading it."

"Okay, honey. Thanks."

On my next visit De was in a chatty mood. I was there over three hours. We talked about A.C's bluntness. I told him what A.C. had told me the morning he called to tell me about him: "De's dying."

De said, "He has always been that way. When I fell off a horse, he'd come rushing over in a sweat and ask me a dozen times, 'Are you all right? Are you sure you're all right?' I'd say, 'Yes, A.C. I've fallen off horses before; I'll fall off them again. I know what OK is, and I'm OK.' He'd say, 'I'm

271

worried about you, De.' I'd say, "Then go somewhere else and worry, will you?'"

He told me the history of his tumors. I put some Internet-gleaned articles re: new tumor therapies into his shirt pocket after he decided he wanted to share them with his off-site oncologist. I asked him to find out the name of the new drug so I could research it on the Internet at work.

We talked about his important meeting on Tuesday with his attorney, accountant, and consultant. He decided I should drive over and sit in on that. "If there are things you want to discuss privately with them, you can kick me out and I'll go visit Carolyn until you want me back."

He mentioned two doctors who had written him recently asking him to attend important events in their lives where they would be receiving awards. They wanted him to be there because his portrayal of Dr. McCoy had inspired them to enter the profession. De said, "One of them is a gastroenterologist. Naturally I had to turn them down, but when I told my gastroenterology doctor about the invitation, he recognized the name of the doctor who was being honored and about flipped! He said, 'Here I am taking care of you, and one of your biggest fans is famous at what I do for a living.'" De laughed.

I said, "You should call him back and tell him to get his butt out here and take care of you."

De grinned and said, "I should! But it would hurt my present doctor's feelings. I can't do that. He's wonderful, too."

When he started to look a bit weary and the topics were exhausted, I said, "Before I let you go for the day, you left me a voice mail earlier today asking me to put lotion on your upper legs."

"Oh, yes! I need it. I called to remind you because I keep forgetting to ask when you're here."

I got out the lotion and first put it on the usual areas—his arms and lower legs and feet; then I did his upper legs and inner thighs. While it soaked in, we talked a little more about his love for Carolyn, my folks' marriage, my reason for never marrying. As I applied lotion and massaged it in, he mentioned how comfortable he felt with me doing that.

"Oh, good. I feel comfortable, too. I should have done this as a career."

"Yes, you should. I've always wondered how people can do something like this day after day."

"I'm sure it has to be a calling more than a career. People who are attracted to this kind of service are nurturers, pure and simple." He agreed.

On March 28, De called to ask when I'd be out again. I said, "Tuesday, unless you have something for me to do before then. I don't want to just drive out and visit. I figure you need rest more than you need visitors."

He said, "I don't consider you a visitor."

I guessed that meant he wanted me out there, so I asked, "Do you want me to come out today, or tomorrow at lunch time?"

"Why don't you come out today?"

I grinned, "I'd love to."

He asked, "How soon will you be here?"

"About an hour and fifteen minutes. Have a nap until then. I'll give your back a loofah scrub when I get there."

He said, "Okay."

I said, "I look like a street urchin. I just walked with my neighbor and am in jogging pants and a ratty shirt. I'd better change before I drive out."

He said, "I don't care how you look."

I said, "Maybe you don't, but they might not let me in the door when they got a look at me, so I'm going to play it safe and change."

He said, "I guess you're right. Show a little respect around here!"

"Yes, sir. See you in about an hour." I took a quick shower and drove out. I got there thirty minutes early, so stopped at Carolyn's room. She was in a great mood and wanted to visit, so I stayed for forty minutes. Then she said I'd better go over and see what De wanted, so I told her I'd be back afterward.

I went over to De's room; he was still asleep. I woke him so it took a while for him to get with it. I got a warm cloth; he washed his face. I pulled out the loofah scrub and wash and an aromatherapy spray I'd bought and sprayed that into the middle of the room.

He reiterated that he wanted me to attend Tuesday's meeting. I assured him I would. We discussed his upcoming doctor appointment outside the hospital; I asked if he'd like me to fax the Internet information over that he was going to hand carry to the doctor.

"That's a great idea. Then he'll have it ahead of time and be able to look at it before we get there."

I asked, "Do you want me to go with you to your doctor appointment? I can help you remember what was said; take notes, ask questions."

He said, "Why not? Yes, we can meet there."

He got nostalgic and started to tell me about a number of people who had been pressuring him to let them write his biography. He said, "I know you wanted to do it, too. I'm going to tell you where, in the garage, my history is. I'm going to let you know where everything is, in case something happens to me." He said he kept letters from Jake Ehrlich, the lawyer he portrayed in 333 Montgomery Street, and that there were scrapbooks

273

starting in 1945, perhaps even earlier, which would chronicle his career. He said, "I graduated from high school at 16."

I said, "I know, De."

He said, "Oh, that's right. You do. So, enough about me; what do you think of my career?" We both laughed. He added, "There are important papers—not many—in a safe deposit box at the bank. You can have the historical stuff regarding my career."

I protested, "Not now!"

He said, "No, not yet. I just want you to know where it is, in case I get incoherent later and can't tell you. There's a lot of private, personal, sentimental stuff in there. You can use it however you want. I never agreed to let anyone else do a book because I felt I couldn't contribute to it..."

He got up at one point, saying he had to use the bathroom. I stood very near him in case he became weak and needed an assist as he used the walker to get into the bathroom, then I went out to the nurses' station to let them know he was in the bathroom. I asked if they'd change his bedding while he was up. The head nurse came in and we changed it. Once during the process, the nurse called in to De, "De, how you doing?"

"I'm doing wonderfully. How you doing?" She went in to help him and stood by as he got himself back to the bed.

I said, "Before you get back into bed, De, will you just sit on the edge of it for a few minutes? I want to wash and oil your back."

"Certainly." The nurse started to leave and De joked, "I don't know if I can trust this girl! Perhaps you'd better stand by here and keep an eye on her!" I heaved a fake sigh of exasperation, and he chuckled.

As I cleansed, oiled and massaged his back, then helped him back into bed by lifting him, he mentioned how strong I was. I said, "I lifted Mom completely, and she weighed 145."

"My God, you are a strong little shit!" Then he practically did a soliloquy on my wonderful mother.

"I knew the minute I laid eyes on her that she was a beautiful woman. She was a wonderful, wonderful soul." He asked where she's buried.

I said, "She isn't. She was cremated, at her request. She said if there was such a thing as reincarnation, she wanted to come back as one of my pets. She also said that she didn't care what we decided to do with her ashes, but that she wanted part of them to be next to Deaken's in my bedroom, so I did that." I paused and then went on, "I didn't know if I'd like it, but it's okay with me...doesn't bother me...because I know it's what she wanted, so her spirit can keep a close eye on me."

He said, "She was pure love, wasn't she."

"Yes, and I always marveled at it. She did not have an easy life or an easy life partner, but by golly she understood him and stayed by his side from beginning to end. They were beautiful together at the end. I understood then—and only then—what they had going. It never looked like much until Mom got sick."

De became weary. I told him I'd go back and visit with Carolyn for a while.

I sat with Carolyn for almost two hours. She was in the mood for a chat and companionship while she watched a special on Carole Lombard.

Soon after the show finished, De came ambling over, rejuvenated and in fine spirits, pretending he was perturbed by absolutely everything—his nurse, Carolyn, me. He sounded like McCoy quarreling with Spock! It was very cute and very entertaining.

His nurse said, "If you're going to start arguing, I'm leaving!"

Carolyn said, "I don't argue with De!"

I said, "Neither do I. I'm outta here!"

De said, "It's about time! Gawd Awmighty, I thought you'd never leave!"

I drove to their house, did some chores and visited Don for nearly an hour, until it was pitch black outside and I was very weary and hungry. I excused myself and drove home.

On March 29 I was at work. At close to 11:30 I called De to see how he was doing. He said he'd had a bad night and a pretty lousy morning again."I threw up a few times."

"Oh, I'm sorry to hear that."

"I'm feeling better now, though, thankfully."

"I'm calling to ask if you're okay there until the meeting tomorrow, or f I should drive over."

"Why don't you drive over—unless it's a real drag."

"It's never a drag. It's a delight. I'll get in the car right now and be here in— oh, about forty minutes, unless the traffic is bad."

He said, "If the traffic is bad, forget it."

I arrived wearing a copper penny shirt and brown slacks. De mentioned how nice I looked in it. I responded by telling De how good he looked with his weight coming back and his skin re-hydrated and glowing. I asked if he wanted me to wash his back again, and he said he did. "I'll sit up straight in a little while, and you can do that."

It was such a beautiful day that I asked De if he'd like me to throw the door open for a while. He said, "Yes, let's get some fresh air in here."

The nutritionist came in and surveyed De on his meal plans. He said he'd had a rough night, throwing up, and couldn't even think about eating yet. He also mentioned that he'd asked for two soft-boiled eggs that morning and a blueberry muffin but only the muffin had been delivered "and there was no one nearby to ask about it".

275

The nutritionist said, "I need to know when things like that happen, De."

I reminded De, "That's what your call button is for."

De said, "Everyone here is so busy, I hate to stop them for something so small."

The nutritionist said, "That's not small. Call."

De said he thought the supplemental nutritional drink was too rich and that's what made him ill, possibly. The woman asked if he'd had other bouts of nausea.

"I did once, at the other hospital. I don't think they ever decided what caused it."

I reminded him, "Yes, they did, De. They had found your potassium level too high and had given you something to bring it down. They said it might make you sick to your stomach, and sure enough!"

De said, "That's right. I remember that now. It's a good thing you were there, Kris! I don't know my own story well enough to relate it."

The nutritionist asked how often I was at the hospital visiting De. "Oh—every day or every other day usually."

"That's good."

De said, "It sure is! She has all the information you need stored in that computer brain of hers."

I asked her if De could have Sustacal or Boost if I bought it for him. She said, "Certainly."

De said, "No. You have enough on your plate already."

I said, "De, there's a Sav-On right across the street. It'll take ten minutes, max."

He said, "It really isn't necessary."

I said, "If it'll keep you from getting sick, it is necessary...and I'm going to do it."

De then mentioned he'd like a mixed fruit plate. "They have wonderful ones at Ralph's or Gelson's." The woman agreed that would be fine.

At one point, the nutritionist was quizzing him on what he wanted as far as palatable meals—what sounded good to him. De responded, "Freedom sounds good to me! I want freedom!"

The woman said, "You and me, both!"

De joked, "When I get out of here, we'll go lay on the beach together!" and grinned.

She said, "You bet we will."

After the woman left, I told De I'd run over and get the drinks at Sav-On and be right back. I went over to Carolyn's room to report that I was on a mission to get Sustacal and Boost for De, and asked if she wanted anything. "No—but would you open the door to the outside before you leave?"

I said, "Sure!" I did that and then drove to Sav-On.

When I got back to De's room, I cleared off the table.

Carolyn called and asked De if he'd send me over to wheel her over to his room for a visit.

He said, "Certainly. Kris, please go yonder and bring my lovely here." When I got Carolyn to his room, she stood, leaned over and kissed De, then settled down and put her foot on his bed to elevate it. De was confused as to what day it was. He thought it was still Sunday, so he was surprised when I said, "I'd better head back to work."

He said, "You didn't tell me you were at work when you called."

I joked, "Do I have to tell you everything?"

"I guess not!"

I said, "I only work for you part-time right now, remember? A new employee is starting today, so I need to be there this afternoon to show him the ropes and get him settled in."

De said, "You'd better go do that, then."

"Yep, duty calls!" I kissed them both and left.

On March 30 I got to De's room at 8:45 a.m. in case I needed to rouse him before the attorney and consultant arrived. I didn't; he was wide awake in his white robe, having just finished breakfast. He said he'd had the best night's sleep since this whole ordeal began.

I cleared off his tray table so there was room for paperwork, then put lotion on his arms and legs. While I was applying the lotion, De pondered with a fond smile, "I wonder if your dear mother is sitting somewhere right now watching these goings-on and saying, 'Never, in a hundred years, would I have imagined Kris one day putting lotion on DeForest's feet and legs.'"

I laughed and said, "Probably!"

De chuckled. He added, "I'm not a praying man normally, but I sure did pray for your mother."

When the associates arrived the three of us, without De, went to Carolyn's room with her will and power of attorney papers so she could sign them. Then I wheeled her to De's room and propped her broken leg on his bed. The gentlemen explained the document carefully. At one point, De told them, "Wherever Bette or Anne have rights or responsibilities in the documents, I want Kris to be listed, too."

At first the attorney objected, thinking the situation would very likely become unmanageable with three people in the decision-making process. De said, "No, I just want them to be successive choices; if Bette can't serve, and Anne can't serve, then Kris can." The attorney asked me if I was all right with that.

277

I said, "Yes. Whatever De wants is fine with me."

At that point De made it a point to tell the attorney and the consultant, "I want you both to know that I trust Kris completely. She is completely honest and straightforward. If you have anything to tell me, you can tell me through her and I will know I got the message exactly as you intended it. She's a gem, and I trust her with all my affairs."

When the meeting ended, I kissed De and Carolyn goodbye and went to their house, made a few phone calls on Kelley-related business, and then went back to work. De phoned me at work and asked me to help him recall what had transpired during the signing earlier in the day.

On March 31 Carolyn called later in the morning while I was away from my desk and left a voice mail saying that De didn't sound or feel well. She asked me to call her back, so I did. As soon as she picked up the phone and said, "Hello," a nurse came into her room with a message from De. I said, "Go ahead and get the message. I'll wait."

I overheard the nurse telling her that De was about to have a blood transfusion, so not to call him; that he'd call her back when it was over and he felt better. She said okay.

I told her I had heard the message and wouldn't call or visit that day unless De called later to tell me to come in, as I wanted him to be able to rest as much as he wanted. We talked about the previous day's events.

Carolyn said, "It was tiring for him and emotional for me."

I let her know, "I have Friday off—Good Friday."

"Oh, good, you can rest. You need it: you've been so busy!"

I said, "But it's been a good busy, and I'm loving it, so don't give it another thought. I can come visit or work any day you want over this long weekend, for as long as you want me there."

She said, "That's up to De. You need to relax some, too."

She mentioned being anxious about De. When she said, "He's getting a blood transfusion now" I said, "He gets those occasionally."

She said, "He does? I didn't know that. Why?"

I said, "I'm not really sure. I didn't ask. But you can ask his nurse."

She was feeling frantic about De.

I said gently, "Sweetie, that doesn't help and it harms you. Try to occupy your mind with pleasant thoughts instead of imagining those damned worst case scenarios."

"Easier said than done."

"I know. It happens to me, too, but then I remind myself I'm imagining things, and that things are certainly a lot better at the moment than I've been fearing for him all along. He's even having some fun! You should visit more often, and see."

TWO COWBOYS AND TWO STRAIGHTS

At nearly 5 p.m., De called. "I'm calling to check up on you."

"I'm glad you did, because that way I can check up on you."

He said, "I'm doing better. I got a blood transfusion today. I had a couple of bad nights there. I'm going to call Carolyn in a minute and see if she wants you to bring her anything from home." Then he told me, "If you ever feel the need, fall into bed at our house and sleep there, rather than driving home tired after a busy day."

I said, "I haven't been there enough yet to feel the need, but if I do, it's good to know. Thank you."

I asked if I should drive out the next day or give him another day off.

"No, I think you should work for Dan tomorrow. I don't want to take advantage of his generosity."

I said, "Tomorrow is my last day of work there for three days. Friday is a holiday—Good Friday."

He said, "Oh, in that case, for sure go to work tomorrow. We can catch up on Friday and through the weekend."

When I got to work, De called again. He asked if I'd bring in four more photos, plus his white pen and two more manila envelopes when I returned. I said, "Sure. Which photos do you want?"

He said, "Two cowboys and two straight."

I was confused by the terminology and inquired, "Two cowboys and two McCoys?"

He said, "No, two cowboys and two straight."

I said, "Straight. I don't get it…Oh! You mean two De's—studio shots of you as you!"

He said, "That's right. You got it."

I said, "I'm learning new terminology, here!"

He chuckled.

I asked him, "When I come by tomorrow, do you want me to bring you a fruit plate from Ralph's?"

He said, "It sounds good now!"

"But it may not sound as good tomorrow. I'll call just before I drive out and see if it still sounds good, because as you know, it won't last if you don't eat it right away."

He said, "Good thinking, Ollie!"

On April 2 I called De at about 9 to let him know I was on my way out to his home. I asked how his night had gone.

"Pretty well."

"You sure sound good."

He said, "This sounds silly—they'll think I'm about to go out over the wall—but will you bring me the new green corduroy trousers that are in my bathroom closet?"

"Sure! How are you feeling about a fruit plate this morning? Still interested?"

"Yes. Get a little one, though. You know my appetite."

"I'll get the smallest one that has a good variety."

"Yes, do that."

I drove to their house and looked for the photos I thought De wanted. But as I surveyed the selection, I noticed there were very few non-McCoys left, so I grabbed some of them, plus a few of De with motion picture information printed on them, hoping they were in line with what he wanted. Then I drove to Ralph's for the fruit plate.

When I got to De's room, I called out, "Knock knock!" He responded enthusiastically: "Come in! Come in!" I stepped into the room. He was lying in bed with his hospital gown draped solely over his midsection!

Surprised but grinning, I exclaimed, "Well, hello there, gorgeous!" He grinned.

I asked if there was anything else he could think of for me to do at their house.

He said, "Would you vacuum the carpets in the closets?"

"Sure."

"There are shoes and other things on the floor in the closets; you'll have to pull them out first."

"That's no problem."

A nurse came in and said she was sorry I had walked in on a "naked" man; she hadn't known anyone was on the way in.

I said, "Well, I said 'Knock knock', and he said 'Come on in!' so in I came. What the hell!"

She joked, "Typical of any man!"

She said she was going to find him a gown that snapped, and took off. I said, "Before she comes back, and while you're totally exposed, I should put lotion on you!"

He said, "Yes, go ahead."

His skin was very dry again. His chest had never been done and it was caked with the iodine solution they'd been putting on parts of it, so I worked a lot on that area until it was saturated, then worked on his legs, feet, and arms. At one point, as I was helping lift him to a sitting position, he asked if the exertion would give me cramps or anything else adverse. "No."

"Are you sure?"

I reminded him, "I lifted Mom, and I've baled hay: I'm fine!"

He mentioned how well Mom's neck pillow was working for him. "I don't know what I did without it. I hope dear Dorothea doesn't mind me using her neck pillow."

"Not a chance. She's loving it."

When De was positioned comfortably on the side of the bed, I presented his fruit plate; he loved it. I was surprised when he ate more than a third of it, and when lunch arrived forty minutes later, he also ate half of a large cup of tomato soup with crackers and some ice cream and drank some coffee. De said he'd like to stop by the house after his doctor appointment to check things out.

I said, "I hope the transportation people who bring you out will let you do that."

I showed De the photos I had found, but said there were so few of them at his house that I thought they were the wrong ones. He confirmed that.

I said, "I don't see many other straight ones. There's one of you with Fancy, but that's just about it."

"I have a lot of them in the costume."

I queried, "The costume? Oh! You mean the Starfleet uniform?"

"Yes."

"Oh! I was calling those McCoys, and you told me you didn't want McCoys, I thought."

He said, "I'm sorry I confused you."

I said, "That's okay, as long as we're on the same page now. I'll bring them in tomorrow."

He said, "You may as well bring twelve or fifteen. If I have to sign more than that at once, I'll croak!"

At one point, I went over and got Carolyn to sit with us for a while. Later, when we were alone again, De said, "Every time I look at Carolyn, she seems to be looking at me as if she's thinking that perhaps she's seeing me for the last time."

I spoke softly then: "I know. I wish there was some way to help her not think like that, but I don't know what to say or do that would—"

He interrupted, "There's nothing you can say or do. It's just the way it is. She's going to think whatever she thinks to think, and no one is going to talk her out of it."

At about three I thought he was beginning to look like he could use a nap. He said he wouldn't sleep, "but you can go if you want to or need to."

I said, "If you want me to get to the bank today, I'd better leave here pretty soon, or it'll be closed."

He said, "Oh, that's right. You go ahead."

281

At 8:15 that evening De called. "When you come out tomorrow, I'd like you to take some of this stuff out of here. I keep trying to clear off my tray table and it just gets piled higher and higher."

I said, "I almost mentioned that today, and then promptly forgot when we got going on something else."

He continued, "Don called me about thirty minutes ago. He just went on and on about how impressed he is with you. I told him, 'Yes, Don, we've been impressed with Kris for years—but on and on he went!'"

I said, "Well, I'm impressed with him, too. You've said for years what a sweet and helpful guy he is to have nearby, and it has been borne out. We've had a number of great visits together."

De said, "His reaction to you put me in mind of that movie with Nicolas Cage and Cher, where Cage says, 'I think I'm falling in love with you,' and Cher slaps him and says, 'Snap out of it!'" I laughed heartily at that.

He asked, "When will you be out tomorrow?"

I said, "I don't know. When do you want me out?"

He said, "I don't want to rush you."

I joked, "So…8 AM, right?"

He said, "Right!"

I asked if the air mattress we were trying for his comfort was working for him.

"It's better than the other one."

He again asked when I'd be out the next day, and I said, "I'm really not sure. I should vacuum those closets. I didn't get to them this afternoon; I figured the bank deposit was the priority and I was getting weary. I got up at 4 a.m. today for some ungodly reason, so it was a long day."

De said, "Just forget about those closets."

I said, "I don't mind doing them, De. I'll get to them sometime this weekend. I hope you have a good night and get lots of good rest."

He said, "I hope you do, too. We'll see you tomorrow."

I said, "I love you."

He said, "I love you, too, Kris…"

On April 3 I got to the Kelley's house at about 9 intending to call De to let him know what was happening and where I was in case he wanted to reach me. Indeed he did: I arrived to find a voice mail message for me waiting on his answering machine. Part of it was, "Remember to look for the pen I told you about." The other part was about whether he was bothering me too much, calling me at home late at night and so forth.

I called him right away and told him, "Absolutely not; you're not bothering me. It gives me a chance to find out how you're doing. I feel

282

uncomfortable calling you, as I'm afraid I'll catch you when you're trying to rest, so when you call me often, my mind gets its report and I can relax."

He said, "Oh, good. I have to call when I'm thinking about something, or it leaves me and then I may not think to remember it again—and that could be dangerous, if it's something important."

"You call any time. I don't care when, or for what." I let him know I'd be at their house for at least an hour, and while there, I'd clean the closets.

"Bless your heart."

I asked him how his night went.

"Very well. I finally got to sleep at about 3 or 3:30; I managed to read everything I wanted to read last night." Then he reported, "I got up twice to use the bathroom and fell both times."

I said, "Oh, no! You were doing so great in the hallways yesterday. I'm surprised."

He said, "I was, too."

I asked, "Was anyone there to catch you?"

"Yes. The first time it was a gal. The next time it was a male nurse. They had to dig me out of my walker."

I commiserated over that, but he didn't seem unduly disturbed by it, so I joked, "Well, in a little over an hour, I'll be out there and I'll hold you up!"

He said, "You may have to!"

I cleaned all three closets and then drove to the hospital. I stopped in first with Carolyn to show her the checks that De would be signing for deposit that day.

I offered to take her over for a visit, but she was still ensconced in bed and said, "Oh, no. I heard that De had a bad night and I'm not sure he wants me or anyone over there right now."

I said, "Well, if he doesn't, I'll be right back for a nice long visit, if that's okay with you!"

She said, "That's fine with me!"

"Okay, I'll be back sooner or later, depending on whether we can get our work done quickly, or if he'll even see me right now!"

She said, "Okay. When you get back, will you give me a report on how he is?"

"Certainly."

She asked, "An honest report?"

I assured her, "Of course, an honest report."

I walked over to De's room. He was asleep, leaning way over to the right side. I got his neck pillow and another pillow and said, "Here, sweetie, let me get you straightened up a little so you can be more comfortable." He continued to sleep so I propped him up straight and placed the neck pillow behind his neck. In just a couple of minutes, he realized who had helped him and awoke with, "Oh, that's you, Kris…" He tried to chat, but he was still very doze-y so I just waited while his mind cleared. At one point he realized he wasn't making a whole lot of sense, and he joked about it. "Am I around the bend yet, do you think?"

I assured him, "You're just fine, De. As soon as your brain gets the picture that you want to wake up now, you're going to be just fine." Very shortly thereafter, it did. I put lotion all over him except for his back, asking if he ever slept on his stomach.

"No, I never have."

"It's too bad. It'd be good to get you off your back for a while, but the air mattress is probably doing all right for you, anyway."

He again recounted falling in the bathroom as he showed off his new gauze bandages. I just kept applying lotion, not reacting much, as I didn't want to seem overly concerned or anxious about his occasional weakness. He said, "I knew I was going to go down, but not soon enough to let anyone know."

I asked, "Did you pass out?"

"No, it was weird. I just—" Words failed him so I guessed, "You just got weak suddenly?"

"Rather like that, I guess. I'm not sure what happened."

I started to clear off his tray table and put stuff in my bag that he wanted taken home, and followed that by making a list of all his pertinent, oft-used numbers so he would have only one piece of paper to refer to. He told me he'd eaten every last bite of his breakfast, and at close to noon, just before lunch, he started on the second fruit plate I'd bought for them the day before.

I said, "If you get started on this, when the heavier meal comes along, the juices from the fruits and your stomach will help the heavier stuff process and digest more easily."

He said, "You're right about that. I've noticed that I don't have nauseous inclinations when I eat this way—haven't for a few days, anyway."

He was relishing his fruit plate like gangbusters when Carolyn called. De said, "I'm eating your fruit plate. Do you want to come over here and help me finish it?"

Carolyn said, "No, my lunch is about to be served."

De said, "Okay, I'll see you later, then." He hung up and a nurse brought in his lunch tray. I took the uneaten balance of his fruit tray and placed the lunch tray in front of him, to see if any of it intrigued him. It all did; he was ready for more food! He sliced everything right down the middle except for the half peach, and said, "Get a plate. You're going to help me eat this." I took half and two crackers.

Just as he was finishing and grabbing the ice cream and coffee, his long time friend John Stecko and his pal came in for a visit. The phone rang, too; it was Carolyn. De said to me, "Let's get Carolyn over here and have a visit together."

I wheeled her over.

They visited quite a bit, reminiscing about old times, old movies, how good De looked…I kept taking stuff from De as he'd finish it to get it off the tray and near the door to be picked up.

Finally Carolyn joked, "Have you been working here long?"

I joked back, "Not long, but I'm getting the hang of it, huh?"

De told John and his friend how one of his nurses had built up his appetite by saying, "You don't have to eat everything. Just have a le-e-tle bit of this, and a le-e-tle bit of that…He was right! Leetle by leetle, my appetite came back!"

John and his friend didn't stay more than about forty minutes, and shortly thereafter I left, too, as I had to stop by Don's house for the day's mail and by the Kelley's again to get the black and white McCoy photos.

Don was chatty, cheerful and friendly as usual, talking a lot about his wife and son, both of whom had been dead for many years.

On the way home that night, tears welled up in my eyes; for many blocks, I was engaged in sad thoughts: *If I consider who I'm about to lose from my life, it more than half kills me. But then I think of Carolyn and realize she's losing even more. How will she ever survive this? She has had him in her daily life for over fifty-five years. I know that's what De is fighting so hard for—he doesn't want to break any hearts. It isn't his fault; he can't help it. He wants to prevent heartaches, not cause them. I wish everyone could have met and known him in the way I have!*

STAR TREK MEMORIES: A HEALING TOOL

On Easter 1999 I went star polishing and to the grocery store, then to the Kelley's house to enter into their black book the various residual payments De had received since I began keeping his books. As I was doing that, I called him to see how he had passed the night. He said he'd had a good night. I told him where I was and what I was doing. I asked if he'd like another fruit dish before lunch; he said he would. "Just get a little one, though—or you can eat half." Then he said, "Oh, here's a little bit of good news! They weighed me yesterday, and I'm up to 112 pounds!"

I practically shouted, "Jesus, De! That's fantastic!"

I drove to Gelson's. They had a plate with a large variety of fruit in it, so I got it. I figured the nurse could refrigerate it and De could have some the next day, too.

I got to the hospital at about 11:30. De looked well rested. I gave him the fruit dish right away, since I knew lunch would be along soon and he'd have time to process the fruit before it arrived. As he ate, we discussed some of the items I'd been dealing with—checks and insurance primarily. He was very chatty and told a few stories about his acting days.

His nurse came in packing a lunch plate and told me that not only had De's weight been improving like gangbusters, but his blood sugar level was rising as well. It had gone from 93 to 123. After the nurse left, De said, "That's good news. When he told me—he doesn't mince words, that one—he said 'Only dead people have a blood sugar level of 93!'" De ate a few bites of ham and perhaps one bite of the au gratin potatoes then shoved the plate across the table to me. He ate about a quarter cup of the cream of potato soup, then passed it to me. I joked, "I was losing weight!" as I swallowed his abundant leftovers.

Then I lathered him up with the new skin lotion I'd bought. I got his back this time, too. It looked very good. He said it itched, so I massaged it until he said it was okay and that the lotion would take care of the rest.

De went into his most recent call from Don. Again, Don had regaled De with statements such as, "Do you know what you have in that girl?"

"Yes, we do, Don."

"Do you see what she drives?"

"Yes, I know—a little red jewel."

Don shot back to De: "She's the jewel!"

I was laughing and feeling acutely embarrassed. De just would not stop—he was on a roll, telling me "Don said this, Don said that…Don asked, 'How long have you known her?' I told him 'About twelve or fourteen years well…' 'Well, you just don't know what you have there. She's just amazing!'"

Excruciatingly embarrassed, I finally joked, "To quote Mark Twain: I can live for a week on a compliment!" Then I got a little philosophical: "I'm awfully lucky in that way: I get compliments at work—two or three times a month at least, I think. I think poor Dan gets sick of hearing it from his vendors and work associates."

De said, "Well, I guess you know it, then. We talk about you all the time, but we forget to tell you about it."

"That's okay. It embarrasses the hell out of me—but it is great to think back on—later."

He said, "You know, we all tend to think we have all the time in the world to tell people what they mean to us, and then one day we find out we don't."

I said, "I know. I'm only forty-eight, and I'm beginning to get that message loud and clear already."

"You're way ahead of me, then."

About half an hour after he finished his meal, I said I'd go visit Carolyn until she got tired of me. "Shall I stop back by afterward or just go home after that?"

"Oh, stop back by. I'll be here!"

I went over to chat with Carolyn. She wanted to know what De and I had talked about; I gave her a report on that. At about that time, Dr. Kaaren Douglas, a frequent guest, came by with her dog Sammy for a visit with Carolyn.

Then Kaaren went over with Sammy to visit with De. I spoke with Carolyn for a few more minutes, and then asked if she had seen De yet today. She said, "No, and it's getting kind of late for that today, anyway." I said, "No way! You gotta see him; he's looking so good! Let me take you to him."

I wheeled her over. She and I basically listened while Dr. Kaaren and De chatted. De recounted a few stories about his career. A particularly funny anecdote involved Christopher Plummer in Star Trek VI and the fact that both he and Plummer had worked with Burt Lancaster and Kirk Douglas in different pictures, and what selfish actors they were, wanting the best lines, the best angles, what-have-you. Then Plummer and De got into doing shtick the next day on the set of Trek VI along those lines, with Plummer calling De "Burt" and De calling Plummer "Kirk"! It was hysterical!

THERE'S NO PLACE LIKE HOME

The next morning I called De at about 9:30 to see how he had passed the night. "Very well. I'm putting on my pants now for the doctor appointment."

"You're being awfully pre-punctual, aren't you?"

"These things take a while. And I had a problem. You know those new green trousers I had you bring out to me? What a difference six or eight pounds make: I can't get them on this morning."

I laughed. "That's wonderful! Getting too big for your britches, eh?"

"I guess so!"

"That's okay. You still have the other pair you wore the night you came to the hospital. You can wear those."

"Yes, I can, but the green ones would be warmer."

"Just throw the white robe in the vehicle with you, to have it along in case you're not dressed warmly enough."

At 10:15 I drove to De's house to pick up his sweater and turn up the heat in the house so it would be warm inside when he visited after his doctor appointment. Then I watered the roses for about ten minutes and drove to the clinic.

I met up with De at 11:35 in the lobby, along with the transportation coordinator, who was stationed with us so she could call for the vehicle when we again needed it—but we didn't know this at the time. We went up to the oncologist's office. Several cheery nurses immediately started bantering with De. There was a long form to fill out, so I did that while a technician drew blood from De's arm. Then we went into a room and waited for the doctor to arrive.

It wasn't long before the doctor entered and performed a cursory check of De's lungs and leg edema, which was slight but getting worse as the day progressed. Then they launched into a discussion of De's current status. De handed the doctor the two articles I had found on the Internet about ways to try to thwart liver cancer.

The doctor said one wouldn't work at all, as De's cancer has spread beyond the liver and colon, and there was just no way to pinpoint and attack all the spots that would need to be addressed. The other idea was a viable option. I asked about drug therapies that cut off the blood supply to tumors, and he said there are 16 or 17 drugs that do that; plus other clinical trials for other things they could try. The doctor listed De's three options:

Do nothing at all, De's current election: no chemotherapy, radiation just keep him comfortable and perking for as long as possible.

Chemotherapy: there were several options here, with a 1 in 3 chance of shrinking the tumors 20 to 30% and giving De a better quality of life and greater longevity. "If it works for you, you'll feel better."

I asked about the side effect of nausea.

"We can limit nausea significantly with drugs."

De said, "The stuff I'm on now works wonders in that way."

Clinical trials: the doctor knew about two trials just off-hand that offered some promise, one at UCLA and one in Houston. He had called the facility in Houston and said he'd follow up on that call. I was put in charge of calling UCLA and getting an appointment for De as soon as possible. 60 Minutes had just run a segment on the trial the previous evening and good results had been seen there. So I said I'd call first thing in the morning from work.

The doctor said to make another appointment with him in two weeks and said also to call him back on Thursday to see what he had found out, or to report any changes. We were then directed to get De's monthly Sandostatin shot. There was a slip up there, because the chart didn't get into the nurse's "to do" slot, so everyone went off to lunch. De and I were planning to drive to his house anyway—where he had some of the drug in the fridge—so a nurse told him, "Go ahead, and call us from there to be sure the drug is the right dosage. If it isn't, come back here after you've been to the house and we'll give you the shot then."

We went downstairs. The transportation coordinator advised us that the driver had gone on another call and wouldn't be back for forty-five minutes to an hour. We were chagrined, to say the least.

About forty-five minutes later, De's doctor came back into the building and we mentioned that De hadn't received his shot, so we went back up. The doctor said he couldn't give the shot—it was a specialty shot—and we'd have to wait for the return of a nurse. So we sat and chatted with the insurance coordinator for the facility.

By this time, thirty minutes more had passed. Finally, a nurse popped her head in and said she could give him the shot. Then she said, "I'm so sorry! I've been back here for a good twenty minutes, but no one let me know you were waiting." De said, "Nothing surprises me today." The shot was a real ow-ee, but he did fine with it.

Then we went back downstairs to find that the driver had again been called away and would not be back for an hour. We were sitting in the chilly lobby, and De was beginning to get weary and deeply frustrated. I said, "I'll take you over in my car, and the driver can come there to pick you up." De said, "Good idea. Let's go." The transportation coordinator said, "No, no, you cannot do that. I must call my supervisor!'"

I said, "Okay." She called the supervisor, who at first denied the request for me to take De to his house. Furthermore, she denied the request to have the driver take De to his house afterward.

"We are supposed to deliver patients only to their doctors, and then back to the hospital."

I asked De, "What do you want to do? You're my boss."

He said, "I want to go to my house." I felt that if I violated the hospital's transportation rules and just took off with their patient without permission, I could get into trouble. So I was quite hesitant to do as De wanted. On the other hand, I knew it was the fondest wish in his universe to see his home again, and I was willing to risk all to fulfill it. So I tried again with the transportation coordinator:

"I have my orders. I'm taking him to his house."

She was frantic, and asked, "Will you speak to my supervisor, please?"

I said, "Certainly, I will. I'd be happy to." So the supervisor was dialed again.

I got on the line and said, "Mr. Kelley is six blocks from his home. His doctor appointment has been over for more than thirty minutes, and transportation took off to get another patient, so we are pretty much stuck here in a cold lobby for the next forty-five minutes to an hour. This is no good for Mr. Kelley, and he wants to go home for a brief look-see before he returns to the hospital. Can I get your approval to drive him the six blocks to his house? We can wait for the driver there."

The supervisor said, "Certainly."

I gave De a thumb's up. We couldn't leave the transportation coordinator stranded, so I asked her, "Would you like to come along?"

She nodded, "Yes!" So I told her supervisor, "She'll come with us."

The supervisor said that would be fine.

We piled into my little Mazda, wheelchair and all, and drove to De's home. I wheeled him into the house. The transportation coordinator called the driver and gave him the address, so he'd know where to come to pick De and herself up when he got around to it. By the time we got to the house De had to use the bathroom, so I decided to wheel him into Carolyn's bathroom because the wheelchair access was slightly better.

I lifted him out of the wheelchair and was figuring out how best to support him as he headed into the bathroom. After I got De back into the wheelchair, I pushed his wheelchair slowly around the house, so he could check everything out. He asked me to turn more water on the roses, so I did that. He dialed Carolyn and told her, "Here we are, looking out the window into the backyard." They spoke for a few moments about the crazy, time-consuming day then hung up.

At about that time, the driver showed up—too soon, as De had wanted to stay a while and savor the ambience of his home—so I told him and the coordinator that they could leave and I would drive De back to the hospital in his Lexus.

I said, "Your supervisor gave me permission to drive him. So you're in no bind in going on ahead without us." So they left.

De was emotional in his home. He told me twice that he had hoped to spend time there alone that afternoon. "You could go out and have a bite to eat or do the banking or something."

I told him that, as much as I'd love to respect that wish, I felt completely responsible for him now and would worry my fool head off if I left him there alone.

He said, "I understand completely. You don't have to explain. It's all right. You're doing the right thing. Stay put."

I went out into the yard to put water in the birdbath and do some other miscellaneous chores so he'd have a few minutes in the house alone. I could keep an eye on him through the window, so he wasn't unattended—we were just separated by glass.

When I got back inside, he said he was ready to head back. I wheeled him to the car and put him in it, then loaded the wheelchair. I drove to the hospital and helped him back into the chair, then wheeled him to Carolyn's room.

They spoke for about fifteen minutes. De reported on the doctor's appointment, and then mentioned what a strong champion I had been all day: keeping at the issue of getting him to their house against the protestations of the transportation folks until they finally relented.

Carolyn asked what it was like to go back to the house. De got emotional. "It felt like our house…but it was…odd. It was a weird feeling."

I said, "You probably felt like an exiled visitor, since you weren't able to stay."

He teared up at that.

I wanted to say, "Don't worry, you'll be back," but I didn't want to say it in Carolyn's presence, as I was aware that her return home was highly questionable.

After a few more minutes, I wheeled De back to his room. He was extremely weary by then. I helped him into bed and propped him up with pillows and then put lotion on his legs. His feet and lower legs were puffy. Two nurses came in and took his vital signs and asked how the day went and what had transpired at the doctor's office. De told them part of it; I told them part as he began to run out of steam.

I stayed for about ninety minutes massaging his feet and legs until the edema started to resolve. Just as I had kissed him good-bye and was about to leave, the dinner tray came in. He felt a little nauseated and didn't want to eat anything. I reminded him he hadn't had any lunch, and he said he hadn't had much breakfast either: "They forgot my eggs this morning."

I exposed the dish of food and asked him to have "just a leetle bit of this and a leetle bit of that"—which he did. He had one bite of fish and one bite of rice and then about half of the green beans and about half of the ice cream cup. That was plenty for him; he told me to eat the rest. I declined. He again thanked me sweetly for all my help. I reiterated how much I enjoyed doing it.

I went over to Carolyn's room to visit for a while. She said how glad she was that I was willing to go through everything with De. I told her it was a big thing to me to be able to show how much I love and appreciate them. "You have been so kind to me for so many years."

She said, "We have known you for a long time, haven't we?"

I said, "Yes, and every day has been a big blessing for me." I left there at about 6:30.

On April 6th, I called UCLA Medical Center and left voice mail messages at two numbers. I gave a brief history of De's situation and asked someone to call me back as soon as possible. Within a half hour a doctor's secretary called back and told me the doctor would accommodate De's schedule; that he would make himself available to see him. I called De's room twice, but there was no answer, so I called Carolyn to see if he was with her. He wasn't, and she hadn't seen or talked to him all day. So I called the nurse's station and gave the nurse the information. I asked how De was. "He's a little out of it today; he tried to reach for the phone when it rang but he didn't get to it in time. He's getting better as the day goes along. I think they gave him a sleeping pill last night, or else he's just still wiped out from yesterday." I said, "I won't call him again. Will you pass along the message?"

De's physician in residence called me at about 4:30 that evening to get more information than the nurse had taken down as to what I'd learned and arranged for when I called UCLA that morning. He wanted to know my relationship to the Kelleys. I said, "Long-time friend and presently assistant." I asked him how De was doing this afternoon and he said, "He's improving." I said I'd heard earlier that he was pretty low this morning, and he confirmed that, saying "He was awful this morning, but as the day goes along, he's coming back." I told him that De had a very long, rough day yesterday due to transportation glitches and he said he had heard about that.

At about 5, I gave De a quick call, based on his doctor's indication that he was bouncing back. De answered the phone slowly after several rings. He spoke slowly and without much energy.

"Hi, De. This is Kris."

"Hello, Kris."

"I heard you had a bad day."

He confirmed that.

"Did you sleep last night?"

"Not much. Oh, I did get a little sleep, I guess. What's new out here?"

"Did your nurse tell you I called UCLA and opened the door for you to see the doctor at your convenience, any time, whenever you're feeling up to a drive again?"

"She told me something. I don't think I'm going to be going to UCLA for any seminars, though."

I could tell he wasn't getting the picture—still a bit dazed—so I said, "That's OK. We'll talk more about this on a better day."

"OK, honey. I love you. Have a good night tonight."

De called me at home at about ten and asked if he had awakened me.

"No."

"Oh, good. I thought twice about calling you at this late hour—"

"Don't ever think twice. Don't hesitate: If you want to call, call."

"I was wondering if you have any extra photos of me at your place."

"Not many."

"Oh."

"I did get twelve or fifteen of the black and whites you want, but in all the craziness yesterday, I forgot to drop them off with you when I took you back to the hospital."

"Oh, for heaven's sake. Well, remind me next time you come out to get them. I have two here to sign, but I need some more."

"They're here, and you'll have them soon."

I asked De if he remembered me telling him about his invitation to meet and speak with the UCLA doctor about what they may be able to do for him.

He responded, "With the energy I have right now, I don't think it will ever happen. But I may feel differently about it later."

I said, "Perhaps he can come to you."

"I just don't know if I want to get involved in anything like that. I haven't up until now."

"I understand that, and it's totally your decision."

"A number of times, they've told me they can't help because of what has already been done to me."

"Well, your oncologist and the UCLA doctor are discussing your history, so they'll reach some sort of consensus before they'd think to involve you in a trip down there, so that it won't be a waste of your energy or time."

"That's good," he said. Then he reported, "I've had a bad day. I'll just get to sleep and someone will come in and awaken me. It just happened again, and I thought, 'Well, I think I'll wake KRIS now!'"

I laughed and said, "Any time, De."

"So I'll let you go now."

"Okay. Goodnight. I love you."

On April 7 I drove to the Kelley's house, arriving at about 10:40 after having deposited checks at the bank. Then I called De. He picked up the receiver after about six rings and answered sleepily, "Hello?"

"Hi, De. Kris. Did I wake you?"

"Almost."

"I'm sorry."

"Well, it's time to wake up."

"I'm here at your house. I'm planning to drive over and see you in a few minutes and bring you the photos you've been waiting for."

"Oh, good."

I asked, "Is there anything else here at the house you want me to bring along?"

"Let me think. No, I don't think so."

"Okay. I went over to Don's for the mail, but he isn't there, so I'll stop back by this afternoon and get whatever he has gathered."

"That's fine."

Then he said, "When will you be here?"

"Oh, about twenty minutes, I guess."

"That's good. I look forward to seeing you again."

I said, "Take a nap until I get there."

I walked into De's room and found him groggy. I pulled out the envelope of photos and showed him that I had them and would leave them. Then I checked out his feet and legs and said his edema was all gone. I asked if he'd like lotion and a massage, and he said, "Oh, yes. I'd like that." So I put lotion on his feet, legs, arms, back, chest, and neck. I told him his skin was looking great, and he said, "Thanks to you, it is. You really stay on top of it, and it shows."

About that time the head nurse on shift could hear us conversing, and she came in saying to De, "Well, you're awake now, so let's get your blood pressure and other vitals checked out. Lunch will be along soon, so I'm glad you're with us again."

Scarcely a minute later the nurse returned bearing a large pill. She said "Here's a new pill for you. Bactrim. You have a little bit of a urinary tract infection this morning."

De said, "Yes, I noticed that the tip of my penis is a little puffy this morning."

I was embarrassed to be an ear-witness to this conversation, but there I was, and so the situation seemed right for an infusion of humor. I piped up, "I've had that before—a urinary tract infection, not a puffed penis!"

De mused drily, "In this town, nothing would surprise me."

The nurse laughed and said, "Well, swallow the pill and I'll leave you two alone with your urinary tract infection and your puffed penis!"

De looked at the pill and said to me, "Good Lord. Look at the size of this thing, will you?"

The nurse said, "Let me break it in half for you." She did that, and the pill went down easily.

I asked De if he'd like me to raise the head of his bed a little more, since lunch was due shortly and he wasn't elevated enough to partake safely. He nodded, so I did that then noticed that his body was so far down in the bed, it looked as if the bed was trying to fold him at his chest instead of at his hips! So I smiled and said, "I think perhaps we need to find you a new position in the bed."

He shot back, joking, "This certainly isn't it!"

That cracked me up, so—laughing—I headed around the end of the bed to get into a position to push him upward when he lifted his upper body off the bed using the "monkey bars" they had recently set up for him. I took hold under his legs and behind his back and said, "Okay. On three! 1, 2, 3!" and I hurled him upward toward the head of the bed.

His body weight was so negligible that he practically sailed into position. The neck pillow shot right off the bed.

"Wait! Your pillow just developed legs and walked! It's gone AWOL!"

"How did that happen?"

"Danged if I know! We are awesome powerful, we are!"

Another sweet nurse came in and asked if De's menu for the next day had been filled out, and he said, "Not completely."

She said, "That's okay. You two can work on it together. I'll come back in twenty minutes to get it."

As soon as she left a volunteer came in with her companion animal dog, Mitzi, and De was one happy camper. Mitzi and De visited for a good twenty minutes, with Mitzi sharing his bed and giving him a few kisses on the hand and chin.

Just as Mitzi and the volunteer left, lunch arrived and so did the nurse, hoping for the menu. I apologized, saying we were interrupted by a doggie visitor, and she was very understanding and patient. She said to De, "You have a good friend, here." Then she said to me, "You're here every day, aren't you?"

"Just about. As often as I can be, I am."

"That's important."

De said, "It sure is."

The nurse said, "I'm happy to see it. You're a fortunate fellow, Jackson."

I said, "He's a wonderful fellow. I think you should call him DeForest, though. Only his Army buddies call him Jackson."

At the mention of the name DeForest, her eyes opened wide, and I think that's the first moment she realized who this Mr. Kelley was. I continued, "He didn't know his first name was Jackson until he was in the Army Air Corps and saw his birth certificate for the first time. His family always called him DeForest."

That led De into, "I can still hear my mother calling to me from the front porch: 'De Fo-rest!'" His eyes filled with tears at the reminiscence. "I could hear her down in the school yard: 'De For-est'!' I had a little brown dog named Sandy. At 3 every day, I would go near the window to sharpen my pencil, mostly to let Sandy know I was nearly ready to leave school for the day. That little dog's tail would raise up, and off he'd go, down the street, in through the window without the screen, and all around the house; then he'd come back and lead me home."

The nurse tapped me on the shoulder, and I stood up and hugged her. She said, "I'll be back in a little while for the menu."

I said, "It'll be ready."

She said, "I'm really in no big hurry. He's my last patient, and I'm patient!"

De laughed. "It's amazing what pops into my mind! I just thought of that funny little box you sent to Carolyn because she had been confined to the hospital for so long. The box that looks like someone's in a crate and it yells, 'Get me out of here!'"

"Oh, yes!"

"I could sure use it right now!"

I remembered to tell him that his "Decision" episode was going to air on BONANZA the next day. He said, "Is that the one where I poisoned a bunch of Indians?" I said, "No, that was Honor of Cochise." He said, "You have an amazing mind for stuff like that." I gave him an outline of the episode and said it was a great portrayal and asked if he wanted to catch it.

"Yes, I might do that."

"You might have company—a whole roomful of nursing fans—if you let them know it's coming on." He smiled. I told him I'd put a note on his bulletin board to remind him when it would air and on what channel. "A nurse will spot it and be sure you tune in, I imagine. And I'll try to remember to call you just before it comes on to be sure you're awake and aware, if I don't get swamped at work and forget to look at the clock. I'm recording it at home, so if you don't see it, you can see it later."

During lunch De was having trouble cutting the crust of the pizza because it was so tough, so I cut it for him. Then I cut the cherry pie into a few small bites for him so he could concentrate on eating instead of dissecting food. He said, "If I let you keep doing this, you're going to spoil me." I said, "If I thought you'd let me spoil you, I'd do it."

He asked, "What would you do to spoil me?" I said, "Well…I'd cut up your food…"

"You're already doing that!"

"Once! I've done it exactly once! I'd do it all the time. And I'd massage you… Hey, I guess I am spoiling you." He said, "Yes, you are!"

I said, "Good! You deserve it!" De said, "I wish Carolyn would take advantage of the massages, too."

"So do I. I did it once, and she really liked it, but then she never let me do it again. She told me, 'It doesn't turn me on.' I told her if it turned her on, I'd get pretty nervous!'"

De threw his head back and laughed.

While he was eating the last few bites of his meal, the phone rang. De said, "That sounds like Carolyn's ring."

I said—because his hands were occupied by a soup cup—"Do you want me to get it?"

"Yes. Tell her I'm finishing lunch and will call her back in five minutes." I picked up the receiver and gave her the message.

She said, "Oh, okay," but fewer than two minutes later she called again, telling me, "I'm sorry to call again, but I'm very anxious about De."

I said, "Oh! Then by all means, here he is, sweetie!"

I handed the phone to De, who told her he was fine and that he'd had a couple of rough days, but that he felt better and would see her again soon. I motioned to him to let me speak to her as he was finishing up, so I could calm her fears by telling her, "The nurses gave him sleeping pills real early yesterday morning and this morning; that's the reason he's lethargic. The pills allowed him to get some really good rest. There's nothing to worry about over here, sweetie. He's doing fine."

She said, "All right. I was just concerned." I told her I'd be over in just a few minutes to visit, and she said, "Okay, then," and we hung up.

In a few minutes, I left De and went to Carolyn's room. I put lotion on her legs, and while I did, she asked how Dad was, so I gave her the run-down on that. She asked if I had put lotion on Mom's legs.

I said, "Oh, yes. You bet. She loved it. She'd say, 'I'll give you two hours to stop that.'"

Carolyn laughed and said, "I'll bet!"

Her nurse came in to take her for a walk, so I bid her farewell, and then remembered to tell her about De's Bonanza episode. Then I remembered that I hadn't left De the note about the episode, so I had to stop back by and pin it on his board. I thought, *He'll probably be asleep, so it will just take a second. I won't wake him.*

I went back to De's room, intending to sneak in and pin the message on the board. To my surprise, he was sitting on the edge of the bed thinking about getting to the portable toilet next to his bed. I said, "You're not supposed to be getting out of bed alone."

"It's not far."

"Never mind how far. Ask for help."

He said, "Yes, nurse."

A male nurse came in and helped him onto the commode, so I wrote the note about the Bonanza episode and taped it below his TV set, where he or a nurse would be sure to spot it. When he was finished, I helped him back into bed and handed him eyewash. After using it, he told me, "The last time I saw your dear mother was the first time I realized I was probably doomed."

That brought me up short. I said sadly, "Really?"

"Yes. No one had told me yet, but I just felt it."

I almost cried. He added, "I'll tell you more about it when I think I can get through it without crying."

After a time, he said, "We thought long and hard about who we should involve in our troubles."

I said, "You protected me for the longest time."

"Yes. Perhaps we should have been honest with you from the outset, though."

I only half-joked, "It did come as quite a shock a few weeks ago, the way A.C. brought it to my attention. I was hearing about conventions you were attending, and I was figuring you must be all right. But the calls were fewer and shorter and I began to get a feeling that all was not as rosy as you had been telling me, so I started to ask you again if there was anything I could do. You kept saying no, so I finally figured—just to keep myself from going crazy—that you probably had somebody else lined up and just didn't want to risk hurting my feelings."

De said, "No, we didn't have anyone else lined up. I was handling everything pretty well up until recently. I regret keeping you in the dark for so long, though. I guess it's always better to know what's going on than to have to wonder about it."

He seemed genuinely remorseful for having kept the devastating news from me for so long, so I finally assured him, "De, you made the right decisions for yourself and Carolyn all along the way. Don't try to second-guess yourself now. Don't even worry about it anymore. I'm not upset. I love you for having protected me for so long. I know you did it out of concern for me." He knew I had been dealing my mom's terminal illness. "I completely understand."

He said, "I'm glad you do."

Then he asked me, "If you could start over—be anything in the world you wanted to be—what would you do?"

I laughed. "De, I have been a very lucky person. I have pretty much done all I ever wanted to do. I worked on a horse ranch when I was crazy about horses; I worked at a wildcat sanctuary and other places when I was not on wild animals; I worked at API when I wanted to make a difference for animals; I came down here and got into the entertainment industry because I wanted to. There really isn't anything I haven't done that wasn't a real passion of mine." I paused and then said with utmost sincerity, "Right now, I'm living the epitome of my life's dreams—doing something meaningful to help you and Carolyn, because you have done so much to help me all these years." I gave his hand a quick kiss. I paused again, then continued: "I feel, now, that my life is pre-destined, like the course of a river, and if I'll just jump in and go with the flow, I'll be carried to the spots where the greatest contributions can be made. I trust the process. I'm spiritual in that way. God knows what He's doing, even though I don't always know what He's doing. I'm just—I don't know—I feel lucky and happy! I'm doing exactly what I want to be doing."

He said, "I'm very glad about that."

On April 8 De called me at 7:15 a.m. and asked "Were you in the shower?"

"No."

"I didn't wake you, did I?"

"Nope."

"I'm wondering when you'll be by today."

"Noon-ish—or do you want me sooner?"

"I'm going to have a shower at 8 this morning, and then you could put lotion on me. I need to get my butt out of bed and get going today!" He sounded so strong, with it and energetic.

I said, "So! When do you want me? 9:00? 9:30?"

"Either is fine."

"Okay, I'll be there."

I drove by Don's place to get the mail he had gathered the past few days, as he thought there were important things in one or more of the envelopes. We chatted for a few minutes about De's amazing progress. Don said, "I'm hoping, now, that De will be home soon."

After we chatted for a few minutes, I traded cars and drove De's Lexus to the hospital. He sounded so wired I thought he might want me to drive him somewhere.

299

When I got there, he looked fantastic. He was hooked to the nutrition bottle again, as the thought of food made him feel ill. He was otherwise just fine—chatty, funny, with it.

He asked me to take an envelope and letter over to Carolyn and then come back. I did that. I asked Carolyn if she wanted to go over and visit with us while I was there, and she said, "Sure, why not?" I put the brace on her leg and wheeled her over. De was happy to see her. Carolyn got up and kissed him, then sat down in the wheelchair and put her leg on his bed next to him, so he could pat it.

He asked the nurse for a pain pill, saying his lower back ached. I asked if he'd like me to put lotion on his lower back and rub the achy part. "Yes. I think that would help." So I put lotion on him and rubbed the areas he specified. It took about four minutes, and then he leaned back on the pillow and said, "Wow! What a difference."

I said, "Sitting all the time, you probably just needed some circulation there."

At about that time one of De's doctors came by. We had spoken on the phone before but this is the first time we'd met. I remembered to tell him that De had his monthly Sandostatin shot. De mentioned that he used to have to inject himself twice a day.

The doctor said he'd been in touch with De's other doctors and with the doctor at UCLA and that they were putting their heads together to see if there was anything in clinical trials that would be of significant benefit to De. De reiterated, "I don't think I'll be taking in any seminars down there."

I clarified, "These aren't seminars. They're clinical trials. They have drugs there that haven't made it to market yet. No one here has access to it until it's tested. If there's something there that's a wave of the future, state-of-the-art drug to help you, they'll look it over and let you know, so you won't be wasting your time going down there."

De said, "Oh." Then he sighed. "I'm just not sure I want to involve myself in that."

The doctor said he wasn't pushing the idea, or discounting it, and he would honor De's wishes. De said, "Well, I feel confident with the treatment I'm receiving now, so I'll respect your judgment as to whether I should give the trial thing a shot."

Not long after, he confided to me, "I got in so easily at UCLA that I'm a little afraid it'll just become a celebrity thing; that I'll be making an appearance whether or not they have anything for me there."

I nodded my awareness regarding that possibility.

He said, "Isn't that awful? I shouldn't be pessimistic like that—"

"Well, it's certainly understandable."

"I've had only a very slight taste of what Elvis or Michael Jackson had to deal with; it's really a double-edged sword. On the one hand, it's flattering and can be a lot of fun, but on the other hand…"

I concluded for him, "It's invasive and un-fun."

"It can be. Most people are very nice and perhaps once or twice per trip to the market, I'll be stopped, which I don't mind. But when you're rushed, or don't feel well…." He didn't finish the sentence.

I again nodded my understanding.

I told them then that I had been called to do another Walk of Fame interview about being De's star polisher next week, "but I didn't know what we'll be doing next week, and if we're doing nothing, I should be at work, working. I can't think how to ask Dan for more time off to do an interview."

De said, "No, I wouldn't push my luck. He's done an awful lot for you—for us all—recently."

De asked, "Of your five days at work, which are the busiest?"

"I used to make them all as busy as could be. I'd look around like a maniac for extra stuff to do when things got quiet—almost to the point of dusting and washing the windows. But then I realized I was wearing myself to a frazzle, so I just slowed down. I told myself, 'It's going to take you eighty years to get to age 80 whether you walk or whether you run, so you may as well slow down and enjoy the trip before it's all over."

Carolyn—who considered me hyperactive—joked, "You told yourself that? When?"

De guessed, "When Dorothea got sick, I'll bet."

I said, "Yeah. Right around that time."

Then De said, "I keep coming up with springtime things that need doing, a whole list of things, and then a doctor comes by and reminds me that my time is so short. It kind of takes the wind out of my sails."

I said, "I'll bet. But don't let the doctors tell you what to think or do. They aren't God. Live your life exactly the way you want to; don't limit yourself to the prognostications of others."

"Good advice," De nodded.

As De became wearier, Carolyn and I decided we should leave and let him nap.

I took her back to her room, and then went back and put extra pillows underneath him so he'd be comfortable. I gave him a warm cloth to wash his face and cleaned his glasses for him. Then two nurses and I exchanged the monkey bars above his bed so they wouldn't dangle as close to his head. It was a much better arrangement, although by the time we finished, he was nodding like crazy, about to fall asleep and wishing mightily we'd get lost.

I finally said, "Okay, I'm outta here!"

He said, "It's about time! Get going!"

De called me at work later in the afternoon to share a few moments of banter. Then he said, "I awoke and remembered the Bonanza episode. I only caught the last twenty minutes, but it was a good one. I called Carolyn and she tuned in and enjoyed it, too."

"I wish you had seen it all. You seemed to be such a snake in the beginning, sitting in jail, but as the episode progresses, you find out why. It was a terrific portrayal."

"Let me tell you a little secret about actors. Sometimes we get a chance to experiment. This episode was just such an experiment."

"Well, it was sensational. Whenever people say they haven't seen you in anything besides Trek, I always recommend that they catch two of your Bonanzas—the one you saw today plus Honor of Cochise—and then Apache Uprising, and The Law and Jake Wade."

He chuckled. "Awww…Apache is one of my favorites."

"Mine, too. I even had a dream about you one night as the guy in that portrayal. I wouldn't want to meet that guy in a dark alley!"

He chuckled and said, "We may have to try that—resurrect that hombre!"

"What? And ruin your reputation?"

I drove to the hospital to get a check from De to give to his accountant for the tax services. De was waiting to have his shower, impatiently.

He said he had to wait until an IV drip finished before they'd take him in—"and I've been waiting since 7:30."

I could tell he was really frustrated. This predicament reminded him of the six-hour, transportation-plagued day he'd had on Monday and he groused about that again. I just listened and nodded, since I couldn't do a darn thing about either situation and figured he just needed to vent.

I reported, "It's cold outside this morning. If you could see a little farther northeast than your viewpoint allows you'd see that the entire mountain range is white with snow."

He said that had happened a time or two the past year when he drove out to visit with Carolyn, and it was always a glorious sight.

I didn't stay long, as I was due at the accountant's at 11:30. I told him I'd get gas in my car then go by the accountant for the paperwork and then come back for him to sign it. I asked if he'd like a fruit dish when I got back. He said that sounded good: "But just a little one."

We got started on the IRS paperwork. Just after De signed and was about to get back into bed Carolyn came over. She took the paperwork and proclaimed she didn't understand it, but wanted to look it over anyway before she signed it.

De said, conversationally, to both of us, "Who does get this tax stuff? Our accountant is the only one who has to know what it all means."

I chuckled and agreed.

On April 10th De called me at close to nine a.m. and said he had tried to reach Don, but got no answer. I told him Don was at the market. He asked if I'd keep trying to reach Don.

"Please tell him to call me. I want you to bring him out here this morning. I want to have a personal, private talk with him."

"Sure! I'll keep calling until he answers and will have him call you right away."

I called every fifteen minutes or so, but De was the one who managed to reach Don first. Then De called me to report he'd reached him.

"Don said you were planning to wait until the mail comes this afternoon to come out."

"No, those were yesterday's plans. I told him they could change at the drop of a hat if you wanted something else."

"Yes, that's too late. I want to see you this morning."

"I'll call Don right now and tell him I'm on my way to pick him up. We'll be there soon."

I drove to Don's, picked him up, and we drove to the hospital. We were both pretty nervous. This sounded real serious/almost urgent!

I led Don to De's room, kissed De hello, and then said, "I'll be over with Carolyn. Give me a buzz when you want me to come over."

After ninety minutes or so Don came over to get us. We went back to De's room with him. Don and I both mentioned how great De looked. I said, "Every day, I can see an improvement." De joked wryly, "That's why I called you out here, so I could hear that."

I put lotion on De's arms, feet and legs and told him the new mail could wait until tomorrow; there was nothing in it that was a show-stopper.

Don, Carolyn and De talked about old movies and other times gone by. Then Don said he'd like to get back home soon, so I asked De if he wanted me to take Don home and come back, or just come back the next day. De asked, "Do we have any work today?"

"Nope. Nothing that can't wait."

"I hate to have you come all the way back here if there's nothing to accomplish."

"It's not far. It's just up to you."

"Let's just do it tomorrow."

"Okey dokey!" I kissed them both and we left.

As we drove back to the house Don said there were only a few minutes of confidential talk; the rest was just guy stuff. "It sure felt good to have a good old- fashioned chat with De again," he said. "He's looking so good, I'm beginning to have hope again."

"Me, too! I wish the doctors would stop reminding him how sick he is and let him feel as good as he feels while he's feeling it."

"I do, too. He doesn't need to be reminded."

I did about an hour's work at the Kelley's house then Don came over with new mail. I put it with the other mail I'd be taking out the next day. Don said, "When we spoke today, De told me he thinks the world of you."

I said, "He thinks the world of you, too. It's just one huge Mutual Admiration Society, isn't it?"

"Yes—and isn't it wonderful?"

"It sure is."

De called at about 7 that evening and asked, "How's the Number One Girl?"

"Huh? Me? Oh! I'm fine." I asked if he'd had any naps that afternoon. He said no. "I don't really want to. I'll sleep better at night if I don't." After a pause, he said, "I hope I get to feeling better. I'd like to have one day—better, two—at home."

"I think you will feel better soon. You're looking great and you have more vim and vigor daily—perhaps you can't notice it, but I sure can see a daily improvement. Your energy is a lot better recently."

"Energy! You've got energy!"

"Good thing, huh?"

"Yes! Good thing! But I wish you'd sit down once in a while."

He asked when I'd be out the next day.

"I thought I'd leave that up to you."

"Don't leave it up to me. Come out whenever you want. Tomorrow morning is star polishing day, isn't it?"

"Yes, but I'll do that real early, if it isn't raining."

"It's so cold right now, why don't you just skip it tomorrow?"

"Not unless it rains."

"I don't want you going out there and getting stove up."

"I won't. I dress warmly, and it only takes five minutes." Then I said, "Besides, if I shiver, just think of all the extra calories I'll burn!"

He said, "Just keep doing what you're doing; it'll happen."

I told him I'd watered the plants indoors and under the eaves at his house, checked in on Myrtle, who was still lethargic, and aired out the house while I was there.

On April 11th after star polishing, I carried a vase of De's home-grown roses to his room. He was still asleep when I arrived at 8:20 a.m. so I put them and the other materials in his room and went back out to the obby. The head nurse was working at her station, so I went over and patted her on the back to tell her, "De is crazy about you."

Then I asked her to put me down as the person to contact in an emergency. "He listed me as the emergency person at his regular doctor's on Monday, so I thought I should be listed here that way, as well. After all, he's here, not there." She agreed, and let me fill in the information.

At about 8:50, the nurse decided she'd better rouse him "before his breakfast gets too cold."

She went in and jostled him awake. He looked so cute and unstressed asleep, I wished she could leave him alone longer.

We raised the head of his bed. He said, "Kris, you're here early. What time is it?" Then he looked at the clock and said, "Good Lord. You're not early; I'm late!"

I got him a warm wash cloth for his face. The nurse brought in the tray; it just about turned his stomach. "I can't eat just after I've come awake."

She said, "I can't either. Don't worry about it. It's here for when you want it."

I asked if a little of the fruit from the fridge sounded manageable.

He said, "Yes, it does."

So I got that out and he had a few bites of that. I hoped it would whet his appetite for something a bit later—and it did.

I showed him roses I'd picked at his house, and he just about flipped, saying they were the most beautiful things he'd ever seen. At almost that exact moment, Carolyn called. De picked up the phone and said good morning; said he'd just been roused, and "Kris is here with a vase of flowers from our garden." He asked me to carry them over to her to see. I did so while they continued to chat on the line. She loved them, and I said I'd bring her some too if she'd let me—a week earlier she had declined the offer—and she said, "If you'll take care of them, I'll take some."

I took the roses back to De's room. He was still on the phone with Carolyn, saying that he had called A.C. the night before at about 10:15 and chatted for over an hour "all about the night I almost died."

De started to get teary-eyed and said, "He said he was there holding my hand. He said they thought they were losing me…I remember seeing A.C. as if from a distance, across the room, dressed so well, the way he always is. The room was all white. It was not peaceful or placid at all. It was very scary. It scared me." Then De told her, "A.C. and I also were talking about how fortunate we are to have Kris…"

Again De started to get choked up and was unable to continue, so I responded, loudly enough so Carolyn could hear me at her end, "No! It is how fortunate I am to have you two!" That made the tears spill down De's cheeks and I grabbed his hand, nearly in tears myself, and kissed it and rubbed my cheek on it. He put the phone down, and I picked it up and said, "Carolyn?"

She said, "Kris, I want to tell you, too, how lucky we feel to have you in our lives at a time like this, so willing to help with everything."

I looked up at teary De, and repeated, "I'm happy to be here, and happy you allowed me."

De took the phone back, and sniffled, "I'll come over and get you later, after I've tried to choke down some breakfast." He turned his attention to me. "After A.C.'s call last night, I didn't get to sleep until about 2 or 2:30. I just kept thinking about that night when I almost died." His eyes were far away, thinking about that awful night. Then he said, "I'm sure glad we're here now, and not there anymore. It was scary and awful."

I said, "That's because it wasn't your time to go. That isn't the way it happens, De."

He said, "I sure hope not." He was still haunted by the memory.

I told him, "I had a similar experience that time I developed bronchitis. I couldn't even stand up without the room becoming black; it felt as though I didn't have enough breath in me to stay alive. I was going to call 911, but Emese said she'd come and get me. It seemed to take forever for her to get to me, but it was probably only about thirty minutes. I was so scared. When your body betrays you, it's a terrible feeling."

He emphatically nodded his agreement.

Then I added, "We think earthquakes are scary. They're nothing compared to a feeling like this!"

"You have it exactly right. There's nothing scarier."

Carolyn called and said she had to go to the bathroom and no one had come in to help her. So De said, "Go help her. I can wait."

I jogged over to Carolyn's and spotted her while she got into the room; after she finished, I piloted her back and asked if she'd like lotion on her legs before I put on the brace. She said yes. Then she told me that one area on her leg had recently gone numb, so I massaged it and said I would tell the nurse about it. Then I remembered that De had been thinking about getting into the bathroom, and said I'd go help De to the john and back and be right back to put her brace on. I went over to De and helped him into the bathroom. The phone rang, and I picked it up. It was Carolyn, saying she had to go again. So I told De to stay put—"Promise me!"—until I go back. He said he would. I ran to Carolyn and helped her back to the bathroom. She had more success, so I helped her back into the bed and then went and got De back into bed. Then I went back and put Carolyn's leg brace on.

As I was whizzing back to De's room for the umpteenth time, the head nurse asked me, "What are you doing?"

I said, "I'm running a bathroom relay between these two."

She said, "You don't have to do that."

I said, "I'm loving it!"

She said, "Then carry on!"

After that, De was going to shave, but suddenly decided, "You shave me."

I said, "Ho boy! This is a first. This makes me nervous." I shaved his sideburns with the trimmer and then ran the electric razor over his face and neck. After I'd had a shot at it, he took the razor and got the nooks and crannies I had missed for fear of injuring him. I said, "I think I'd have done better with a razor than with the electric."

While he was shaving, I asked if he wanted a mirror; after a little bit he said he did, so I handed him the small compact Carolyn had loaned him when he was admitted. He affected a gay blade lisp and said, "I feel a bit femme using thissss compact."

I laughed and said, "You're getting in touch with the softer side of De."

De said, "Yesssss, I am." He was so good when he assumed a role— any role.

He mentioned that Mom's neck pillow had been a real blessing and then said he'd appreciate it if I'd take it home and wash it. I said I would. I said I'd wash his two pairs of dirty socks at the same time. He said his socks were too tight. I told him about diabetic socks, which are loose and expand as needed, and asked if he'd like me to get him a pair to try. "Yes, I would. They sound like just what I need." I told him I'd get a pair on the way home.

Edema had put a few pounds on him, "Up here high, they tell me. They're going to start me on something today to relieve it, I think. I'll probably be peeing my brains out once I get going on that."

We discussed two convention offers he had received. He dictated to me how to respond, and asked me to call Joe Motes and get more information on an upcoming convention because he wanted to make an appearance at it if he felt up to it.

As he was reading an invitation from actor John Hertzler about appearing at a Berlin, Germany convention, he looked at me and said, "See? If I was feeling up to it, we could be traveling all over the place."

I said, "Keep the faith, boy! Perhaps you will, yet."

De got ready to go for a walk. We walked around the "block" and ended up in Carolyn's room for a rest, at which time De said he'd love a donut. I said I'd run across the street and get him some and some black coffee.

When I returned, he was in his own room, and ate a few bites of a donut and drank some of the coffee. Then he wanted to get back into bed.

He confided, "I'm almost afraid—as is Carolyn—to ask what the status is on her leg. I'm afraid they're going to tell me she'll never walk again on that leg." He looked as if he might cry when he said it.

"De, someone here told her that this kind of thing could take up to two years."

He frowned.

I continued, "So yes, it's a long haul, but that doesn't mean it's a hopeless cause."

Later on, with Carolyn over for a visit, we talked about our upbringings, and Carolyn said she was spoiled by her dad; "All little girls are spoiled by their dads." She asked De if he was spoiled by his dad.

"No. Never! He was very strict with me."

I said, "Boys are different. Their dads expect big things from their sons."

De said, "Mine sure did." Then he mused, "When I told him I had decided to become an actor, he was sure I was going straight to hell."

The nurse came in and De asked when the doctor would be in that day, as he had a question to ask: he wanted to ask about Carolyn's new numbness in her leg. The nurse found out where the numb spot was and said it was a good idea to tell the doctor about anything new that occurred. Then De said he was curious as to what was going on with Carolyn's leg. The nurse explained that Carolyn's type of arthritis was causing her bones to mend very slowly. "It's a long process and she's still very fragile."

De began to look tired, so Carolyn said she'd go back to her room. I wheeled her back and got her long sock so I could wash it, then went back and straightened De's tray table so everything he needed was easily within reach and tossed the trash away and kissed him goodbye.

He looked good. He was talking about wanting to go home and getting stuff done, even if it was just in a series of drives whenever he felt up to going out. I thought he'd be able to do that and possibly more.

On April 12th, I called De at about 11:00 to see if he wanted or needed me to come out.

"Yes, by all means, come out."

"Okay. I'll be there in about forty minutes if the traffic is moving. I washed the pillow and Carolyn's sock, plus your socks, but I think the neck pillow is still a wee bit damp."

"That's all right. It can finish drying here."

"Oh, okay! I'll bring it along then."

I went into the Kelleys' house momentarily to be sure everything inside was good and that there were no important phone calls; then I drove to the hospital. De was in bed, with his gown hanging down from his chest. He was lying almost prone, so I asked if he wanted to sit up more; he said he did. I raised the head of his bed.

Then he said, "I called you twice, but you were already on your way. I wanted you to bring Bill Shatner's phone number with you."

I said, "I always have your phone book with me, so I have it, if it's in there."

He asked me to dial "Willie Boy's" home number for him. "Say it's DeForest Kelley calling."

I called Shatner's house. A housekeeper answered the phone. She said he wasn't there, so I asked for his work phone number. I called and reached his assistant Stephanie. I said, "Hi, this is Kris Smith calling for DeForest Kelley. Is Mr. Shatner there?"

She said, "No, he isn't. He's out of town until Wednesday night. This is Stephanie."

"De, do you want to speak with Stephanie?"

"Sure." I handed him the receiver.

"Hi, Stephanie. Would you have Bill call me back when he gets a chance? I'm here in the hospital, just where nobody likes to be." She asked what for and he said, "Oh, I've been fighting this cancer thing for over a year now." It was news to her, and when he hung up, he mused, "Bill didn't tell Stephanie anything about my cancer."

"Well, maybe he thought that the fewer people who knew about it, the better the chances it would remain a secret."

"Perhaps. But Bill is strange; he can't talk about cancer or death or dying."

I said, "Neither can A.C. He gets real squeamish."

He asked, "Where's Dorothea's pillow?"

I grabbed it for him and said, "Right here. Do you think it's still wet, or just cold?"

He felt it and said, "It's a little damp, but it will dry in no time." Then he mused again, "I wonder what Dorothea thinks of this."

I smiled and said, "I'm sure she's happy to share her pillow with you."

"I hope so."

At about that time, De's lunch was delivered. He said he wanted a cola to go with the ham sandwich, so I went to the cafeteria and bought one for him. He ate more than he had in days and really enjoyed it, and said that late the night before he'd had some more of the fruit. Then he talked about the places we could go for his favorite foods after he got out of the hospital. These cues to his renewing health were music to my ears. Chili cheese dogs, pastrami sandwiches…A week earlier, if he'd have mentioned them he probably would have become sick to his stomach. He seemed to be on the mend.

I ate half of his sandwich and some of his soup. Then I ate his ice cream and the balance of his cola.

De said, "Oh, by the way, before I forget again…I was going to say— I'll never get through this—I was going to say that the last time I saw your dear mother, and I embraced her…twice…I somehow felt a communion with her…as if we were going to be sharing the same fate. I just felt—even though no one had told me yet; I hadn't been diagnosed yet—that I had the same prognosis as she did. And it seemed almost as if she knew it, too! It was just…very weird, and just…very much like a communion, of sorts."

I said, "You know, my Mom and you would have gotten along like gangbusters had you known each other better."

He said, "I know that. I felt it then and I know it now."

I added, "I have to say this: of all the people I have ever known in my life, there have been only three—Mom, you and my Grandma—who seemed to me to be God's prototypes for what He had in mind for us as a species. You three have always epitomized to me what it means to be truly and wholly wonderful."

He got a little teary all over again.

I continued, "I don't think any of you had it easy—far from it, in fact—and yet you managed to keep your love flowing through it all."

De said, "My mother was like that, too. She had a tough, tough life as the wife of a poor preacher. She never got the chance to see me make it big—she saw the start of it, but she wasn't here for Star Trek."

I quickly said, "She was looking down—she still is—and she knows."

He joked, "She's probably yelling, 'Where's the money, De For- est!'"

He and I both laughed then he added wistfully, "I wish I could have made her life a little easier…"

I told him, "Although I really feel that Mom is looking down on me and is happy for me, the past month or so I have wanted in the worst way to just pick up a phone and talk to her."

De said, "I know exactly what you mean. I felt the same way about my mother. Still do, at times."

"It's nice to know they don't need phones now to hear us."

"Yes, but I wish there was some way they could let us know that they know."

I nodded in complete agreement. We were both in tears before the conversation ended.

On April 13, I drove to the hospital, arriving at about 11:25. De and Carolyn were in De's room, as were two doctors. De's usual physician

310

motioned me into the room when he spotted me and I shook hands with both of the doctors and then said hello to De and Carolyn.

De mentioned, "This is a work day, isn't it?"

"Yes, but I escaped."

He said to Carolyn, "Wouldn't it be a hell of a thing if she lost her job over helping us?"

Carolyn said, "I somehow doubt that will happen."

Following a short visit, I wheeled Carolyn back to her room. When I returned to De's room, he told me that Carolyn had again asked when I'd be out today. That cheered me, to know she was asking for me.

I said, "I didn't even know if you wanted me out here again today, but I figured I'd drive out anyway and if you were sick of me, you could send me home."

He said, "I could never get sick of you. I'm glad you came out." Then he added, "As a matter of fact, just this morning Carolyn said to me, 'You miss Kris when she isn't here, don't you?' and I said, 'Yes, I do.'"

I said, "Awwww. That's so nice to hear! Thank you!"

He said, "Well, it's true."

I added, "I miss you when I can't be here, too."

I pulled out an e-mail response I had received from actor John Hertzler, who had recently invited De to Germany for a convention, because it was such a great note. In it, he revealed that Bones was his favorite Trek character of all time and that he hoped he would be able to work with De sometime in the future.

De read it and said, "Isn't that something? That's a wonderful little letter." He was deeply affected by it.

I said, "This letter is a keeper!"

"It sure is."

The lunch arrived not long after and De couldn't eat much of it, since he'd just eaten berries, so he pushed the plate to me and said, "Eat. I ate every bite of my breakfast this morning, and every bite of those berries. That's all I'm going to ask of Jesus today." He talked about going to one of his favorite haunts for lunch or an early dinner after his doctor appointment on Monday. He also said he wanted to go by the house again for a while.

I said, "Cool. I'll get permission to drive you around in your Lexus from now on, so there won't be any more transportation headaches."

I put lotion on De's legs and feet. His physical therapist arrived to walk with him. We walked around the "circle" and ended up in Carolyn's room. There I put lotion on her legs then massaged her legs and feet until she said, "That's enough. That's fine, Kris. Thank you very much."

Then he confided, "I think the nurses are a little jealous that you're here, and that you do everything for me that needs doing while you are here."

I looked at him, incredulous, and said, "Really?"

"I sometimes get that feeling."

"I'd think it would relieve them, having an extra pair of hands and legs for a few hours; give them some breathing space."

"I would, too." But then I reminded myself he's such a pleasure to help—such a light in everyone's life—that they may be jealous when I show up and take over their duties!

I joked, "Maybe you should pull a Toby Jack Saunders on them! That would make them happy I'm here!"

He laughed at that. Then he said, "I want to tell you how I got the role as Jake Ehrlich. I was doing a test with a fellow actor. In the scene, he turns away, not looking at me, so I grabbed his shirt and pulled him back—[he almost did it to me; if I had been closer, he would have]—and said, 'You look at me when I'm talkin' to you!' Jake Ehrlich chose me after he saw that. He said, 'That's the guy I want portraying me! That's exactly who I am!'" Then De said, "Jake was a hard man—a hard man."

I said, "I could tell in the pilot, 333 Montgomery Street. I think you have to be hard as nails to be a criminal defense attorney."

He nodded, "I think so, too."

"You stayed with him for a while, researching the role, didn't you?"

"Yes, I did. We went to a different restaurant every night, Gene Roddenberry, Jake and I. It was an intense period of time."

I stood up, and he said, "Sit down for a while and relax, will you?"

"I'd love to, but I can't stay long today. I don't want Dan getting the idea I'm abusing the privilege."

"Oh, that's right. You're right. He has been so good to let you get away like this. Go on back."

"I need to go by Carolyn's again and sit with her for a while, too. I don't want her to feel left out. So I'd better go right now."

He agreed and thanked me for coming out.

I said, "I wish I could stay."

He said, "I do, too, but get going before you lose your job."

I walked over to Carolyn's. At that very moment, her walker came by to walk with her. I frowned. The walker quickly put Carolyn's sock and brace on, then her shoes.

I asked, "I don't suppose you'd walk someone else first, and then come back for Carolyn?"

"Yes, I would. It will be a half hour."

"Perfect—if that's all right with you, Carolyn."

Carolyn said, "That would be just fine!" So we sat down and spent forty minutes together.

I wandered back over to say a final good-bye to De for the day, but he was asleep, so I walked back and told Carolyn he was. I dropped a card on Carolyn's desk as I left. It was a sweet card about not having to be brave all the time…

I added, "If you'd like me to go get Florene this weekend or some other weekend—I know she can't drive herself—I'd be happy to do that."

"You don't know where she lives."

"I have her address, and you can give me directions easily enough."

"Let me think about that. It would be fun."

"I could do it this weekend if you ask her and she can come out then."

She said, "No, I think Bette and Anne are coming out this weekend."

"That's why I mentioned it. Perhaps you'd like them all at once, like a big party."

She said, "No, I would like them spaced out."

"Okay. Whatever. Do they know each other?"

Carolyn said, "I don't think so. I'm not even sure Bette and Anne know each other. They're an entirely different set of friends."

"Oh, okay. I thought maybe you hung out together, playing cards or whatever, and it would be a treat for everyone to get together again."

She said, "No, I don't think so. I'd like to see them individually."

I said, "That's cool."

On April 14 De called at 6:30 a.m. I was in the bathtub but had taken the phone into the bathroom just in case he called, luckily. I jumped out of the tub, picked up the receiver and said, "Good morning."

"Is this Kris or her answering machine?"

"It's me, in the flesh." He had no idea how accurate a statement that was!

"Oh, good. Good morning, Kris. Did I get you out of bed?"

"No."

"You weren't asleep?"

"No."

"Say, can you find me a larger calendar? The ones out here are too small to see from the bed."

"Sure."

"Also, will you bring out those size 32 trousers when you come out today? The ones I told you about, that are in the closet?"

"Sure. No problem."

"They're the beige ones. I have two pairs in that size, I think—a beige pair and a dark pair— almost black, if not black."

"How soon do you need the pants?"

313

"Oh, I don't need them. I just want them here so they'll be available for the doctor appointment next Monday. No hurry."

"Okay. I'll be out at around noon."

"Okay, honey."

I went to Don's for the mail, clipped four rose buds for Carolyn, and then drove to the hospital. De was sitting in a chair in his room, looking good.

"Good morning, Kris. You'll have to unload the wheelchair to sit down this morning."

"No problem." I showed him the trousers. Then I showed him the wildcat calendar I had brought from my home. He said he had one larger than that at his home.

"I don't think so. I think you brought that one in for Carolyn."

"Oh, that's right. This one is fine—it's larger than the one I have." I showed him the large photo of serval kittens on one of the pages, and he said, "That's perfect."

"I guess you know why I chose this calendar!"

"I do, indeed...Oh! I straightened the thing out about you."

I queried, "The thing?"

He said, "I spoke to the head nurse this morning about your visits here. I didn't want there to be any animosity about your being here among the nurses. There's no problem with you being here. She said it's a big help."

"Oh—good. I wondered why it would be considered anything other than helpful, but then I remembered who you are and how much fun you are to help, and then I really did begin to wonder if you were right about there being some jealousy."

"I did, too. I wondered if they wanted to keep me all to themselves. But that isn't the case. I like to clear the air if I feel there is a problem."

That led me to ask, "Are you psychic at all?"

He said, "Sometimes I think I am. I know my mother was as least a little psychic. She would call me from Georgia and tell me things I was doing in California, and there was no way she could have known."

"I think that's pretty common between parents and children who are really tight with each other." I tried the diabetic socks on him; he swam in them. I said I'd get a smaller size for him to try.

The phone rang. Stephanie had Bill Shatner on the line. I gave the phone to De. De spoke with him and found out that he was calling from the airport in Atlanta and that he'd be out to visit with De on Friday. De said, "That would be great. I love you, Bill." He hung up and gave me that news.

I said, "Okay. I won't be out on Friday, then, so you two guys can talk."

De thought about that for a moment and then decided, "Yes, I guess that would be best."

It was a warm, beautiful day, so I threw the door wide open. De could hear the birds and was loving it. Overcome by the juxtaposition between the beauty of the day and the tragedy of the situation at hand, I said to De, "I wish I could take on your cancer and Carolyn's broken leg so you two could go home and have more time together."

He quickly responded, "Oh, don't say that; you'll make me cry— because I know you mean it."

I assured him emphatically, "I do mean it!"

He said, "I know you do. Bless your heart." He grabbed a Kleenex and we sat there sniffling.

I went to Carolyn's. I rubbed her knee because she told me how much it hurt whenever she had to move it. I told her that it was probably going to hurt for a little while, since it had been held immobile for so long. "But each day, I think it will feel a little bit better. Your knee has to learn how tough it was before, and work to get that way again."

I gave her two rose buds that she put into a bud vase and admired.

She said she wanted to go over and see De, so I wheeled her over. De told us a funny story about sitting in the lobby that morning and having two girls stare at him for at least ten minutes.

Carolyn said, "You should be used to that after about fifty years of it."

De said, "No, that wasn't it." He said they stared and stared at him, and then his nurse said something fast in Spanish to the other nurse, and De, who could understand a respectable amount of Spanish, told the nurse, "That one went too fast. What did you say?"

And the nurse admitted, "Those girls are staring at your family jewels!"

"I guess I had my gown hiked up enough and my legs open enough that everything was in full view!"

I cracked up; De chuckled, thinking it was plenty funny. Carolyn was just mortified.

After a co-piloted trip to the bathroom, De washed his hands and then uncapped the toothpaste tube to brush his teeth. I stood there as a spotter, of course. He observed as he brushed, "When you're in the hospital, so much for privacy!"

"I'd leave, but they want you to have a co-pilot."

"I know. I'm not complaining, just mentioning how different life is once you become ill." I spotted him back to bed and asked if he wanted a back and kidney massage before he laid back down.

"Yes."

As I massaged his back, I asked, "Feel good?"

He said, "Wonderful…"

On April 15 De called everywhere he could think to reach me, but I was already on my way to his house. When I got there, there were two messages from him asking me to call. "It's nothing terribly important, but if you get this message, please call me before you come out."

I called from his house and he said, "Something very funny happened this morning; I have to tell you about it. I called your house—or thought I did—and someone answered the phone who sounded just like you. So I started out joking, 'You know, this has happened once before, and if you're late reporting to work one more time, I'm going to have to fire you!' The gal said, 'I know, but….' I figured you were just playing along, so I said, 'No excuses, now. I have to be able to rely on you, or I have to let you go.'" He chuckled. "I went on like that with her—I thought it was you—trying to defend yourself. Finally, about a minute or more into the conversation, the girl asked me, 'Who is this?' and I said, "Well, I don't know who this is, but I hope you're Kris Smith!' and she said, 'No, I'm not!' We both hung up! I probably gave her a heart attack!"

I loved it, laughed and then said, "So, am I fired?"

"No!"

"That's good!" Then I told him I was walking into his garage to look for the archiving box we'd be using to file some necessary paperwork that Carolyn had saved for years.

"I'm also going to look for the tennis balls for her walker that are out there somewhere."

De said, "I can describe which cabinet they're in."

I said, "OK, I'm taking you with me. I'm using your new cordless phone. I'm walking out into the garage now."

He said, "You can put the phone down and come back to me if you can't find them."

I said, "No, I'll just take you along, and we'll find them together."

He chuckled and said, "All right."

I reported as I advanced, "O.K. I'm entering the garage now, opening a cupboard drawer on my left. Here is fertilizer and garden food."

"It's the next cabinet over, to your right."

I opened it and said, "Aha! Here's the archiving box—cool—and here are the tennis balls. I got 'em!"

He said, "That was fast!"

I asked, "Shall I bring two balls for you, too?"

He joked, "OK, but Christ, if I have four balls for people to look at, I'll never get out of here!"

I walked back into the house and said, "I'll go to Don's and get the mail, then come out. It'll probably be about a half hour."

"Okay, honey. I'm looking forward to it."

I visited with Don for about fifteen minutes—he wouldn't let me get away any sooner than that—and then headed for the hospital. There was a slight traffic snarl on the way in, so there was a delay getting there.

I walked into his room and said, "I probably really am fired, now."

"Not a chance." I gave him a hello kiss and then he noticed the **Touched By An Angel** T-shirt I had on. He commented, "Boy, that's appropriate for you to wear. You are an angel!"

I looked at it and then at him and said, "Well, thank you! I'm an angel in training."

"You're an angel in fact."

"Well, it takes one to know one. Anyone who isn't a fellow angel would probably say I'm just a goody two shoes."

He chuckled, "You're probably right."

Then I showed him the newest pair of diabetic socks, which he tried on and flipped over. "I have to show these to Carolyn. I've been looking for socks like these for years."

I told him I'd wheel him over.

I wheeled him over to Carolyn's room. He got up and gave her a kiss and I gave her the tennis balls and the two black clips she had requested. She, too, mentioned the **Touched By An Angel** T-shirt and said, "That certainly is a good shirt for you to wear. You are an angel!"

De grinned, "I just told her the same thing."

I said, "Stop, now! Or I'll get a big head."

De remembered to tell me he'd lost two pounds, but it was water weight, not fat or muscle. He weighed in at 114. That was a tremendous gain from when he was in the ICU in the other hospital not long before. The added pounds really showed. He looked, acted and felt so much better. It seemed to be a miraculous, wonderful recovery. I thought hopefully, There's plenty of life in the old boy yet"—and no one was any happier than I was about it.

John called and told De that his nasal cancer had completely disappeared following radiation and chemotherapy treatments. De was ecstatic. When he got off the phone, he related to me what John had said, then said, "Hand me a Kleenex. I'm going to cry!" He was so happy for John. Just then the phone rang; it was Carolyn. I gave her the good news, and then handed the phone to De. He cried again telling her how happy he was to hear John's great news. He told her, "See? It can happen! You can get better and I can get better."

After he hung up, I asked, "Have you pursued the UCLA thing any further?"

"No, the doctor and I pretty much decided against it."

317

"But your oncologist said they might have something there that can help you. If he calls there and feels confident about something, don't you want to try it? No one would think to drag you down there and put you through it if there wasn't a real chance that it will make you feel better and perhaps even stop the spread of the tumors."

De said, "The oncologist is the one researching it. I will abide by what he suggests."

Not long after, De's physical therapist came by to take De on his walk. De looked so sturdy that I mentioned, "I don't think he even needs a walker today."

The therapist said, "I agree. Do you want to try it without the walker, De?"

"Sure." The therapist dragged the walker along behind, in case De got tired, and I dragged the bottle rack. De didn't tire at all. We wound up back in Carolyn's room, and chatted a bit. Carolyn said De looked good, strong and sturdy again.

Not long after that, Carolyn's physical therapist came by. De and his P.T. headed out so I could prepare Carolyn's leg for her walk. I did that, and then Carolyn's walker and I went over to De's room. De was sitting in the lobby in an easy chair, so we sat with him for about four or five minutes. De was sure to keep his gown down so he wouldn't cause a riot again with the family jewels.

I joked, "Girls learn early on to keep their legs together and their skirts over their knees, but it isn't exactly second nature to guys who wear gowns late in life."

Carolyn got up to walk some more. I asked De if he wanted me to stay and help him into his room. "No, I'll sit out here for a while longer." I got up and walked with Carolyn back to her room, commenting on how well she was doing and how strong and normal her stride was suddenly.

Her P.T. said, "It's a big improvement."

Not long after, I went back to De's room. He was almost back in bed but was standing next to it without a spotter. I cautioned him, "De, you aren't supposed to be moving around on your own."

He looked real tired and said, "Someone helped me come in."

I said, "OK, then, I won't swat you. But get into bed. No traipsing."

A nurse trainee came in and told us that she was going to disconnect De from the bottles. He said, "Hallelujah!" She said she was going to give him his meds, too. "Yes, I thought it was about time." They discussed that she was just about to graduate from nursing school. She was eager and De told her she was very good and would be a wonderful nurse. He signed a photo for her. She was delighted. After she left, he commented on the

318

edema in his feet and legs, and wondered if it would be more effective for him or me to call his doctor in to check on it.

I said, "I don't know."

"Why don't you go ahead and call?"

So I did. The doctor said he'd come by at around four.

While we waited for his arrival, De mentioned, "I think we [the original Star Trek cast] still have another movie in us. I have a couple of ideas for a movie. I've told Bill about them, but nothing has come of it yet." He added, "I've told you about one of them, I think."

"Oh, yes—the one where Uhura gets kidnapped."

He smiled. "Yes. I have another one, too…"

I didn't hear his other story line other than a mention that it had a post-retirement theme.

Not long after, I told De, "I'd better get going pretty soon and make another appearance at WB today."

"Oh, yes. Before you go, will you straighten my tray table; throw out anything that isn't essential; and that list of phone numbers looks terrible now, too."

"I'll re-write it for you, and then I'll computer-generate it at work, and bring you a great one when I come in on Saturday."

"What day is this?"

"Thursday."

He looked a bit perplexed by that, and I figured it was because he was wondering why I wouldn't be back before Saturday, so I reminded him, "Remember, Bill is coming out to see you tomorrow."

"Oh, yes!"

"There isn't much point in me coming out if he's going to be here at one—unless you want me early in the morning or after work tomorrow night."

"No, that isn't necessary. Take the day off and have your lunch time at Warners tomorrow, but we'll be in touch tomorrow, probably more than once."

I said, "I hope so, or I'll have withdrawal symptoms."

Not long after that I gave him a kiss and told him I loved him. He thanked me for coming and said, "I love you, too, Kris."

De called me that night at 11:15. "Last call of the night! I just called Carolyn and she asked if I'd ask you to bring her a pair of scuffs next time you come out on Saturday?"

"Scuffs? Are those slippers without heels?"

"Yes. She said she doesn't remember where they are, but I do. They're in her bathroom closet on the south side."

Then I said, "I'm glad you called back, actually. I wanted to ask you what the doctor said about your edema."

"Oh, he didn't seem at all concerned by the edema; in fact, he says it's less than it has been."

"Great! Did he think some of it was weather-related, because it has been so warm?"

"He didn't say. They don't give you a lot of information, do they? He says mine is a result of my albumin levels, which they're working on. But he didn't seem at all alarmed. Perhaps he's just staying calm to keep from alarming me."

I said, "I don't think so, De. It probably is nothing to worry about. I think they're being straight with you." Then I added, "Oh! I also found out about the upcoming local convention that you asked me to check on. It'll be July 30, 31 and August 1."

De said, "If I'm feeling up to it, I want to go out there. I need to ask the hospital consultant about that, see if that will cause any problems." Then said, "I'll try not to call you any more tonight."

"Please don't worry about that, De. It's OK to call me anytime."

He added as an afterthought, "If I go to the convention, you have to go along, too."

"Sure. No problem."

"You will have to wheel me into the bathroom, like you do when we go to the oncologist. You'll have to stay in there with me, so I don't fall on my face."

"Yep. I know that. You might have some splainin' to do to the men standing at urinals, though!"

On April 17 I got to the Kelleys early and watered the roses, put Miracle Grow on the indoor plants and put the archive box together with the files I'd made earlier. When it was time to leave, the Lexus wouldn't start. I had left a door slightly ajar and the battery had run down. I called De to let him know I'd be in as soon as I could get the Auto Club to give me a jump.

More than an hour later than originally planned, I walked into De's room joking, "Am I fired now?"

He shook his head, "No."

I could tell he'd had a bad night. He told me he was having breathing problems that were making him anxious.

I said, "I know this sounds nutty as hell, like the opposite of what you want to do, but if you will just breathe more slowly and take deeper breaths from the abdomen, you'll feel better and your breaths will do more for you."

He nodded and tried that for a moment, but soon reverted back to the earlier, less effective breathing pattern. I let him know that his color was

320

good and that even though he felt he wasn't getting enough air, he was. I pressed the tip of one of his middle fingers, to determine how much time it took for the blood to return underneath the fingernail; that little test was normal. I assured him he was all right. He still didn't look convinced, so I told him I'd tell the nurse, and he nodded that he'd appreciate that. I went out and told the nurse, and she said she'd be in to give him something to help him breathe better. I went back and told De. The nurse came in real soon and told him exactly what I had, about how he should breathe more slowly, deeply and from the abdomen.

He looked at me as if to acknowledge, "You were right!" and adopted the new breathing rate more religiously than he had previously.

When he had a handle on his breathing and felt better, he told me he had been sick to his stomach again the night before. I sympathized mightily. He said he had called for a nurse when he felt the sickness coming on, telling her he was feeling nauseated, but no one responded soon enough, and so he got sick twice into the little plastic basin before anyone arrived. "I rang again, telling them I was throwing up, and then someone came in, right away. Good thing—because there was no room for anything more in the basin."

I said, "Next time, be sure to tell them you're about to throw up. Saying you're nauseous doesn't necessarily mean you're about to vomit. They need to know. I'm sure they would have come right in had they known you were that close."

I told him I could stay all day and also overnight on weekends to be sure he got the assistance he needed whenever he needed it.

He said, "I appreciate that, because I know you mean it. But you do enough with all you do already. I just have to let you know I was never so happy to see anyone walk in that door as I was you this morning." I almost cried, and so did he.

De told me about the visit with Shatner. Then he said, "It's sure nice having you around, someone I can discuss dying with. I can't do that with Shatner or with many other people, it upsets them so. They'll talk about anything else, but not dying."

I said, "Well, I used to be the same way."

De said, "So did I. I understand it completely. Still, it's good to have someone I can talk to about it."

On April 18, I got there at 9:15 a.m. De had breathing problems again. I told the nurse. She gave him more Lasix and we added oxygen to his medical regimen. He ate melon and berries and for lunch had almost half of a grilled ham and cheese sandwich. He drank ½ to 2/3 of a soda.

De mentioned that the yard and roses probably could use a good dousing of water again. I said I'd get it done in the next day or so. "No

321

hurry—just whenever you happen to be out. It doesn't have to all be done in one day."

Nichelle Nichols came for a visit at about 2:45. De, Carolyn and I waited in De's room for her to arrive. When she was overdue by almost twenty minutes, De said he hoped they wouldn't be waiting much longer. He was beginning to feel and look tired. Luckily, just moments later Nichelle arrived, and she stayed only about an hour. Her visit perked him up considerably.

Not long after Nichelle left, De said he was beginning to feel a little nauseated, so I told the nurse and then went back to press the reflexology points in his hands until the anti-nausea drug could take effect. A male nurse came in and asked what I was doing. I told him. De told him, "I thought she was making this stuff up, until another nurse knew exactly what she was talking about." The nurse nodded and said that acupuncture works wonders, too, when all else fails.

I left the hospital as soon as De felt comfortable again, to let him sleep, but by the time I got home, he called and asked me to remind him to call the doctor in the morning. I said, "I'm going to be on the road very early in the morning, on the way to you; I won't be able to call and remind you, I don't think."

"Okay, I'll remember to call. Can you get here by 8 tomorrow?"

"Sure, I can get there any time you want me."

"I think the earlier, the better. If I can have your help to get ready, things will go more smoothly. I won't have to wait on the nurses to help me dress, or to shave."

"No problem. I'll do everything so you can conserve your energy and save it for the doctor appointment and the stuff at home afterward."

"Yes, that's the best plan."

"I'll be there," and we hung up.

About five minutes later, I called him back. "Since you want me there so early in the morning, I think I'll drive to your house and stay the night, to be past the 405 rush hour crush in the morning."

"Good idea."

"So…if you need me again tonight, remember I'll be at your place."

"Okay."

I got some stuff together and drove to the Kelley house, arriving at about 8:15 p.m. I decided to water the lawns and work in the office on filing. I worked from 8:30 to 11:45 and then fell into bed and slept like the dead until 6:30 a.m.

On April 19, I drove out to get De, arriving at about 7:40. I was amazed to find him awake already. He had already shaved but that task had taken most of the starch out of him. He was moving very slowly. I helped him into the bathroom for a bath and washed his armpits and upper body. As I washed him, I realized he was very weak and I let him know we didn't have to go anywhere but to the doctor, if the trip home afterward seemed to be too much for him.

"No, I really want to get home today. I need to talk to Joe about what needs to be done."

"You can tell him over the phone."

"No, I have to walk around and show him."

"Okay, but just remember, this doesn't have to be done today. We have permission to take you out again any time you need to go."

He nodded.

I mentioned to him that I felt a little nervous, taking him out when he was feeling so low-energy, then said I figured the nurse wouldn't let me take him if it was dangerous for him.

De agreed with that assessment, but then added, "Listen, I want you to know something: If ever I should happen to die while I'm at the house with you, I don't want you to feel guilty about it. That's where I'd prefer to die, anyway."

I took a quiet, deep breath at that. "Okay, I won't feel guilty—but if it happens, I might die, too, so don't you dare!"

I got him back out near the bed and helped put his clothes on, then got him into the wheelchair. We were ready very early, but the IV drip had to be slowly shut down, so we sat and he ate breakfast while we waited to be cut loose for the trip.

I called the painter for De to confirm that he'd meet us at the house after De's doctor appointment. His wife answered; De talked to her. She told him they were very sorry, but that Joe wouldn't be able to meet with him that day. De was horrendously disappointed, and let her know that getting out to the house was a tremendous effort and that he didn't know when or if he'd be able to do it again. She said she'd try to reach her husband and let him know how important it was. De said, "Please do, and call us back to let us know." She said she would. When she didn't call back, I called again and only got voice mail. I left a message saying that we were leaving for the doctor appointment and that I hoped Joe would be able to make it out, but if not, to please call De's house and leave a message letting us know. I finished with, "We'll be there at noon. We very much hope Joe will be, too."

When De was finally cut loose, we went to Carolyn to tell her good-bye for the day. De looked like a whipped puppy; he didn't feel well.

When Carolyn bid him farewell, he cried, and she wondered why.

"I'm just emotional today."

"You're stealing my stuff!"

I said, "That's okay. It's okay to cry."

Carolyn said, "It sure is. Have a wonderful day, honey."

I wheeled him out of there and got the car. After I got De into the car, and while the door was still open to let heat out, a reed-thin, frail young man approached the car. He, too, was quite obviously a patient. He apologized for imposing —"I would normally never do anything like this"—then told De how much joy De's career had brought him and how important he was to him as a human being. De asked him what his malady was, and they spoke for a minute or two. De became teary-eyed again and told the young man that his kind words meant a lot to him. He wished the young man well and thanked him for stopping by. As we drove out, De said, "I wish I could have thought of something more helpful to say to that young man."

I assured him, "Just spending the time with him was helpful, De. It made his day."

He said, "I hope so. He sure made mine."

We drove to the oncologist's office and waited ninety minutes to see him. De and I tried to leave twice, but received assurances that the doctor would be right with him, so we waited. We were told that the doctor had some hopeful news for De, and that it would be a productive meeting. When we finally got in, the doctor mentioned a few more things he had tracked down—other options to consider—and said he'd research them and get back to us. He asked De to return and see him again in a week, so we scheduled another appointment.

When we got inside De's home, we discovered that Joe's wife had called and left a message, saying that they were very sorry, but that Joe was unable to meet with him that day. De was very disappointed, but there was nothing we could do about it. He decided to call his friend John, who was a retired hairdresser, and let him know he was at home for a while. John offered to come out and cut his hair, and De jumped at the chance.

I went back to the garage and heard Myrtle rattling around in her box. I lifted her out and lowered her to the patio, then reported to De that Myrtle had emerged from hibernation to welcome him home. He mentioned what a dear thing she was and said he wondered if there was anything in the fridge to feed her. "I have cantaloupe and honeydew in there."

He exclaimed, "Those are her favorites!"

I pulled them out and took them to her. She started right in eating. We watched her for a while.

While we waited for John to arrive, De wandered around the house using a cane, and I cooked two small pizzas. It was a horrendously hot day but De wanted the doors and windows thrown open, so I did that. It quickly became even warmer in the house. I was sweltering. De was happy as a clam.

He talked about the possibility of Carolyn and himself eventually coming home, if they got better. I said that would be terrific.

"We'd have to get you a bed."

"Yep, I guess so. Or I could stay with Myrtle—most of the year, except during the rainy season!"

He laughed at that.

I said, "I stayed in a tent in the back yard with Deaken a lot in Encino."

"Yes, I remember you did that."

He called a couple of neighbors and chatted with them. Soon after John arrived and De sipped on half a beer while John and I ate berries and melon. Then we went outside so John could cut De's hair.

After the haircut, John said his goodbye and De decided he wanted to have a shower in his very own shower. I told him that after he got out of the shower I wanted to put lotion on his back and neck and upper arms, because they were so dry and two nurses had mentioned it that morning. 'Okay, when I get out I'll let you know."

He got into the shower and bathed for such a long time that I began to get a nervous about his status, so I called in, "De? Are you okay?"

Absolute silence. I almost panicked and tried again, "De?"

He heard me the second time. "Yes?"

"You okay?"

"Yes. I'll be out in a minute."

"Okay!"

He came out and called me in to put lotion on him. It was sweltering in the house already, but the second I walked into the bathroom, he asked me to turn on the wall heater. I did that and immediately began to baste in a veritable torrent of perspiration. I very quickly doused him with lotion and then asked, facetiously, "Are you warm enough?"

"Yeah, it feels good."

"Well, before I die of heat stroke, I'm getting the hell out of here, boss!"

"Go!"

I escaped to a cooler—98 degree—part of the house and waited for him to emerge, but pretty soon he said, "You can come in and turn off the heater now. I'm not strong enough to do it anymore."

He came out, put on underwear and then flaked out on the bed. Within a minute he was fast asleep. I worked in the office for close to an hour, cleaning it up after my night of activity, figuring he needed the rest. At 4:20 I tapped him on the shoulder and roused him a little.

325

"I'll let you sleep longer if you want, but if we don't get going pretty soon, you'll miss dinner back at the hospital."

He sat up. "How long have I been asleep?"

I looked at my watch. "Almost an hour."

"That's the best sleep I've had in a month."

I put his clothes on him as he sat looking out the bedroom door, marveling, "This is a beautiful, beautiful place."

De walked into the workroom again, commenting on how much I'd done already.

"I did most of it just last night, and that's why the room looked pretty disorganized just before you fell asleep. But now it looks better because I took out the trash just now while you were sacked out."

He said, "My angel deserves a big hug for all the work she has done for me recently."

I said, "Awright!" and collected the sweetest hug, right there on the spot.

We went back to the car. We drove to the hospital and I wheeled him most of the way in and then asked if he wanted to walk into Carolyn's room and make her day.

He said he did, so I helped him stand and he sauntered into her room, newly groomed and looking dapper. He told her about the wonderful, productive day and she just beamed. After a few minutes of reporting to Carolyn all that had gone on, De and I went back to his room. He mentioned how he hated the air mattress so I put in a request to have a nurse remove it.

As I got ready to leave at about 8:15 p.m. he seemed hesitant to let me go. He kept asking me to do last minute things for him. I was so sweaty from the hot, busy activities all afternoon that I hated to get very near him to help him undress, go to the bathroom, get into bed, and the like. He said he didn't care about my perspiration—it had all been for him—and that I could take a nice long bath when I got home. "You can bet I will!"

As I was leaving, he got teary-eyed again, saying, "I just can't begin to express to you how wonderful it is having you so willing to help do anything we need."

"You don't have to, De."

He finally said, "You're the best."

I countered with, "No, you're the best!"

That blew him away. He lost it entirely.

I rushed over to him, took his hand, and said, "Oh, sweetie, don't cry!" Then I said, "Oh, go ahead. It's okay! It's okay to cry." I kissed his hand, cried a little with him, and left soon after.

On April 20, I got to the hospital at about 11:30 and stayed until 2:10. De told me, "I slept great last night." He wasn't as full of energy as he had been the day before, but I could tell it was a happy, comfortable tired, not a sick kind of tired. He mentioned what a great day it had been; I agreed. He asked if I'd had my bath.

I assured him, "God, yes!"

He chuckled and said, "I thought about you last night."

I joked, "Why didn't you call?"

He said, "I didn't want to electrocute you. That's all we'd need now!"

I laughed.

He told me that Shatner wanted to read one of his poems at the Pasadena convention that weekend, "but I'm not at home to find one for him."

"I have copies at my house of all of your Trek-related poems."

He joked, "Boy, I hired the right girl, didn't I?"

I told him I'd get them to Shatner via fax. I called Stephanie and got the fax number so I could do that. De said he wondered how, exactly, Bill planned to use the poem, and so we put in another call to Stephanie. Bill called back not much later and they discussed the plan. De told Bill I'd fax the poems to him the next day so he could choose which one he would read on the weekend.

Carolyn called; I went over and brought her to De's room. We discussed De's effect on fans. Carolyn sometimes thought it was a little silly.

I said, "Usually it's a really heartfelt, wonderful thing. That's why I love going to conventions when De appears. I love how the audience loves and interacts with him." We discussed the number of doctors and nurses that De's career spawned.

Carolyn mentioned how wonderful he was with the fans, saying, "De is a sweet man. A good boy!"

De got tears in his eyes over that. I agreed wholeheartedly. De again mentioned the sick fan he'd met outside the hospital the day before, saying he wished he could have done more.

On April 21, I faxed the three Star Trek-related poems to Shatner's secretary then received a voice mail message saying that the poems were too long and that they wanted something shorter, if De had something. I called De and gave him the scoop, and he said, "Well, I'm stuck here and can't get to the shorter ones."

I told him I could get them and bring them to him, and he told me where they were in the house. He asked how soon Shatner needed the poem.

"This weekend."

"It would be good if I could get them early this afternoon,"

327

"My gang at Warner Bros. is taking me to lunch for Secretary's Day."

"Oh, forget it, then. It's really not all that important."

I told him I could bring them out that evening when I planned to visit again.

He said, "It really isn't necessary."

I told him I'd call Stephanie back and let her know we'd look for a shorter poem, and that if we found one, I'd fax it to her no later than Friday.

He said, "Okay."

I went off to lunch. When I got back, there was a voice mail message from a social worker at the hospital asking me to call her back, "since you're a longtime friend and know so much about Mr. Kelley." Just as I was retrieving her message, she called back and related that Mr. Kelley wasn't forthcoming with her on some issues.

"Different people feel differently about social workers, and I honor that, but just as a precaution, I wanted to know if you know if there have been any final arrangements made in the event he should pass away while he's here at the hospital."

I said, "Oh, yes. He has that all arranged and paid for. He's to be cremated and his ashes scattered at sea by the Neptune Society."

"Can I get copies of those instructions?"

"Not unless he releases me to give them to you. But I know right where they are and can put my hand on them if it becomes necessary."

"Oh, okay. That's good enough. That's all I need."

"Incidentally, his doctor recently gave him some hopeful news, so all of this is premature."

"I hope I haven't misled you. The information I'm gathering has nothing to do with any thought that he is close to death. It's just preliminary in case something unforeseen would happen."

I said, "I see. And I understand."

She said, "Thank you very much for your help. Since Mr. Kelley was so hesitant to speak with me about less grave issues, I certainly didn't want to address this one with him."

"I understand. If I can help in some other way, please give me a call."

De called in the evening at 9:00. The first words out of his mouth were, "I missed you today."

"I missed you, too!"

"I'm having a procedure done next week at another hospital."

"Is it the liver embolism procedure?"

"Yes, I think it is."

"Is your oncologist doing it?"

"Yes. I will be there for a while—probably a week."

"Oh, really? He said it wasn't very invasive."

328

De said, "There will be some pain."

"He mentioned that—a degree of discomfort for a few days."

De said ruefully, "I love that term—'discomfort.'"

I told him there was a phone call from Bob Justman on his answering machine at home. "I'll bring his phone number with me tomorrow. I don't know if you want to call him back, or not."

"Yes, I do."

I told him I tried to feed Myrtle more melon, but she walked away.

"She usually just eats grass the first few days. Don't worry about her. I suppose we're going to fall in love with her again and want to keep her instead of giving her to the neighbor across the street."

I asked if he'd had a good day.

"I can't remember." Then he said, "I'm trying to decide if there's anything else I wanted to tell you...Let me think...I guess not."

"If you think of it later, you can call back."

"What time do you go to bed?"

"It depends on what I have to do. Tonight I had mail to go through, ours and mine, and some of mine to answer, so I just got into bed about twenty minutes ago. Some nights I'm up until midnight. It just depends."

He said, "Well, I'll let you go. I'm going to call Big Mouth now."

I queried, "Big Mouth?"

De said, "A.C."

I chuckled. "Oh! Big Mouth!"

"I'll try not to call you again tonight."

"Call any time you want, De. It's fine. Bye bye, I love you."

"I love you, too, Kris. Goodnight."

On April 22, I drove to the hospital, arriving at about 11:30. I arrived with perfect roses from their garden. De marveled at them and then said I would have to take them to Carolyn later for her to choose which ones to keep.

He told me about the following week's surgical plan. I showed him the liver embolization paper I had written up; he thought it was amazing that I had remembered so much of what we were told. I asked if I should give his doctor a copy of it, and he said I should, so I carried him a copy and handed it to him. He started to read it.

I said, "I heard the information twice, and then wrote down what I remembered of it that night."

The doctor was reading it and said, "This is very good."

I pulled out the poems I had collected from De's house, and while De went through them, I went to Carolyn's room for a visit; ended up staying more than an hour. I massaged lotion into her legs. We chatted for quite a while then I wheeled her over to be with De.

The Kelleys were affectionate, lovey-dovey. De's hands were cold, Carolyn noticed, and he said, "I don't have my body warmer in bed with me the way I used to." She took his hand in hers.

De was very emotional again that day, becoming teary-eyed whenever anything was said that would touch the heart. Carolyn and I both told him it was all right to be emotional; "We are too."

He asked, "Then why do I always seem to be the only one crying? No one else is crying."

Carolyn said, "I used to be just like that. Hated it."

Then I reminded De that I had cried with him a time or two last week, and he nodded, remembering. I told them I cried at night.

Carolyn said she did, too, sometimes…

De read some of the poems I had brought and picked one of them, "The Yellow Balloon," for me to fax to Shatner for the convention. He said, "When I wrote these, they didn't seem to me to be depressing, but now that I read them again, most of them are."

I asked if he wanted me to fax the poem to Bill in its original hand-written form, or to fax it after I had typed it.

"Type it first."

"Okay."

I had a terrible time faxing De's "Yellow Balloon" to Shatner. After that herculean effort, I returned to De's room and asked him where he wanted me to put the extra copies of the liver embolization paper.

Carolyn asked "What's that?"

I said, "It's my report of what we heard in the oncologist's office the other day, about the procedure De is having done."

She asked, "May I read it?"

"Sure. You can have your own copy."

De quickly told her, "It's my fault you don't have one already. I told Kris I didn't think you'd be that interested in the documentation."

She said, "Well, let me see it…" Then she said, "I would like to keep this copy, if I may."

I said, "You bet."

Just before 3:30, Carolyn decided to go back to her room. As soon as she left, De reported that he was beginning to feel nauseated, so I informed a nurse and then went in and pressed the reflexology points until the shot was administered. It hurt this time. He was also feeling chilly, so I covered him well.

He fell asleep for ninety minutes soon afterward. When he awoke, he ate a few bites of dinner. He was still tired. We watched the news about the Littleton Colorado shootings and cried. Then he said he was still very tired so I kissed him and went over to sit with Carolyn for another forty minutes or so. We watched Wheel of Fortune together and I explained the following week's liver embolization procedure further, so she'd fully understand the benefits he should reap from it. She said wistfully, "Perhaps he'll outlive us all, then."

DE'S POEMS

On April 23, I called De at 10 a.m. He told me he'd had a helluva morning. When I got to his room, I showed him his computer-generated poems and let him know I could re-do them in script font or any other font or size he wanted in a jiffy. I showed him where a couple of the poems didn't look finished, and he said he'd work on them.

He told me about his morning of showering and medical treatment. I called John for him and they chatted for a while, then I went over and got Carolyn to come over for a visit. De didn't want lunch, so I had a few bites of his. After that I excused myself to go back to work. De thanked me for everything.

"You're welcome. See you tomorrow."

During our next visit De showed real signs of weakness. I told De I'd call the oncologist's office first thing on Monday and schedule a Tuesday or Thursday appointment. His eyes were getting droopy, so I said I'd let him sleep. He nodded and went off to dream land.

While De slept, I went over to Carolyn's to sit with her and watch television. A couple of hours later, De called over to Carolyn's wondering if I had gone home. Carolyn said I hadn't; I was right here, and that she'd send me over.

I went over to sit with him. He was sick to his stomach in the evening a number of times and the vomit smelled foul, so the nurse put in a call for the doctor. It took two hours for a doctor to come in; he ordered an x- ray for first thing in the morning.

As we sat all that time waiting for the doctor, De mentioned to me, "I'm sure glad you're here. Sometimes I think you're here too late at night, but when things like this start to happen to me, I'm so glad you're right here. It's a comfort to know I have help."

I said, "You bet you do."

De began to look more comfortable and unlikely to vomit again at around eleven, but I offered, "I'll stay all night if you want."

"No, you go home now and get some sleep."

On April 25 I got to the hospital at about 9 a.m. De still felt puny and asked me to call a long-time friend of theirs and cancel the visit they had planned for that day. I did that. I didn't stay on long and was speaking quietly, as De's eyes were closed and I didn't want to disturb him.

De slept away most of that day trying to escape his discomfort During his waking moments that evening we talked. He did a lot of appreciating. We had been watching Touched by An Angel in his room for several weeks running by this time, and both of us had been brought to tears by each of the episodes. De became curious, and then asked—very sincerely truly questioning me—"Are you an angel?" His question touched me deeply, and had I been able to somehow manufacture a halo, a la Roma Downey, I may well have succumbed to the enormous temptation to say, "yes," so great was my desire to reassure him that he was, indeed, surrounded by angels. I took his hand.

"No, but I'm trying to be."

He said, "I think you are."

I said, "From what I've read about angels, they're an entirely different species. We never become angels and our guardian angels aren't people who have gone before us. But one quote I just love, by Og Mandino, goes something like this: 'The trouble with full-time angels is that they are completely unpredictable and you cannot just send out for one. That is why part-time angels are so important. Part-time angels are you and me.'"

He liked the quote so much he had me repeat it.

Carolyn came to De's room for a short visit. De was sweet to her, and explained carefully that his pain, discomfort and reduced energy level were what kept him from wanting to visit. She understood and was sweet in reply to him.

At nearly midnight, I decided to go home. I told De, "Since your doctor appointment has been re-scheduled, I'll plan to report to work tomorrow and then take the day off when your appointment is set."

"Okay, honey."

"So, I'll see you at noon."

He said, "I'm going to make this up to you. I don't know how I'm going to do it, but I am."

I said very sincerely, "De, forget it. You made it up to me long before I even started doing it. I love you. Have a good night."

The next day I got to work at about 7:50. At 8:10 De called and said he'd had a terrible night and that he was going to have a terrible day.

"Do you want me to come out?"

"Yes, if you can."

"I'll be there in forty minutes. Sooner, if the traffic allows."

"Okay, honey. See you then. I appreciate it."

When I got there, De told me about how nauseated and uncomfortable he had been all night. They had given him the routine treatment for the situation, but it hadn't done anything to solve his problem.

De's male nurse described a procedure—brief but painful—that would result in swift relief. De agreed to it. As the nurse prepared the way to do the procedure I asked De if he wanted me to step out of the room while it was done.

"No. You've been through the rest of it; you may as well be though the worst of it."

Mercifully, the procedure lasted only brief seconds. De swore mightily then quickly apologized, saying, "I almost never swear using those words. I just couldn't help it. I have been through a lot of pain, but that was the worst ever." Not long after, his system began to respond. He was comfortable again and soon enjoyed a restful nap.

On April 27 when I got to the hospital, De's first words were, "You've received a lot of compliments."

"I have—from whom?"

"From the staff here."

"Oh, that's nice."

The head nurse came in, checked De's lungs, and told him he had some lung involvement. De agreed: "I can feel it."

She said, "You were lying down most of the weekend because of your discomfort. Try sitting up straighter today, and when you're out. That will clear your lungs."

De and I got to his oncologist's office and had to wait a good ninety minutes again. De was miffed and said, "He's always overbooked. This happens every time." His strength was waning and waiting in the office always wore him out, so he hated it.

Toward the end of the wait, De decided, "Let's just go. We have people waiting for us at the house, and I don't want to tie them up." I started to push him out of the office. The doctor noticed us leaving and entreated us to come back, saying it would be only five more minutes.

When we finally got into the office, the doctor again explained the liver embolization procedure. He did it in such an unattractive way this time that De decided against the procedure.

The doctor said, "I don't even know what decision I'd make for myself if I were in your shoes, so I honor your decision."

De asked how he would die.

The doctor said, "You're dying already. Your energy is becoming less and less, as you know. You will begin to sleep more often day and night. Eventually you will slip into a coma, and you will pass away from there."

De said, "That sounds good. That's the way I want it. No pain."

The doctor said, "We will do absolutely everything possible to be sure you don't experience any pain."

"That's good."

The doctor shook our hands and said, "I'll see you again in a week or two."

De said, "I hope."

"If you can't get here, I'll come out there and visit you. I don't have privileges at your facility, but I will come out just as a friend, to visit."

De said, "All right."

334

As we left the exam room, De said he wanted to stop by the nurse's station and thank the nurses "and say good-bye. Then I want you to take me to another office in this building, to Dr. Shaw's office, so I can tell him and the nurses there good-bye. Everyone has been so good to me."

I said, "Okay," and we did that. Dr. Shaw wasn't in, so De said he'd call him later from the house to say his good-byes.

I was very upset that De had decided against the liver embolization procedure, but tried not to show it. I was nearly in tears.

I helped him into the car and we drove to his bank for some cash and then to his house. He gave me $100 of the cash—against my protestations—saying, "I'm not paying you enough for all you do for me."

"You're paying me enough to pay my bills. That's all I need."

"But it's not all you deserve. Take this. Don't upset me."

So I took it.

Not long after we arrived at the house, the painter Joe arrived and De showed him what needed to be done to the house. Then Tony Kirk, the mailman, stopped by. It was at this point I learned, from listening to De on the phone to Dr. Shaw, that he thought his oncologist had told him he had only a week or two left to live. My head came up in a hurry and I quickly whispered to Joe and Tony, assuring them that De was mistaken. As soon as De hung up, I told him, "De, your oncologist didn't tell you that you only had a week or two to live!"

He looked at me and said, "I heard what he said."

"Sweetie, he didn't say that. I promise."

De said, "I heard what I heard."

I asked, "Will you let me call him right now, so I can find out which of us is right?"

De said, "Okay."

I called the oncologist from another room and told him that De had misunderstood his comments and thought he had only two weeks to live.

The doctor said, "Oh, for heaven's sake. Let me speak to him."

Before I carried the phone to De, though, I asked the doctor, "Do you know how long he has left?"

The response was, "I can never be sure about these things, but based on what I'm seeing, I'd say he has another month and a half to three months."

"Okay. Thanks. I don't think De wants to know how long he has, unless he asks you, but I need to know."

I carried the phone to De and the doctor straightened him out promptly, telling him that he would never be able to say when. "It depends on so many factors."

De hung up, relieved, and told the guys he was mistaken. Then he looked at me. "Why do I ever argue with you? You're always right. I won't argue with you again."

I asked, "When have you argued with me before?"

"Not much, because you always end up being right!"

"I'm sure glad I was right about this."

He said, "So am I! Don't tell Carolyn what I thought I heard."

I said, "I won't, believe me."

Greatly relieved, De's mood lightened. He told the men a story about his role in the pilot of Steve McQueen's television show, saying that when he walked in for the audition, McQueen looked at him and said, "You're not what I have in mind for the heavy."

De said, "Well, perhaps I can convince you I am." He threw McQueen around a bit, snarled, and McQueen quickly agreed, saying,

"Okay, I was wrong. You're just right for the part!"

The guys got a big kick out of their vision of gentlemanly De throwing his weight around and punching McQueen out.

When we got back to the hospital, we went to Carolyn's room and reported the day's events. De told her he had decided against the liver embolization procedure, and she didn't argue with him over it.

I took De back to his room. He said he wanted to do something for my boss, Dan. He asked what Dan would like.

I said, "I don't think he wants anything."

De said, "I want to sign a photo to him, at least. Please get me a color photo."

I got one out of his photo envelope and handed it to him. He signed it, 'To Dan, With deep gratitude for you know what! DeForest.' I told him Dan would love it.

I went over to see Carolyn after leaving De for the evening. She was having a lot of issues about De's decision. She wanted to know how long De would last without the procedure, and I said I didn't know for certain, but that I guessed he'd probably pass away in under three months.

Then she began to grouse, "And I don't have any say in the matter as to whether or not he has the procedure."

I said, "You have every say in the matter. You need to tell him how you feel, if you feel differently; if you want him to undergo the procedure and be with you longer."

She said, "I can't do that. I can't make that decision for him."

I said, "Okay, then. That's the way it will be—the way he wants it."

She said, "I want what he wants."

I said, "You're a brave little soldier, sweetie."

She said, "I'm not brave. I'm just realistic."

On Wednesday April 28, I went for a visit at noon to let De know how much Dan loved the signed photo. De was happy about that. He dictated a few letters that were intended for friends, as he didn't feel up to writing them himself and yet felt he owed them a letter.

De said, "Before I do this, I want to tell you I'm not a good dictator." He did a fine job of dictating the letters.

De was very tired. We didn't talk much. At one point, he asked me, "Do you think you're fired yet, at Warner Bros.?

"No, De. Even if I was, it would be the most honorable firing ever."

De agreed, saying, "I guess it would—fired for helping a dying friend during his last days." Then he said, "I really hate being in the hospital, even though it's a wonderful hospital with good people. I miss being at home."

I discussed with De the possibility that he could return home under Hospice care for the duration of his life.

He said, "Carolyn would hate it if I went home. She wants me here, near her."

"You could still visit her, while you're able. And she could come home on three day leaves, and be there with you, watching the birds and squirrels in the back yard."

"Oh, you couldn't take care of two of us. It would kill you."

"It would not. I'm willing to give it a try, if you are."

He said, "I don't know if I am. I know what it would entail."

I said, "Okay," and let it drop.

THE ONLY THINGS CERTAIN ARE DEATH AND TAXES

I had to go to De's bank first thing Friday morning, June 11 to get his estimated tax checks mailed to the IRS that day, but I dreaded having to leave him, as I didn't know if he'd be alive when I got back. A nurse assured me that if he passed away while I was out, it might well be because he wanted to: "Often it's easier to let go when there is no one else in the room. A loved one's presence can sometimes hold them here when they'd prefer to go."

I said, "Okay," then went back into the room to tell De where I was going.

"De, I have to go to your bank and to the post office to get your estimated taxes out. Is that okay?"

He nodded yes.

"Will you be okay while I'm gone? Can I leave you for a little while?"

He nodded yes.

I then asked, "Shall I stay here with you a while longer instead?"

He nodded an emphatic no, and then whispered almost inaudibly, "I can't talk."

I said, "Okay, then. I'll be back as soon as I can. You just rest; a nurse will be with you all the time, so don't worry."

He nodded and shut his eyes, so I'd go.

I said, "I love you. I'll be back soon."

I drove to the bank, where I got two checks for estimated tax payments. I drove from there to the post office and mailed the checks, then drove back to the hospital.

I had no more than started down the long hallway to De's room when the nurse I had spoken to earlier came rushing out and said, "Oh, Kris, thank God you're here. I think he's waiting for you. Hurry." I started to run toward his room.

"Don't run," she cautioned me. "Don't run."

I ran anyway.

When I got into the room at close to 11 in the morning I spotted Carolyn and Chaplain David Grant at De's bedside.

Carolyn said, "Oh, thank God, you're back!"

I set my stuff down and took a seat next to Carolyn and David, close to De's head. I took Carolyn's right hand—she had De's hand in her left hand—and David's right hand.

De was lying on his left side. I had read that hearing is the last sense to go and that comatose people can hear, so I told him, "Hi, sweetie. I'm back I got your taxes all taken care of. Everything is taken care of and will be taken care of, De, so you can relax. We'll take good care of Carolyn, so don't worry about a thing."

Carolyn said she'd had about 25 minutes alone with him and had said all she wanted to say to him. "I told him he could go; I told him I love him."

The chaplain asked Carolyn to recount some of their life and times together as we waited and the minutes ticked by, so Carolyn told a few cute stories. Occasionally she would laugh or giggle at the remembrance. Each time she did, I would look over at De. I could see the pulse in his neck becoming less and less pronounced and the breaths coming less frequently. I prayed that he was hearing her laughter and feeling that she would be okay, if she was okay at a time like this.

As the time drew very near, I told David, "De loved hearing the Lord's Prayer the other day."

David said, "Oh, really? Shall I offer it again?"

I said, "I think so."

Carolyn said, "That would be nice."

So David stood and placed his hand on De's forehead and recited the Lord's Prayer and then the 23rd Psalm, finishing with Numbers 6:24. It was poignant, almost beyond endurance.

With tears threatening to flood my eyes, I said, "Go with God, De, whenever you feel ready. It's okay, sweetie."

I believe these were the last words De ever heard. He slipped away at 12:15 p.m. June 11, Pacific Daylight Time—peacefully, never regaining consciousness.

So…where from here? Those of you who love De can extend yourselves to others, De-fashion, if it's within your personality and character to reach out and touch others in ways that heal.

If that path doesn't resonate within you, surely it's enough just to remember the Physician's Oath: "Do no harm."

Filmography
Film

1947 *Fear in the Night*
1947 *Variety Girl*
1948 *Canon City*
1949 *Duke of Chicago*
1949 *Malaya*
1950 *The Men*
1953 *Taxi*
1955 *House of Bamboo*
1955 *Illegal*
1955 *The View from Pompey's Head*
1956 *Tension at Table Rock*
1956 *The Man in the Gray Flannel Suit* (unbilled)
1957 *Gunfight at the O.K. Corral*
1957 *Raintree County*
1958 *The Law and Jake Wade*
1959 *Warlock*
1964 *Gunfight at Comanche Creek*
1964 *Where Love Has Gone*
1965 *Black Spurs*
1965 *Marriage on the Rocks*
1965 *Town Tamer*
1966 *Apache Uprising*
1966 *Johnny Reno*
1966 *Waco*
1972 *Night of the Lepus*
1979 *Star Trek: The Motion Picture*
1982 *Star Trek II: The Wrath of Khan*
1984 *Star Trek III: The Search for Spock*
1986 *Star Trek IV: The Voyage Home*
1989 *Star Trek V: The Final Frontier*
1991 *Star Trek VI: The Undiscovered Country*
1998 *The Brave Little Toaster Goes to Mars*

Television

1949 *The Lone Ranger* (as Bob Kittredge in episode "Legion of Old Timers")
1960 *Richard Diamond, Private Detective* "The Fine Art of Murder"
1952 *The Lone Ranger*, as the Doctor

1953–54 *City Detective* episodes "Crazy Like a Fox" and "An Old Man's Gold"

1955 *Science Fiction Theatre* (As Captain Hall in episode "Y..O..R..D..")

1956 *Gunsmoke* (appeared in various episodes)

1957 *M Squad* (Appeared in the episode "Pete Loves Mary")

1958 *Wanted: Dead or Alive* (as Sheriff Steve Pax in "Secret Ballot")

1959 *Wanted: Dead or Alive* (TV series) | *Wanted: Dead or Alive* (as Ollie Tate in "The Empty Cell")

1959 *Rawhide* (as Slate Prell in episode "Incident at Barker Springs")

1959 *Mackenzie's Raiders* (as Charles Barrons in episode "Son of the Hawk")

1959 *Mickey Spillane's Mike Hammer* (as Eddie Robbins in episode "I Ain't Talkin'")

1959 *26 Men* (appeared in episode "Trail of Revenge" with Leonard Nimoy)

1959 *State Trooper* (as Graham in "The Patient Skeleton")

1959 *Richard Diamond, Private Detective* (as the Sheriff in "The Limping Man" and as Ken Porter

1960 *Two Faces West* (as Vern Cleary in "Fallen Gun")

1960 *Johnny Midnight* (as David Lawton in "The Inner Eye")

1960–61 *COronado 9* (as Frank Briggs in "Loser's Circle" and Shep Harlow in "Run, Shep, Run")

1961 *Perry Mason* (in episode "The Case of the Unwelcome Bride")

1961 *Shannon* (as Carlyle in "The Pickup")

1961 *Lawman* (as Bent Carr in "Squatters")

1961–66 *Bonanza*, (appeared in various episodes)

1962 *Have Gun – Will Travel*

1963 *The Dakotas* as Martin Volet in "Reformation at Big Nose Butte"
    1965 *The Fugitive*

1966 *Death Valley Days*

1966 *I Happened*

1966 *Laredo* (as Dr. David Ingram in "The Sound of Terror")

1966 *Ride the Wind*

1966–69 *Star Trek*

1970 *Ironside* (appeared in various episodes)

1972 *The Bull of the West* (telemovie based on two episodes of *The Virginian*) (as Ben Tully)

"When he shall die take him and cut him out in little stars and he will make the face of heaven so fine that all the world will be in love with night and pay no worship to the garish sun."
— Shakespeare,
Romeo and Juliet

Kristine M. Smith, Author & Copy Writer

Author Kristine M. Smith has been a fan of DeForest Kelley for five decades. She has also meandered among his fans at numerous conventions and at individual and collective ceremonies honoring him and Star Trek. She writes: "I have witnessed first-hand the enormous love and the respect people have for De. And I continue to see how people have remained enchanted with him, even following his passing in 1999.

Millions of people were immediately and acutely affected by his unanticipated death. Tens of thousands of them expressed outright anguish; feelings akin to losing one's best friend or a family member. A single, cursory visit to just one of numerous DeForest Kelley websites (national and international) proves the veracity of this declaration.

"Categorically and undeniably, De became—and will endure as—one of the most-loved and best-remembered personalities in the world. His Dr. McCoy is at the heart of Star Trek's mythology, and Trek is a tenacious mythology which will last, in all likelihood, until the day humans forget how to aspire to a higher standard for themselves and their progeny.

"De was my friend, but he was also my hero—one of very few heroes whose durability was sorely tested, yet found to be utterly reliable. I wrote his book to show how deeply De influenced my life and to remind you, his fans and friends, how seamlessly and comfortably he fitted into yours.

"I undertook this endeavor for the millions of fans who never had the pleasure of meeting De 'up close and personal.' My sincerest goal for this book is that it will validate every intuition you ever had about DeForest Kelley being one of Hollywood's 'good guys.'"

A Pacific Northwest native, Smith transformed her copywriting business from a struggling start-up (in 2008) to a going concern in near-record time. Prior to launching her own copywriting business, Kris served as a fledgling copywriter for a University Place on-hold script production company, where she won Employee of the Quarter the last two quarters she worked there.

Kris's freelance writing career was launched by actor DeForest Kelley in 1969. It was Kelley and his wife Carolyn who encouraged Kris to try Hollywood on for size, which she did from 1989 to 2003. Kris served as Mr. Kelley's personal assistant and caregiver during the final months of his life and presented heartfelt sentiments about her mentor at Paramount Studios' memorial service for him in 1999. She has written two books about him.

In Hollywood, Kris served as an administrative assistant and secretarial floater to writers, producers and—later—information technology professionals at various studios. Most of her Hollywood career was spent at Warner Bros. Studios in Burbank where she served as an executive secretary

343

for the VP of Software Development and as a Hardware Lease Administrator.

Kris's most notable creative endeavor at Warner Bros. was writing the copy for an intranet website to help newly-arrived secretaries learn the ins and outs of serving on the WB campus in record time. The website earned her a monetary reward and the coveted (don't laugh!) Carrot Award (Bugs Bunny runs da joint, ya know!); the accompanying Certification of Appreciation was co-signed by the head of the Human Resources Department and her boss.

Kris loves dancing with words and interacting with people. You can reach her at hireme.wordwhisperer.net and at kris@wordwhisperer.net.

If you enjoyed this publication please consider the following titles by the same author:

Serval Son. If you've ever wondered what it's like to own (and be owned by) a wild animal—especially a wild cat—get ready to experience it in ways you will never forget. The author does not advocate the keeping of wild pets, especially wild cats, wild dogs and simians. But there are times when adopting a wild one seems like a calling, a part of your destiny. If you've felt the tug, this book will introduce you to what you'll be getting into. Look before you leap. This title reached #2 an #4 in two niche categories at Amazon when it debuted in 2011.

Settle for Best: Satisfy the Winner You Were Born to Be. Loosely based on Napoleon Hill's seminal bestseller, Think and Grow Rich Settle for Best reveals twenty commonalities that all self-made millionaire philanthropists share. By adopting the same mindset and methods, you too can enrich your life in every way. This title sat at #1 for three days running in the Motivational Self-Help category when it debuted in 2012.

Floating Around Hollywood and Other Totally-True Tales of Triumph. Amusing collection of reminiscences by Kris Smith spotlighting her adventures as a "floating secretary" in Tinsel Town. A.C. Lyles legendary producer at Paramount/Viacom, wrote "Kris Smith's entertainment industry career reads like a sitcom." DeForest Kelley's back cover comment is, "A fast-paced book, full of laughter, written with comedic skill. It's a delightful read."

Let No Day Dawn That the Animals Cannot Share. Foreword by DeForest Kelley. A mostly-serious collection of Smith's animal "pros-e-try" which will clutch passionately at the reader's heart and spirit. The book spotlights humankind's deeply-rooted bonds to the animal kingdom and then identifies areas in which we have fallen painfully (and dangerously) short regarding our stewardship of scores of irreplaceable fellow creatures.

The Enduring Legacy of DeForest Kelley: Actor, Healer, Friend. DeForest Kelley's former personal assistant has compiled the memories and reminiscences of fans and friends whose lives were blessed and changed forever the career or kindness of the late actor who portrayed Dr. Leonard McCoy in the original Star Trek series. All who contributed to the tome have realized the immense impact that the iconic "Bones" has had on their lives and careers. Smith reveals that Kelley's legacy includes fans who continue to boldly go where few have gone before, making a difference every step of the way. Available at payloadz.com.

ACKNOWLEDGMENTS

When it comes to bringing a manuscript to life, it can be the loneliest of tasks, until one realizes that standing behind each belabored draft are dozens of faith-filled associates and friends who are expecting nothing less than Something Fantastic. There are, additionally, family members who wonder, fretfully, whether lightning will strike and turn their relative into the talk of the town—or into the laughingstock of the planet.

It's always a crapshoot, for the writer and for those in the peanut gallery, wondering what will come of the seemingly- endless hours in enforced, intense isolation. I'm sure at least a few worried, "Has she died? Why hasn't she phoned or answered my e-mail?"

This is the place to acknowledge the many people I abandoned during the two months I was giving birth to this book. I'm sure they understood the intense concentration it took to create something that would hang together from first page to last. I think they also understood that this book was—for me—an extended de-briefing and therapy session during which I again acknowledged my most grievous losses and counted my many, many blessings. Each and every time I chuckled, laughed, giggled, guffawed or roared while recounting these many happy instances of my life and times with DeForest Kelley, I ended up crying for several minutes, too. That's what happens when the rug is pulled out from under you and there is no way to get back to the place where your life was everything you ever wanted it to be.

At Warner Bros., my bosses, co-workers, and associates in Technical Support had to hold me together without even knowing what was up until the very end. Dan Kronstadt, my boss and supervisor, is the only person who knew what was happening from Day One (March 14, 1999). Al Foitag, Dan Alpern and Dorothy Gelhar, my other bosses, had to largely intuit that Something Was Terribly Amiss and that I was in the throes of some sort of personal crisis. Without questioning me, these stellar supervisors gave me the leeway I needed to "be there" for De during the three months prior to his death on June 11, which meant that they had to do without my services a great deal. They knew I wasn't normally a flake, and that's ALL they knew – and that's what they relied on. I thank them for having that kind of faith in me. I couldn't have done what I did for De without this rock-solid foundation of unquestioning support.

Kim Stephens, the late Greg Heimbigner, Maria Thompson, Carol Ranken and others at Warner Bros. were also kept in the dark as to exactly what was transpiring until days before I took my Leave of Absence on May 4th. Nevertheless, they became "guardian angels" during my travails. They

346

stayed close, creating an atmosphere of love and comfort that I don't think I could have been without, without cracking up.

Also at Warner Bros, Office of Emergency Services experts Mario Guerra, Norma Ruiz de Maldonado and Nancy Mathews held me together a time or two. Their comforting, encouraging words and hugs kept returning my nervous system to "functional" from "frantic." They know their stuff. I'm living proof. Additionally, their incomparable training sessions helped me save my nephew's life. How can I possibly thank them enough for that?

At home, compassionate and concerned neighbors Mario and Amada Abelleira, Harriet Rempel, Nayna Patel and Alice Sandkamp became my frequent walking partners during three mile treks designed to keep me from "stressing out." I lied and told them the walk was for physical fitness; it was actually for mental health. So they became physically fit and I remained 99% sane. In the bargain, I made friends that will endure in my heart forever. Special thanks to th e late, great Alice Sandkamp who—during the course of writing this manuscript—would call or pop her head in the window once or twice a day to ask, "Are you remembering to eat?" On days when I had to confess "No," she would prepare me a delicious, delightful meal! I imagine the Sandkamp grocery bill escalated a bit as a result.

Other friends in deed were Nancy Graf in Carmichael, California, Reggie Holloway in Turlock, California, Sandy Zier- Teitler of Elkridge, Maryland, Melody Adams in Tacoma, Washington and of course my collaborator, Terry Lee Rioux, historian and the author of De's biography. Their love, support and steadfast faith buoyed me and never let me sink. I love all of you beyond expression.

This manuscript first went to two women in the Data Center at Warner Bros., Tasnim Fernandez and Deanna Patellis, and to the forementioned Terry Lee Rioux and Sandy Zier-Teitler. They read the most convoluted version of this saga and helped edit it into a document worthy of being called a manuscript. All they could expect to get out of it was eye-strain and a complimentary copy of the published version. And now this acknowledgment. It is nowhere near enough. Thank you from the bottom of my heart!

I also want to thank Lisa Twining Taylor for proofreading, editing and offering the stylistic changes that make this edition far more professional and less pedestrian than the earlier incarnation. She had to jump through hoops I wouldn't wish on my worst enemy and she did so cheerfully to give me the best result possible.

Cover artist Olivia Vieweg is, as you can tell, sensational! When CBS Home Entertainment signed off on my ability to use the image of De's face on the cover in the way Olivia envisioned, no one was more surprised or happier. So thank you to the powers that be at CBS Homes Entertainment for allowing us to lead with a stunning photo of De.

And special thanks to Breanna Brink, who was willing to dive in and re-type the entire manuscript when it appeared that we would have to do that to eliminate egregious formatting errors interposed by another individual. Fortunately, a Star Trek fan name Brent McAlister knew of a work-around so Breanna didn't have to pinch hit for long, but she was willing to give up her Christmas break to do it, so THANK YOU, Breanna!

I want to acknowledge, as well, my late great mother Dorothea Smith—who you too probably love now that you know so much about her. My father, Jack, passed away just six months after De, and two months before I started this manuscript. I only wish Mom and Dad were here now to read this.

My junior high school English and creative writing teacher, Alpha Rossetti, believed in my talent long before anyone else did. She was the one responsible for my first two- year subscription to THE WRITER all those years ago when all I had to hang my hopes on was a high-falutin' dream that seemed impossible for a kid living in the sticks to achieve.

Kristine M. Smith Tacoma, Washington
December 15, 2015